4/96

BEING RED IN PHILADELPHIA

A Memoir of the McCarthy Era

SHERMAN LABOVITZ

Camino Books, Inc.

Philadelphia

Manufactured in the United States of America

1 2 3 4 5 00 99 98

Library of Congress Cataloging-in-Publication Data

Labovitz, Sherman.
    Being red in Philadelphia : a memoir of the McCarthy era / Sherman Labovitz.
        p.   cm.
    Includes bibliographical references.
    ISBN 0-940159-42-2 (alk. paper)
    1. Labovitz, Sherman—Trials, litigation, etc. 2. Trials (Conspiracy)—Pennsylvania—Philadelphia. 3. Communist trials—Pennsylvania—Philadelphia. I. Title.
    KF224.L28L33 1997
    345.748'1102—dc21   97-14527

Cover design: Jerilyn Bockorick
Interior design: Robert LeBrun

For information write:
Camino Books, Inc.
P.O. Box 59026
Philadelphia, PA 19102

Dedicated with deep respect and sincere appreciation to
Thomas D. McBride, 1903-1965
A staunch defender of the Bill of Rights—
the epitome of the real Philadelphia Lawyer

CONTENTS

Acknowledgments vii

Prologue ix

The Smith Act xiii

Introduction: Setting the Scene 1

1. Arrest and Surveillance 7

2. Locked Up 15

3. In Prison and Out 23

4. Indicted Co-Conspirators 33

5. How I Got There 37

6. In the Army 45

7. Victory and After 53

8. The City of Brotherly Love 59

9. A Gathering Defense 69

10. Rig a Jury and Parade the Informers 79

11. The Colonel Falls 89

12. An "Aesop" Fable 93

13. Perjury Continues 99

14. Six More Sad Excuses 107

15. The Defense and the Verdict. 115

16. Sentencing and Freedom 123

17. Debt-Free 133

18. What the Trial Meant 135

19. Afterword 141

Glossary 151

Notes 159

ACKNOWLEDGMENTS

The publication of this book was assisted by a generous Faculty Fellowship from The Richard Stockton College of New Jersey. Considerable help came from the entire secretarial pool of Stockton's Division of Social and Behavioral Sciences, and while I thank them one and all, I am particularly indebted to Patti Williamson.

Two dear friends, my former student Denise Dowell and her husband Arthur Rosenfeld—an ex-colleague whom I've known since his birth—fortuitously came across a set of weathered but complete transcripts of my trial. Knowing that I was in the process of collecting materials, they promptly presented those documents to me.

I am especially indebted to all of those busy people who so graciously gave me time for interviews. While all, I hope, will see and read this acknowledgment, four very special contributors have died. One was Helen Weiss, widow of one of my co-defendants, Ben Weiss. Two others were major members of the defense team: Judge Joseph S. Lord III and Benjamin H. Read. The fourth was Bernard Segal, Chancellor of the Philadelphia Bar Association at the time of my arrest. His thoughts and the files he made accessible proved to be invaluable. Posthumously, I thank them.

Two interviews with Spencer Coxe, former American Civil Liberties Union Executive Director, were loaded with insights into the period and were buttressed by the files to which he directed me. Jack Zucker, an old friend and former associate when he was the Director of the Philadelphia Civil Rights Congress, helped me immeasurably with his recollections of some of the nuances of the period. While in the final analysis this book is my synthesis, I have also tried to accurately convey the views of the many contributors as to what took place during those tumultuous times. Their thoughts are a very important part of the telling of this story. I thank them all and I hope that I have in no way violated their trust.

Additional information about the general "anti-communist" atmosphere in Philadelphia at the time of the Smith Act trial was gathered from interviews by Fred Zimring and from a paper by Iz Reivich. Dr. Zimring's research, found in the Temple University Urban Archives, was concerned with that university's dismissal of Professor Barrows Dunham, after he had been made the subject of one of several Congressional "investigations" to invade the city. The paper by Mr. Reivich presents a first-person account of the attacks directed at teachers in the Philadelphia public school system.

I found useful materials in the Philadelphia Bar Association periodical, *The Shingle*, and particularly in the Temple Urban Archive Files of the Philadelphia Fellowship Commission, the Philadelphia Teachers' Union and the Philadelphia chapter of the American Civil Liberties Union.

Many friends and relatives listened patiently, offered advice and made suggestions. Two of my older brothers, Harry and Dood (David), were among those who were particularly encouraging and helpful. Dr. Esther Labovitz made time for a professional and skillful reading and provided many appreciated observations. My two sons, Marc and Gary, were humorous, biting, tough and, I believe, very proud critics. They read lovingly while learning still more about their parents.

A colleague, Dr. Paul Lyons, helped me focus some of my thinking with several insightful and incisive questions about an earlier draft. I learned considerably from Gene Bloomfield's observations and in particular from Judith Levine's empathetic editing assistance.

But first there always was, and finally there always is, Pauline. During the period of the arrest and trial, my wife was a constant source of love, support and strength. For the telling of this story she provided the same ambience. She helped make the appointments, she frequented the libraries, she listened to every word I wrote. Pauline fought the computer and helped edit and correct the final manuscript. In reliving those long-ago experiences with me, Pauline demanded truth and accuracy in my recollections, and she helped sharpen the significance of each anecdote. In so many ways, it is also her story.

PROLOGUE

It was the worst of times! In 1948, the Truman administration adopted a strong anti-communist policy with domestic fallout in the form of government employee loyalty and security programs. The anti-communism fanned by Winston Churchill's "Iron Curtain" speech was further inflamed early in 1952, when Senator Joseph McCarthy claimed that 205 "communist traitors" were employed in the State Department. The demagoguery of the fanatical McCarthy spurred other opportunist politicians into a mission designed to discover communists behind each tree and under every bed. Search they did: in theater and film, in libraries, in schools and colleges, even in industry and government service, including the military. Today, 44 years after the indictments in the Philadelphia Smith Act case, we look back upon the "McCarthy era" as the nadir of civil liberties in the United States.

Anyone who believes that the climate of liberty today is so significantly better as to preclude the recurrence of another era of full-blown McCarthyism is probably naïve. After all, we continue to indulge in blame by association and exhibit minimal tolerance for ideological and philosophical disagreement; we still give free course to stereotyping, to bigotry, to bias and discrimination against those of unfamiliar or different national origin, race, religion or sexual preference; xenophobia is rampant. But as bad as the situation may be today, it was much worse in 1953-54. Anti-left rhetoric and anti-communist hysteria throughout the nation were at an all-time peak, and Philadelphia was not to be spared.

It is sobering to remember that early in 1953, while Americans were being arrested and brought to trial only for agreeing and organizing to teach and advocate Marxist theory, the American Bar Association appointed a special committee to investigate lawyers and bar applicants and urged legal institutions to identify and disbar them for any communist affiliations. A few years earlier in New York City, at the conclusion of the first of the Smith Act trials, defense attorneys were jailed for contempt of court because of their aggressive advocacy. To say the least, the atmosphere chilled whatever enthusiasm lawyers might have had to leap to the defense of communists.

In Philadelphia, it was difficult for lawyers with experience in criminal defense practice to fit the Smith Act defendants into our prototype of clients. While they were among the more community-concerned and politically opinionated on the block, they did not seem very different from their neighbors. The defendants appeared to be middle-class, community-oriented employees of a political organization. They were known as activists and they made no secret of their Communist Party activities. The charges against them were outside our usual fare as well, but they sounded ominous enough to capture immediate attention and fascination. Consequently, unlike every other Smith Act experience in the country up to that time, the Philadelphia story took its own special turn.

Professor Labovitz describes the wellsprings of a radically different reaction of the Philadelphia bar to the Smith Act charges and defense, and he rightly traces it to Philadelphia's unique historic, social, religious and political currents. I admit to a twinge of nostalgia here. My recollection is that even in Philadelphia, most lawyers were caught up in the era's oppressive anti-communism and either did not care about what was happening or were afraid of being identified as counsel for communists. However, some of the Philadelphia bar did indeed see themselves as direct descendants of the "Philadelphia Lawyer," Andrew Hamilton. They felt absolutely compelled by that tradition to make certain that the Smith Act defendants would have competent and loyal counsel who were dedicated to their interests, no matter what the charges and no matter what their political creed. And after the trial, the same spirit that had prompted a defense for the communist leaders freed Philadelphia lawyers to represent other left-wing causes and clients with less restraint than they had felt earlier.

The encounter between the Smith Act lawyers and their clients could have been a classic interaction between the proletarian representatives of socialism and the petit-bourgeois protectors of capitalism. However, compelled by the influence of chief counsel Tom McBride, defendants and lawyers quickly focused on the job to be done. Getting to know one another was an on-the-job function as we worked together in research and preparations for the trial. Ultimately, initial mutual tolerance warmed into mutual respect.

Through discussions and interaction, we came to know and understand one another and gradually to respect opinions, observations, and, eventually, each other's integrity and character. The defendants reluctantly agreed not to attempt to persuade a jury that Marxism was an acceptable American alternative and that socialism was both inevitable and right for the United States. The lawyers sought education from the defendants about the early communist philosophers and the meaning of their works. We became colleagues and friends as we focused on what became the principal defense motif, the Constitution and its First Amendment.

Lawyers and defendants alike felt enormously frustrated as the prosecution's witnesses reinterpreted writings of communist theorists in accordance with the government's charges. Today we would see these government witnesses as self-discrediting, self-aggrandizing and false in the tradition of Judas Iscariot. But in 1953 they were lionized by prosecutors and congressmen and treated as darlings of a most profitable anti-communist lecture circuit. The trial was not just a trial of books, but of carefully selected phrases emphasizing inflammatory language that were meant to frighten, rather than inform, the jurors.

McCarthyism produced innumerable defendants through the machinations of the House Un-American Activities Committee, the Senate Select Committee on Government Operations, the Immigration and Naturalization Service, and numerous other organizations that actively sought out and punished left-leaning professionals and employees. These aspects of the McCarthy era caused great hardship and lasting damage to First Amendment freedoms. While this is not the place to detail the aftershocks of the Smith Act, we must remember that it has never been repealed. The beast only sleeps.

In a sound and restrained look at the Philadelphia Smith Act case, Professor Labovitz has skillfully recreated both the history and the ambience of his unique experience and has detailed a triumph of constitutional courage. In giving us an inside and close-up view of the impact of a Smith Act prosecution and by putting flesh and faces on the suffering and anxiety of defendants and their families, he has performed a great service. By keeping our memory of these frightening events fresh, we might hone our vigilance against any potential resurgence of the virulent and hysterical McCarthyism that prevailed in the '50s and '60s. The next victim could be some other unpopular philosophy.

John Rogers Carroll, Esq.

The Smith Act (Alien Registration Act of 1940)

Sec. 2(a). It shall be unlawful for any person

(1) to knowingly or willfully advocate, abet, advise, or teach the duty, necessity, desirability or propriety of overthrowing or destroying any government in the United States by force or violence, or by the assassination of any officer of any such government;

(2) with the intent to cause the overthrow or destruction of any government in the United States, to print, publish, edit, issue, circulate, sell, distribute, or publicly display any written or printed matter advocating, advising, or teaching the duty, necessity, desirability, or propriety of overthrowing or destroying any government in the United States by force and violence;

(3) to organize or help to organize any society, group, or assembly of persons who teach, advocate, or advise the destruction of any government in the United States by force or violence; or to be or become a member of, or affiliate with, any such society, group, or assembly of persons knowing the purposes thereof;

Sec. 3. It shall be unlawful for any person to attempt to commit, or to conspire to commit, any of the acts prohibited by the provisions of this title.

Sec. 5(a). Any person who violates any of the provisions of this title shall, upon conviction thereof, be fined not more than $10,000, or imprisoned for more than 10 years or both.

SETTING THE SCENE

The average price for gasoline was about 18 cents a gallon and a loaf of bread cost 20 cents that summer. For the first and only time in its history, the United States Government had just executed two convicted "spies," Ethel and Julius Rosenberg. A massive form of political and ideological repression was running rampant, conjuring up visions of communists under everyone's bed. It was called "McCarthyism," an intensively orchestrated campaign to ferret out and expose any and all forms of thought, behavior and activity deemed disloyal or subversive. And, as in all witch-hunting, it did not really matter if the so-called evidence was slight, or doubtful, or irrelevant or even downright dishonest. This was July 1953; it was a banner time in U.S. history for anti-communism. Throughout the nation, its ideological and political tactics of pursuit and abuse resulted in widespread investigations, arrests, indictments, trials and imprisonment. This book focuses on one such case: the arrests and trial in Philadelphia of nine leaders of the Communist Party. I was one of those nine men.

We were charged with having joined in a "conspiracy [two or more people making plans] to teach and advocate [presumably for others to understand] the necessity for overthrowing the Government of the United States by force and violence as soon as circumstances would permit [not at the time but at some unspecified propitious moment]."

We were accused of conspiring to violate the Smith Act of 1940, a piece of legislation that remains as one of the most terrible aggressions against the constitutionally guaranteed rights of speech and assembly in our nation's history. The Smith Act, still on the books to this day, does not explicitly ban dissident political parties. Instead, it circumvents our nation's Bill of Rights and, when implemented, it severely limits the constitutionally lawful activities in which a citizen can engage. In essence, the Smith Act makes it illegal to work peacefully within our democracy, as we in the U.S. Communist Party did, for a different set of social, economic and political relations.

The Act had already been used for several years to indict, try and convict almost 80 men and women in other cities throughout the country. Those trials had been long, complex legal, political and ideological battles between indicted communists, represented mostly by left-wing lawyers, and government attorneys with their "expert" witnesses "analyzing" tons of Marxist literature. By 1953, the protection of constitutionally guaranteed freedom of speech and assembly had become perilous. Few representatives of the legal profession would dare to undertake the defense of leaders of the Communist Party for fear of being branded themselves. But this was Philadelphia and more would be anticipated from the Cradle of American Liberty. The Philadelphia Bar Association had passed a resolution approximately six weeks before our arrests that offered support to lawyers who would represent and defend unpopular clients. Yet, despite the bar's resolution, the nine communist defendants, their wives and friends, singly and collectively found themselves unable to obtain counsel to appear in court on their behalf.

After this difficult beginning, something different did happen in Philadelphia. When, finally, the Smith Act defendants were brought into court for what was to develop into the longest criminal trial in the history of the federal courts of the Eastern District of Pennsylvania—the proceedings began on March 22, 1954, and testimony concluded on August 8th, 1954—the nine of us were represented by 11 attorneys, selected from among the most prestigious law firms in the City of Brotherly Love.

The events during the year that followed our arrests marked an important turning point in Smith Act trials, and contributed to the beginnings of the demise of McCarthyism. It was a major defense of our Constitution and its Bill of Rights.

The unique circumstances surrounding those involved in the Philadelphia Smith Act case and their struggle against the malignancy of McCarthyism have not been disclosed. Neither has the significance of this particular defense of free speech and assembly been chronicled. As the trial's sole surviving defendant in the Philadelphia area, I feel both responsible and compelled to share the story.

Following World War II, anti-communism in the United States was carefully nurtured and fanned into an unparalleled hysteria. Reaching its heights by the late 1940s, it continued to blaze for another decade. But the frenzied attack on all things "Marxist" was not limited to wholesale arrests, indictments, court trials and imprisonment of the leaders of the Communist Party. While those arrests certainly marked the period, in actuality membership or leadership in the Communist Party was never specifically prohibited by legislation. The assault was far broader. It encompassed as its victims not only those advocates of an ideology that openly challenged the wisdom of maintaining a capitalist economic and social system; it included even the minimal questioners of the status quo. The inquisitors of the time worked to have everyone believe that since Marxism consisted of a body of ideas in direct opposition to capitalism, it had to be an anti-American conspiracy concerned with and dedicated to the violent overthrow of the nation's most sacred institutions. And since some parts of the world were then led by parties claiming the development of socialist societies, any adherent or believer in socialism, anyone thought to be the least bit sympathetic to the idea, anyone remotely connected with or affected by its teachings had to be exposed. Views did not have to be current. They might have been expressed many years earlier—as responses to or opinions about such objective events as two world wars and a great depression.

During the McCarthy era, people from every walk of life were publicly "investigated" and "exposed" for their alleged beliefs or for those of a "subversive" friend, colleague, or perhaps even a distant relative. Under the pretext of protecting families, communities and the nation's security, teachers were dismissed, lawyers were disbarred, clergymen were removed from pulpits, actors were blacklisted and denied employment, scientists were refused clearance to enter their laboratories, union officers were forced to resign, workers were fired from their jobs and ordinary people were refused their right to travel abroad. Books containing questionable views were removed from library shelves and alleged "communist propaganda" films were taken out of circulation. Newspapers and periodicals from parts of the world believed to be subversive were not delivered and hosts of foreign-born Americans were threatened with revocation of citizenship and deportation.

At its peak, the phenomenon of anti-communism was so widespread that it is very difficult to fix its origins or establish culpability. However, I believe that the November 1946 Congressional election campaign is probably a good starting point. Many political analysts agree that the post-World War II economic recession and the "threat of communism" injected into that campaign by Republican Party candidates, aided and abetted by FBI Director J. Edgar Hoover, resulted in the first GOP victory since 1928. Soon thereafter, a defensive and politically astute President Truman seized upon the rhetoric of Winston Churchill's "Iron Curtain" speech, delivered in Fulton, Missouri, in March 1946. On March 12, 1947, Truman stole the thunder of the Republican Party by appearing before Congress to virtually declare war on international communism. In pursuit of what became known as the Truman Doctrine, hundreds of millions of dollars were allocated to prevent the governments of Greece and Turkey from losing control to their respective communist parties. Additional millions of dollars were spent in France, Italy and Belgium to force the communist parties of those countries out of their governments. The Doctrine's clear aim, cloaked in high-sounding moralistic phrases, was to rescue Europe from developing socialism.

Thirteen days after announcing the Truman Doctrine, the President issued Executive Order 9835. This order required loyalty oaths from two and a half million government employees. Shortly thereafter, the order was extended to include another five million in the armed forces and then to an additional five million employees of defense contractors. Year after year the numbers of secret dossiers of individuals with alleged "membership in, affiliation with, or sympathetic association with any organization, association, group, movement or combination of persons designated by the Attorney

General as subversive"[1] increased dramatically, assisted with accusations by anonymous, protected informers.

The Truman orders were the first manifestations of what was eventually to become known as McCarthyism. The frenzy that turned into hysteria reduced everything in the universe to a struggle between good and evil, where evil was defined as the Soviet Union and international communism, and good was defined as anti-communism and the United States. Its pervasiveness can be measured, in part, by the numbers summoned before investigating committees or placed under surveillance. Caught up in the fever, no one could be sufficiently anti-communist, and both Democrats and Republicans vied to outdo one another. Truman was attacked as "soft on communism" in 1946, and he struck back in 1947. By 1948, the Republican-dominated House Committee on Un-American Activities sought to "uncover communist infiltration in government" so as to explain developments in China, in Czechoslovakia and in Berlin. Everything in history was now seen in terms of American successes or defeats. The Russian explosion of an atomic bomb was not the culmination of their scientific efforts but the outcome of a betrayal of the United States by spies who stole our secrets. The Chinese overthrow of the corrupt Kuomintang government was not their achievement, but our loss, the result of a conspiracy that could have been prevented except for the role of betrayers in the State Department.[2] Senator Joseph McCarthy went so far as to charge a popular and venerated World War II hero, General George Marshall, with having "been part of a conspiracy so immense, an infamy so black, as to dwarf the history of man...a conspiracy directed to the end that we shall be contained, frustrated, and finally fall victim to Soviet intrigue within and Russian military might from without...."[3] Intimidated Secretaries of State, George Marshall and Dean Acheson were forced at times to state that the People's Republic of China would never be recognized by the United States. And in the election campaign of 1952, Eisenhower/Nixon supporters attacked Democratic presidential candidate Stevenson as, "Adlai the appeaser who got his Ph.D. from Dean Acheson's College of Cowardly Communist Containment," charging that Acheson and Truman, for political reasons, "covered up the communist conspiracy."[4]

Mushrooming like its atomic catastrophe counterpart, this deadly cloud penetrated national, state and local concerns. A peace and civil liberties event to benefit the Harlem Branch of the Civil Rights Congress was scheduled to be held in Peekskill, New York, on August 27, 1949. The popular novelist Howard Fast was to be a featured speaker, and the internationally renowned African-American, bass-baritone Paul Robeson was to appear in a concert performance. But the early arrival of a gang of brass-knuckled vigilantes, armed with rocks and clubs, broke up the planned affair. The hoodlums attacked a small group of men, women and children who had come early to prepare for what they expected would be a memorable occasion. Books were burned, cars were smashed and 13 people were seriously injured before the local police arrived on the scene.

The aborted performance was immediately given a new date, and a call went out for support. I was present on that rescheduled day, in Peekskill, New York. It was September 4, 1949, and I will never forget how ugly and cruel an aroused mob whipped into anti-communist hysteria could be. It was a day of terror.

I was the driver of one of 25 carloads coming from Philadelphia. We were responding to the call for support and demonstrating our solidarity with Robeson, Fast and Harlem's Civil Rights Congress. As I drove into the town looking for coffee, donuts and directions, I naively attributed the hostile response we received at a diner to my pre-World War II Plymouth's cargo of interracial passengers. I was hardly prepared for what was to come.

We made our way to the same dell and picnic grove, just a couple of miles outside of Peekskill, where the vigilantes had attacked eight days before. There Paul Robeson and an audience of 20,000 supporters were "protected" by several hundred trade unionists and veterans. Our arms linked, we formed a circle around the small valley and stood guard while Paul Robeson sang magnificently. When the concert ended, we were filled with a sense of strength, pride and accomplishment. We drove in procession out of the dell, onto the main road and into a vicious gauntlet from which very few of us escaped unscathed. We were trapped. Directed by the New York State Police, we were deliberately delivered into the path of hundreds of foul-mouthed stone-throwers who bashed our cars with clubs, overturning many. Close to 150 people were injured.

In other parts of the United States, mothers and grandmothers were arrested and charged with "disturbing the peace" or "inciting to riot" for circulating petitions to ban atomic weapons. In the hallowed halls of Congress, a leading McCarthyite called the Chairman of the Peace Information Center, W.E.B. DuBois, a "foreign agent" and a "Black S.O.B."

Admen were huckstering atomic bomb shelters, and schoolchildren were huddling under their desks during safety drills as alleged spies were being arrested, some convicted and two executed. To prove the reality of an "international communist conspiracy," investigating committees of all kinds subpoenaed witnesses and paid informers to testify. State and local government groups vied with national bodies for jurisdiction. Old and outdated state laws were resurrected to try and convict citizens with leftist sympathies, and imprison some for sedition. Local boards of education conducted "hearings" and dismissed hundreds of teachers who invoked their Fifth and First Amendment privileges. Universities and schools were virtually stripped of all vestiges of "liberalism." Brow-beaten and strait-jacketed, people shied away from all controversy, some even refusing to sign petitions that only carried excerpts from the American Declaration of Independence.[5] The federal government passed ponderous new legislation. The McCarran Subversive Activities Control Act of 1950 authorized the construction of internment camps, and the McCarran-Walters Immigration Act facilitated deportation procedures.

By 1953, when McCarthyism had reached its pinnacle, the hysteria had traveled full circle. The United States Attorney General, Herbert Brownell, charged the former President of the United States, Harry S. Truman, the man who had initiated the loyalty oath, with having knowingly harbored a Soviet agent, Harry Dexter White, who had died following a Congressional hearing in 1948.

That same year, the Department of Justice reached into the storage closet and trotted out the Smith Act. Officially known as the Alien Registration Act of 1940, it was enacted by Congress 18 months prior to the Japanese attack on Pearl Harbor and the U.S. entry into World War II. Passed at a time when Americans were already suspicious of most foreigners, the law was supposed to regulate the movement of aliens in our nation. Most of the Smith Act, however, has absolutely nothing to do with aliens or their registration. And its official name does not reveal its major focus, which is to limit the constitutionally guaranteed freedoms of speech and assembly. Nor does its name indicate anything about how the Act would be enforced, in the years that followed, specifically to harass and imprison members of the Communist Party and those believed to be its sympathizers.

Just how many of us were there to constitute so clear and present a danger to the security of this great nation? I recall taking part in discussions regarding the FBI's assessment of the size of the Communist Party. It was generally acknowledged that there were two peaks in party membership. The first occurred during the Great Depression in 1932, when membership was estimated at about 100,000. During the short-lived era of the Communist Political Association, near the end of World War II, the claim was that there were 80,000 members.

After the war, we often spoke of two kinds of people who would join the Communist Party. The first group joined around specific issues where there was a strong congruence with the party's position. Most of these people would leave when the specific issue or commonality in positions no longer existed. The second group, a much smaller one, joined as a result of our understanding of and commitment to socialism and believed in the party as the vehicle for its attainment. Even with both groups factored in, by 1950 there were fewer than 55,000 dues-paying members. As the party found itself engaged in more and more legal battles and as its opposition to the Korean War subjected it to even greater attacks, a heavy toll was taken. Membership fell to about 40,000 in 1951, and to 31,000 in 1952. At the time of the Philadelphia Smith Act trial, there were probably no more than 25,000 committed members left in the Communist Party of the United States. Perhaps two-thirds of that number were the "inner-party" workers who continued to function in the open. The remainder were those whose efforts would be compromised if their membership were known, because of their activities in mass and community organizations.

That's how it was during the summer of 1953.

Chapter 1

ARREST AND SURVEILLANCE

July 30, 1953.

The only relief from the blistering heat and humidity that night was the occasional breeze sifting its way onto the small front porch of the tiny row house in a crowded narrow street in Strawberry Mansion. The children were sleeping, and as my wife and I chatted with neighbors on both sides of the porch rails for several hours, I sensed a hustle and bustle in the community that was not only unusual but disquieting. I felt that something was wrong even before we made our way to bed after the 11 o'clock news. "This is it," I responded when the banging on the front door awakened us from an early deep sleep. It was 1:30 a.m., and it was the FBI.

The night was scorching and muggy. The large exhaust fan in the kitchen window pulled the steamy air through the open bedroom windows and past my naked body on the bed that sat between them.

I ran past the tiny bedroom, aware of the labored breathing of my infant son, to the bathroom next to the rear room where his six-year-old brother, exhausted from a heavy day of boxball, half-ball and step-ball, slept soundly. The towel I grabbed there was enough to permit me to respond to the persistent knocking by opening the front door without fear of an additional indictment for indecent exposure. "Sherman Marvin Labovitz, alias Sherman Marion Labovitz—you are under arrest for conspiring to violate the Smith Act."

Pauline brought down the clothing I had earlier thrown on the bedroom chair, and three FBI agents watched carefully as I buttoned my shirt and zipped up my pants. One of them, stocky, young and very angry looking, tried to prevent me from passing the few dollars from my pockets to my wife. He was admonished by a second, somewhat older agent who appeared to be in command, to "Let her take it." Along with the money went a slip of paper. On it were several names and telephone numbers I neither wanted to take with me nor have the agents see and, perhaps, add to their list of suspects. The ease with which that bit of concealment was accomplished filled me with a sense of power. I learned a lesson. The "enemy" I saw was not an infallible one. He was every bit as human as I. He, too, could err.

"Hey, you don't have to do that," I complained. "I'm not going anywhere." The angry agent manacled my wrists behind my back and shoved me into the back seat of their sedan while neighbors watched from their porches. "You bet you're not!"

The 10-minute ride into Center City seemed endless. I was a prisoner. The sedan, with no way to open its back doors from the inside, was my cell. The driver and the two who flanked me were my silent inquisitors. I could only imagine what lay ahead and I was frightened.

For those who did not directly experience or were not affected by the tenor of the times, it may be difficult to comprehend how fearful I felt. While the fate of American leftists was never that of our counterparts in other countries who opposed or were critical of their governments, many of us anticipated an American form of brutal fascist terror. My concerns on the night of my arrest were not the result of paranoia; they were rooted in my own experiences and those of friends and comrades.

It was only a few years earlier when I witnessed how easy it was for anti-communists to goad a crowd into an attack upon a street-corner speaker with whom they disagreed. I well remembered how they shouted "better dead than red" and, bent on mayhem, pushed the indignant critic from his makeshift wooden platform, chased him down the street and into Nate Auspitz's Famous Delicatessen where he was fortunate to receive the owner's protection.

I also knew what had happened to many alleged co-conspirators of mine who, while not charged in my particular indictment, had been arrested and tried earlier and were victimized while in prison. Former New York City Councilman Ben Davis was forced to mop the jailhouse floors for speaking out against racial segregation in the penal institution at Terre Haute, Indiana; National Committee and National Board member Johnny Gates was put in the hole at Attica Penitentiary for refusing to lock the cell door of other prisoners; the party's National Organization Secretary, Henry Winston, developed a brain tumor while in prison, and without proper treatment it eventually resulted in his blindness; and New York State Chairman Bob Thompson, while serving his time, had his skull cracked with an iron bar by an anti-communist zealot. Thompson's injuries resulted in his death shortly after he was released from prison.

As I sat handcuffed in the back of the car being driven by the arresting FBI agents, my mind began to race through the previous several years and my many encounters with the same kind of agents as they kept tabs on, tailed or otherwise harassed me and my family. Clearly, they had been developing a scenario for something much more dramatic.

June 1950.

Twelve quart bottles of flavored, carbonated water went into a crate. The truck I drove carried about a hundred of them inside and on top. The bottles were not disposable, and at the dozen grocery stores to which the crates were delivered, there were a similar number of "empties" waiting to be put back in and on top of the truck.

I was very tired and irritable late that summer afternoon. Having just removed and stacked all those crates of empty soda-water bottles, and after properly parking the Sheffield Bottling Co. delivery truck, I was eager to get back to Pauline and the kids. But before I could turn the ignition key of my 1941 Plymouth, I was startled by a well-dressed man rapping on the window of the passenger's side. He looked stocky, yet very trim and muscular, and his dapper suit accented very broad shoulders. He walked around to the driver's side and as I was rolling down the window, he disarmingly requested, "Sherm, can I talk with you for a minute?" In the seconds it took for me to follow him back around the car to the pavement, he opened an album he was carrying. The man then quickly turned so that I could see the photographs of several communist leaders who had forfeited bail after their convictions in the first Smith Act trial, held at Foley Square in New York City, and had "gone underground." "Do you know any of these men?" The stranger demanded. Feeling both tricked and compromised, I turned on my heel. As I moved toward my car I heard, "What's the matter, Sherm? I never thought you were yellow!" Angrily, I spun around and pointed my finger at his nose. "The day you come after me with a warrant for my arrest is the day I will talk to you."

Feeling absolutely violated, I got back in my car and drove home. I was still shaking when I sat down to dinner.

Fall, 1950.

Four women were arrested just before sunset one Friday evening. Two of them, young wives and mothers, lived within a couple of blocks of our first-floor apartment. A third lived in the apartment just above ours. The fourth was my visiting mother-in-law, Jenny. The women were charged with disorderly conduct and inciting to riot because, during the Korean War, some five years after Hiroshima and Nagasaki, they had the courage to circulate the Stockholm peace petitions.

Widespread concern that the atomic bomb might be used again resulted in several international peace conferences. More than 150 delegates from around the world met in Stockholm, Sweden, on March 15, 1950. The World Partisans of Peace asked "all peoples of good will [to] demand absolute banning of the atomic weapon [and establish] strict controls to ensure implementation [and to consider] the first government to use the atomic weapon as committing a crime against humanity and to be treated as a war criminal."

Many statesmen, scientists, Nobel prize winners, religious leaders and literary giants signed the Stockholm Peace Appeal, including George Bernard Shaw and Thomas Mann, the prime minister and cabinet of Finland, eight Catholic bishops, a former premier of Italy and a past president of Mexico. In the United States, a lifelong crusader for Black liberation, the distinguished scholar and author, Dr. William Edward Burghart DuBois, led a campaign to add to the millions of signatures collected throughout the world. For his activity "in battle for peace" (the title of one of his books), DuBois was indicted and tried for failing to register as a "foreign agent."

York Street was one of several shopping areas in Strawberry Mansion. Hundreds of people flowed daily through its stores and onto the street. It was a natural place for the four women to talk about the danger of nuclear bombs and how urgent it was to join with others throughout the world petitioning for an immediate end to the production of these weapons.

As their discussion focused on using the bomb again, this time in Korea, a local politician and private investigator felt that the four women had no right to petition in disagreement. This "patriot," a burly ex-cop, called the police precinct and, timing their arrival perfectly, proceeded to make a "citizen's arrest."

That weekend, I was the only Communist Party functionary in the city; the others were attending a conference in New York. Saturday morning we appeared in magistrate's court. Jack Zucker, on behalf of the Civil Rights Congress Bail Fund, was there, as were the husbands of the three young women, my wife and some friends. Our attorney was the indefatigable Harry Levitan.

After an uncomfortable night in the local police lock-up, the four women were brought before the sitting magistrate who held each in $5,000 bail for disposition in municipal court. We were stunned! We expected the case to be dismissed. Even if the magistrate decided to send the case to municipal court, we anticipated the total bail to be no more than a couple of hundred dollars, but $20,000? In 1950, that was approximately four times the value of the two-apartment house we shared; it was 10 times the price of a brand new Chevrolet. Harry Levitan urged that we permit him to appear in municipal court to seek a writ of habeas corpus and the reduction of bail. But it was Saturday, and that couldn't be accomplished until Monday. Nevertheless, Zucker and I agreed with Levitan and hastened to my apartment to meet and share our collective wisdom with the others.

The absolute fury of one husband at the thought of his wife spending two more nights in jail turned all of us around. We spent the next several hours supplementing the Civil Rights Congress Bail Fund with loans from families and friends. By the end of the day the four women were released. That night and all day Sunday we celebrated their freedom.

The Communist Party's district staff met every Monday at 9:00 a.m. in offices above the old Schubert Theatre, now the Merriam, at 250 South Broad Street. On this Monday the major item on the agenda had to do with why I permitted the posting of excessive bail. After a lengthy discussion, the district chairman, Ed Strong, admonished me, "It's one thing to know the right thing to do. It's still another to do it."

Despite constant pressure, the criminal justice system stonewalled for 18 months. "The Case of the Four Women" tied up $20,000 and an inordinate amount of the time and effort of many peace activists. Eventually, Harry Levitan succeeded in getting the case into the hands of a judge who was willing to move on its merits and not postpone its disposition. When Judge Levinthal finally ruled, he dismissed all charges.

August 1951.

Several hundred people, mainly Philadelphians, were gathering at a large farm some 30 miles northwest of the city for a fundraising picnic. We may have been raising money to publicize the Stockholm Peace Appeal to ban atomic weapons, or for a local election campaign. Most likely, it was to help fund the defense of Virginia's "Martinsville Seven" or Mississippi's Willie Magee—early civil rights struggles concerned with the use of phony rape charges against African-American males that prompted international protest but failed to prevent their executions.

There were about a dozen of us responsible for what we called "securing the grounds," and I was in charge. The narrow road that led into the farm was the only route for the scores of cars making the hot trip. I arrived early, about noon, and placed the others, including Jerry Marshall, in "strategic" positions around the farm grounds. After alerting them to be on the lookout for provocations, I began to circulate among the guests. Jerry was a big, strong, good-looking guy with a gift for gab, a consummate salesperson sometimes mistrusted but always available. He was a natural for the security squad, and I placed him immediately inside the picnic area just off the little road. It was relatively quiet and everyone seemed at ease when a very agitated Jerry found me.

"Sherm, FBI cars are blocking the road and preventing cars from entering," Jerry reported. "The bastards are scaring people!" We hopped into my car and quickly made our way to the problem area. Sure enough, there were two cars parked on each side of the entrance so that there was barely room for another to squeeze through. Outraged, I stopped, got out of my car and walked toward them. One driver stepped out to meet me. "You may have a right to be here, but you have absolutely no right to intimidate others," I shouted at him and pointed my finger. "Move that car off to the side." "Yes sir, captain," he responded, saluting and snapping his heels together. "Whatever you say, sir." His sarcasm was still smarting as I hopped back into my car and noticed two more cars parked one in front of the other about a hundred yards further up the road. Was it the devil or my alter-ego or was it just my impetuous, youthful bravado that took hold? The driver of the first car was leaning into the open window on the driver's side of the second car. He was unaware of my deliberate, slow approach. When I got to within 10 or 15 feet of him, I pressed heavily on the horn. The startled agent jumped and banged his head pulling it out of the window. As I moved by, I noticed that he was young, tall, slim and blond. He was glaring as he shouted an obscenity. That was all there was, but we were to meet again.

September 1951.

We lived a few short blocks from the edge of Fairmount Park. Just about every day we went there to walk, to climb the monkey bars or swing, or to play ball. Late one afternoon, my son Marc and I took a familiar but special trek on the open-air "toonerville," a trolley car that made its way deeper into the park westward across the Schuylkill River to Crystal Pool and the nearby Woodside amusement park. Marc had been described by various people as big, strong, agile, athletic, extremely active and aggressive. He was certainly all of those things, but nastier folk called him "Little Stalin." He was all of four years old. Marc was both fascinated and frightened by the "Laughing Lady" who towered ominously above the entrance to the amusement park's Haunted Castle. She was there just as she had been on each of the dozen or more earlier visits Marc had urged we make. As I finally managed to pull him from her presence, promising we would return before we left the park, I first became aware of "them." From then on, everywhere I turned they were present. Two men in suits, ties and well-shined shoes rode the merry-go-round on horses next to us, sat on the Ferris Wheel in seats above us, stared at us from across the slithering Caterpillar and sat directly behind us on the tumbling, rumbling Tornado. Making no effort to be inconspicuous, they were clearly just what they intended to be—intimidating. They were at our heels at the popcorn stand just before we were to return to the "Laughing Lady" when I "lost my cool." Taking my son in hand, I marched him before the two FBI agents announcing with all of my anger and frustration, "See these guys? They eat little children!" I hurried Marc back to the "Laughing Lady," and I've carried the shame of that confrontation ever since.

December 1951.
Mr. Barenbaum lived two doors up the street. He was old and somewhat fragile. I thought of him as warm and friendly. We always nodded at one another, even if he seemed to avoid conversation, perhaps in fear of his live-in son-in-law's wrath. Barenbaum knew that his daughter's husband was just aching to find some excuse for a fight with me. He almost succeeded following an earlier incident between our respective three-year-olds.

Old man Barenbaum was sitting on his front porch that afternoon. He watched it all. As I parked my old Plymouth in front of the house on 31st Street, the larger car that had been following me home from work pulled directly up to my rear bumper. The two agents remained in the front seat as I entered my home. Home was a first-floor apartment in a house owned by Pauline's parents. Its second-floor apartment was rented at the time by two other Communist Party activists and their three children. For "security" reasons, the husband and father was usually "unavailable." I was surprised to find him home on a conjugal visit and alarmed at what I had brought home with me. Were they there for me, or did they want him? If he was their target, how could we get him back under cover?

What the old man saw over the course of the next hour was a live comedy, at least in retrospect. Ten minutes into the hour I went back to the car. I started mine; they started theirs. I turned off the ignition, and so did they. I returned to my apartment; they waited. Ten minutes later I came out to the Plymouth and sat; they waited. I started the motor, so did they. Again I switched it off, and they did also. Then back into my apartment I went, only to repeat the procedure once more. This time, for some strange reason, I put my car into reverse gear and pushed them back a couple of feet. Remaining bumper to bumper, I turned off the motor and went to my apartment. Ten minutes later, seeing the two cars exactly as I had left them, I returned to my car and started it once more. In anticipation of their decision to ignore me on this occasion, my associate rushed out of the door and into the passenger's seat. Pulling out with only the headstart of pre-ignition, we made it to the corner, rapidly turned right and after one block, sped off left in an attempt to lose our pursuers. There was no plan for dropping my passenger, but the moment we thought we might have lost the agents, he jumped out of the car and popped into a grocery store. I cruised a bit longer and made my way home. When I got to 31st Street, a crowd had gathered across from my apartment to watch the "capture." The FBI agents had already returned to their parking place. I pulled up and waited. The crowd waited. Barenbaum waited. Nothing happened. When I finally left my car and started up the front steps, the old man smiled and raised a clenched fist in salute.

Of course, we learned to deal with "having a tail."

Using the telephone frequently became a game. Despite repeated inquiries and complaints to Ma Bell about static, noise and interrupted service, we remained convinced, her assurances to the contrary, that our telephone lines were illegally tapped. Often the sounds were such that we were certain there were live ears listening. On many occasions our displeasure with wire tapping was marked by some kind of announcement to show our disdain for the eavesdropper. And just as frequently, prior to any conversation, these announcements would be followed with devices meant to be distracting—the rapid clacking of the dial system or the ear-piercing squeal that could be produced by putting together the mouthpiece and receiver of an old-fashioned stand-up telephone.

I recall how we dealt with some news that our corner grocer told us. He had observed that each week on trash pickup day, before the regular city collectors arrived, a special truck would park in front of his store. Its two occupants walked the 50 yards to our house, picked up our trash and took it to the front cab of their vehicle. The regular trash collector's wife and I had worked together on a community project, so I called her for a confirmation. After hearing her tell essentially the same story as had our grocer, I subsequently made certain that the trash we put out for collection every Tuesday morning contained the contents of our infant son's diapers.

July 31, 1953.

My FBI captors had turned right at the corner onto Sedgley Avenue and right again on Montgomery Avenue to 33rd Street and the park. Turning left and south we headed for the Parkway. It was approximately 2:00 a.m. and the usually busy streets were deserted. I was frightened. I gained some strength from knowing there would be others, that my wife, Pauline, was strong and that she and my two children would have support. But the dead silence—the arresting agents said nothing—seemed especially ominous to me.

Where was I being taken? Would Pauline or anyone else be told? Would I be roughed up, tortured, perhaps even "accidentally" killed? The questions swirled around me as we approached Center City.

The offices of the Federal Bureau of Investigation were on one of the upper floors of the Widener Building, and as I was escorted off the elevator through a corridor and into an office for questioning, the atmosphere resembled an Alfred Hitchcock movie set. The office was unusually large, perhaps 25 feet square. It was dimly lit and sparsely furnished. Windows, drapes opened so that the Center City lights were visible, took up the entire wall that I faced as I entered. A large desk was centered about five feet in front of the windows. In the middle of the room and facing the desk was a hard-backed chair to which I was directed. Behind the desk and looking out of the windows, almost hidden in the shadows, was the third FBI agent. The two arresting agents left the room, leaving still a fourth to close the door.

The next minutes seemed interminable. But then the agent in the shadow of the street lights turned slowly and could be better seen. He looked muscular and trim; he had broad shoulders and, despite the early morning hour, he appeared dapper. "Well, Sherm, I have that warrant you told me to get. You ready to talk to me now?" I told him I had nothing to say and asked for a glass of water. "Get Sherm a glass of water," he called out to the agent at the door behind me. A tall, slim blond crossed the room in front of me commenting, "After what he did to me at that picnic?" When he brought the glass of water, I hesitated. There was reason to mistrust these two men; I had encountered them before. The agent by the desk was the man who had accosted me as I finished unloading bottles that hot summer afternoon. The tall, slim blond had been the unwelcome visitor to our farm picnic.

I did not drink the water they brought me. I very carefully wet my lips.

Chapter 2

LOCKED UP

Shortly after their unsuccessful attempts at interrogation, the two FBI agents ushered me into a larger and considerably busier room—much like in scenes from *Law and Order* and *N.Y.P.D. Blue*—bright, unshaded overhead lights, many more hard-backed chairs next to flat-topped desks upon which sat black telephones, and lots of agents with their respective prisoners, my friends and comrades: Tom Nabried, who was picked up around midnight in North Philadelphia as he was approaching his apartment; Ben Weiss, who was about to unlock his car door in order to retrieve a newspaper he wanted to read in bed; Walter Lowenfels and Dave Davis, who had been, as I was, in their respective beds sleeping soundly; and Joe Kuzma, who was leaving a house in the West Mt. Airy section of the city where he had stayed late for tea, cookies and a game of cribbage after a guest appearance at a party club meeting. Each was at one of the desks and flanked by FBI agents.

By now, it was somewhere between 3:00 and 3:30 a.m. and I was told that I could make one phone call. Since my wife already knew what was happening, I satisfied an urgent need to reach out to my mother and brothers by calling the family's cornerstone, my brother Abe. I remember the 30 seconds of startled, absolute silence before one of the agents abruptly ended the call and handcuffed me to Joe Kuzma.

Joe had grown up in the heart of the Allentown/Bethlehem steel area of Pennsylvania. While he had gone to work at an early age in the fur industry, he eventually ended up working in the mammoth Bethlehem Steel plant. Kuzma joined the Communist Party in late 1935, and remained an active trade unionist. From 1941 until 1946, Joe served as an executive officer in the United Steel Worker's Union. In 1946, he turned to full-time party activities and took on many leadership positions. At the time of our arrests, Kuzma was the District Trade Union Secretary. Despite an imposing stature and appearance, Joe was quiet and reserved, difficult to engage in conversation, seemingly uninterested in cultural happenings and not given to speechmaking, either in intimate or public settings. Joe loved to go fishing and was a very private family man. Married to an equally stoic wife, he had a six-year-old daughter and a 10-year-old son. Joe Kuzma was "all business"—hard-working and dedicated.

Handcuffed together in pairs—Joe Kuzma to me, Tom Nabried to Walter Lowenfels and Ben Weiss to Dave Davis—we were shuttled a few short blocks from the FBI headquarters in the Widener Building to 8th and Chestnut Streets, where the Federal Court Building was then located. There, during the early-morning hours of our arrests, the first six of us were brought, without counsel, for a preliminary arraignment and bail hearing. Chick Katz, Bob Klonsky and Joe Roberts, arrested elsewhere over the next several days, were not present at that first hearing.

It was now close to 4:00 a.m. and we were thoroughly exhausted as the "hearing" in the Federal Court Building began. There, and apparently just out of bed and disheveled, the Acting United States District Attorney, Joseph Hildenberger, told the United States Commissioner, Henry Carr, that we were "the hub from which all Communist Party activities stem." And, lying: "these men came out [from underground] tonight and we were in a position to arrest them."[1] He went through the rest of the motions I was too tired and confused to understand, except that it meant a preposterously high bail and imprisonment. The hearing was short; it was not sweet.

Now that this second traumatic event of the morning was completed, we were rapidly transported to the holding cells in "Moco," the Moyamensing County Prison in South Philadelphia. For the next several hours, I shared the filthy concrete floor of a large prison cell with my co-defendant Dave Davis and a dozen or so men who had been arrested for armed robbery, assault and battery, car theft and drunk and disorderly conduct. In the following mid-afternoon, nearly 15 hours after my arrest, the six of us defendants were transferred to Holmesburg Prison.

Dave Davis was married to Sophie and they had two teenaged sons. A feisty five feet two inches tall, weighing no more than 120 pounds, Dave was a fiery orator and activist, a prominent trade unionist and a nationally known figure. He was the long-time leader of Local 155, United Electrical, Radio and Machine Workers Union, lovingly remembered for such malapropisms as "Careful, you'll stand out like a sore thorn." He was also considerably older than I, and I'll always remember how concerned and caring he was about my well-being during those fretfully uncomfortable hours at Moyamensing, even though Dave's intestines were every bit as active as mine.

Holmesburg Prison sits like an impenetrable fortress just off Interstate 95 in Northeast Philadelphia. Its tall, brownstone walls are topped with barbed wire and spotted every 30 to 40 feet by guard towers. It can't be missed, and in the literally hundreds of times I have passed it since my relatively brief stay there in 1953, I have never been able to ignore it. While the incidents I recall, and sometimes relate to others, are not necessarily all that frightening, each time I see those huge stone walls and guard towers, I automatically react by pressing my foot harder on the accelerator to quickly erase the fear awakened by this grim reminder of freedom lost.

There was no Interstate 95 through Philadelphia in July 1953. The stifling sheriff's van that carried the six of us from South Philly to the Far Northeast took the 50-minute trip along the only route those of us who knew the city traffic would travel. We went the working-class, ethnic enclave route: north on Delaware Avenue, passing the many piers; through Irish East Kensington into Polish Port Richmond; continuing north on Richmond Street to the Frankford Arsenal; and then northeast on State Road through German Wissinoming, Italian Tacony and Lower Mayfair; and finally into a small, old African-American section of Holmesburg. I remember my fear being mitigated by my certainty that the people of these communities would support my First Amendment rights and reject McCarthyism. I also naively saw them adopting my Marxist-inspired vision of a world at peace, equitably distributing its resources to each according to need.

Suddenly, there it was; not the least bit different from the way I always knew it—Holmesburg Prison. For seven years, I had lived in its shadow, no more than three miles away, and could tell some of its stories about how guards regularly poured scalding steam into the cells of "unruly" convicts; how the fabled bank robber and safe-cracker, Willie Sutton, had dug a tunnel and escaped. I had passed its ominous walls frequently, never thinking that a day might come when I would be one of its occupants.

It felt like the van carrying us had been swallowed as the gates behind lowered and closed. But almost immediately there was the reality of the burly prison guard who announced to us loudly and clearly, "If I had been driving the fucking van, I'd have backed it up and dumped every one of you communist sons of bitches into the river. This fucking jail is too good for the likes of you bastards." As he was taking roll call, the guard mispronounced my name. I corrected him. An alarmed and knowing headshake from one of the inmate trustees seemed to be telling me not to be baited. The guard deliberately continued the mispronunciation looking for further reactions. When he got no second response from me, he began a tirade about names and numbers that suggested I had no name at Holmesburg. His rage appeared just under control, but about to explode, prompting a second guard to prevail upon him to leave the area. I never saw him again.

After all personal items were taken from me, I was ushered into a de-lousing shower and issued prison garb with such minor inconveniences as lace-up shoes without laces and wide-waisted trousers with neither suspenders nor a belt. I've remained skeptical ever since about the authenticity of newspaper reports of prisoners committing suicide by hanging themselves in their cells.

Three additional co-defendants were soon to join the six of us. On the day after we got to Holmesburg, Chick Katz and Joe Roberts were arrested together, getting out of Joe's car in Atlantic City. Several days later, Bob Klonsky was picked up in Brighton, Massachusetts.

Irvin "Chick" Katz grew up in a family seriously victimized by the Great Depression. A 13-year-old participant in the 1930 Hunger March on Washington, he soon thereafter helped with organizing unemployed councils in his South Philadelphia community. Becoming a student affairs leader and one of the founders of the National Student League, his anti-fascist activities led to an expulsion from high school to which he was reinstated following a student strike that supported him. To help his family, Chickie left school to go to work when he was 16. His working-class and anti-fascist feelings never waned; in fact, they were enlivened by marriage and parenthood. At the time of our arrests, Chick and his wife, Vi, had two daughters, 12 and eight, and a six-year-old son.

Joe Roberts came to Philadelphia early in 1953, to work as the party district's new organizer and chairperson. He was 44 and married to Barbara, who had a six-year-old daughter. Together they had a four-year-old son. Born in the Soviet Union, Joe had become a U.S. citizen in 1931, and for many years was active in the needle trades industry and in the Garment Workers' Union. Subsequently, he became chairperson of the Communist Party in Connecticut and then took on a national task as general manager of the *Daily & Sunday Worker*. At the time, I functioned in a similar capacity in Philadelphia. Joe Roberts was like two different people. In social situations he was loads of fun. He had a Russian love for wine, women and song. Easy-going and seemingly untroubled, his was a free spirit, laughter-filled. Joe's home was always open for a good party. However, in official Communist Party situations that involved policy and decision-making, Joe's countenance changed dramatically and instantaneously. His jaw would tighten, his lips would purse, his eyelids would droop and partially cover a fixed and glazed stare. Appearing as if he was about to deliver himself of something deep and mysterious, he took on an altogether different personality. But when the issue at hand came to a closure, Joe could just as quickly flip into the soul of celebration.

Bob Klonsky was one of several people sent from New York City between 1946 and 1950 to provide leadership to a factionalized Philadelphia Communist Party. When Bob became the party's organizational secretary, late in 1947, it was tantamount to becoming number two in the party hierarchy. He was only about 28 at the time, but he already had impressive credentials. He had participated in labor organizing; he was a veteran of World War II, and even earlier, a very young volunteer in the Abraham Lincoln Brigade during the Spanish Civil War. He and his wife, Helen, already had one four-year-old son, and not too long thereafter a second son was born. One always took notice of Bob. He was bald; he had no eyebrows or eyelashes or any other hair that was visible; he looked extremely strong and he was strikingly charismatic. Bob needed and surrounded himself with people and constantly entertained, singing with gusto in a deep and resonant voice, dancing with flourish and in grand style. Initially, his sharp and droll sense of humor, his creative imagination and his flare for speaking and writing served him well as the "Org. Sect." As the months became more trying and the tasks more difficult and exasperating, functioning in a position that placed him closest to the party "rank and file" leadership, Klonsky developed a reputation as an organizer who was tough, sometimes "insensitive" and, on occasion, even "ruthless."

The anti-communist hysteria in our nation at that time dictated that our group of defendants was so dangerous that we had to be isolated and placed in the most security-controlled corridor cell block of Holmesburg Prison. This corridor had individual isolation cells. Each was approximately 10 feet long and eight feet wide. My cell had a skylight centered at the back of a 12-foot ceiling. It also had a single cot at one wall upon which I slept after "lights out," but was not permitted to rest upon after the early morning wake-up whistles. Immediately to the left of my cell door sat a well-stained commode and next to it a tiny sink. Along the wall opposite the cot was a spoked wooden chair and a small desk/table with two drawers for personal items.

There were approximately 15 of these individual cells on each side of the isolation block. They were staggered so that a prisoner, looking out of the barred open window of his solid metal cell door, saw nothing directly in front of him. The two prisoners on the opposite side of the corridor, in cells at 45-degree angles to the right and left, would be visible only if each came to his respective barred window and provided the window was, in fact, open. The windows could be shut solidly from the corridor if the authorities desired to isolate any individual prisoner.

Entry into our corridor came from a large circular hub that housed the guard station and communication system of the prison and from which emanated all of the other cell blocks like spokes of a huge wheel. The inmates in the cells closest to the hub on both sides of our isolation block were considered to be the prison's most dangerous. At the time of our incarceration, our immediate neighbors included a notorious escape artist, a convicted hatchet-killer and several other alleged murderers awaiting trial. Among the latter was Aaron "Tree-Top" Turner, whose case had received much local publicity. The cells at the far end of the isolation block were used to "protect" a dozen or so Black homosexuals among whom were also the block's trustees. The nine of us were in individual cells next to and across from each other but directly in the middle of this long corridor. We occupied about one-third of the isolation block as we separated the two groups described above. If I looked out of my cell, while unable to see either Joe Kuzma on my right or Chick Katz on my left, I could speak with them. And if I looked across the corridor at the proper angles, I could see both Ben Weiss and Walter Lowenfels and hear them as well. Fortuitously, because my cell was at the very center, I became the conduit for communication from the guards and among the defendants. In turn, I became their spokesperson.

Charged but not yet indicted, unconvicted and awaiting release on bail for trial, we were nine married men without criminal records. Eight of us had two or more children. Seven of us had lived our entire lives, except for military service, in the Philadelphia region, and six of us were owners of our own homes.

Walter Lowenfels had a small country cottage in Little Egg Harbor Township, New Jersey, some 45 miles southeast and 60 minutes from

Philadelphia. He was there with his wife, Lillian, on the night of our arrests, recuperating from one of his bouts with angina. The FBI waited until near midnight before they got him out of bed, handcuffed him and drove him to their Philadelphia headquarters.

Walter was not exactly the typical defendant in a Smith Act case. A poet, he was the first American writer to be indicted under a thought-control act in Philadelphia since the indictment of a descendant of Patrick Henry. In June 1918, John Reed, one of the founders of the Communist Party of the United States, a journalist and author of *Ten Days That Shook the World*, was charged with "inciting to seditious remarks" when he spoke in opposition to World War I at a meeting in the City of Brotherly Love.

Walter was exactly twice my age and had beautiful daughters almost as old as I. He was tall, dark, stoop-shouldered, wore his thick glasses low on his nose and said that he enjoyed an occasional nip of alcohol for medicinal purposes. Walter also had a heavy moustache, sported a beret and looked like a French artist caricature, an affect undoubtedly assumed in the Twenties when, as a young, socially conscious poet, he disassociated himself from his family's Louella Butter Co. fortune and became an expatriate around Montparnasse.

We made national news! A picture of me handcuffed with Joe Kuzma appeared on the front page of the *New York Times*. The caption beneath the picture read, "Sherman Labovitz, left, and Joseph Kuzma, who were among six alleged Communists arrested yesterday in Philadelphia on charges of conspiring to overthrow the United States Government." Perhaps to be certain that readers understood the sinister nature of that conspiracy, the covering story made reference to "force and violence" several times and to a "series of midnight raids" that "netted" the defendants.

The first real notion we had of what the world was being told of us came shortly after a trustee put his head at my window and said, "You guys must be real big shots, real important—making all those waves. You're all over the papers." And then, not waiting for a response, he asked, "What do you need? What do you want? I'll get 'em for you and you'll get 'em back to me when you get your commissary." The few dollars I had when arrested had been put into an account in my name at the prison commissary. I would be permitted to order toiletries and available sundries for delivery by trustees. Very warily I told the man that I could use a bar of soap, some toothpaste, a toothbrush and a razor. Then I added, "Not really all that important, but I'd like to see those papers," to which he responded, "Can't do that...told not to give you anything to read...see you later." On the tray he passed through my window at lunchtime were the toilet articles I requested plus rolled up copies of the *Philadelphia Inquirer*, the *Bulletin* and the *Daily News*.

The *Daily News* carried the screaming headline, "BAIL SET FOR 6 REDS SEIZED BY FBI." Beneath the headline was a large picture of the six of us. The story on page three described Kuzma as "the chief" and the rest of us as his "five lieutenants." So that readers really got the message, the

Philadelphia Inquirer arranged its headline and sublines to read: "FBI SEIZES SIX PHILADELPHIA RED LEADERS; ONE ARRESTED AFTER SECRET PARTY SESSION; ACCUSED OF PLOTTING OVERTHROW OF U.S. GOVERNMENT BY FORCE AND VIOLENCE."

The next day, the Philadelphia *Evening Bulletin's* front page announced, "2 MORE SEIZED IN RED ROUNDUP." The headline referred to the arrest of Chick Katz and Joe Roberts. The news story quoted U.S. Attorney Hildenberger telling Commissioner Carr: "These men are as important as the men we arrested yesterday. It is important that bail be high." The story also emphasized an alleged use of aliases by the defendants. Even though, many years earlier, Joe Roberts and Dave Davis had legally changed their names, the article referred to them as "formerly Samuel Gobeloff and formerly David Dubensky."[2]

The *Evening Bulletin* also ran another story which was headlined, "RED CONSPIRACY AIMS AT COURTS, BROWNELL SAYS." The story covered a dinner meeting of the Philadelphia Bar Association that, coincidentally, was being held just as we were learning how difficult it was to find attorneys willing to represent us. At the dinner meeting, the United States Attorney General, Herbert Brownell, told an audience of several hundred lawyers and their guests that the communists were "no fly-by-night program"; they were instead "members of a closely knit, highly disciplined conspiracy attempting to turn our legal process into a three-ring circus in an effort to bring our judicial system into disrepute."[3]

I read those reports and considerably more news aloud during the first few days of our incarceration, and I don't know if I was ignored or just not heard by the guards. In any event, there was absolutely no attempt to prevent me from fully appreciating and making good use of the special kind of acoustics that our isolation cell block produced.

Chapter 3

IN PRIJON AND OUT

We needed $350,000—in today's terms that would be like asking us to post nearly $2,250,000—in order to get out of Holmesburg Prison. Until we were out, we would be in no position to help search for counsel or plan our defense.

The government clearly wanted it that way, and apparently that message went out to Philadelphia's bail bondsmen. Not one of them would touch us. And contrary to a popular myth prevalent at the time, subscribed to even by one of my own brothers, no one I knew was aware of any "Moscow gold" around to bail us out. While we were marking time behind bars during August 1953, even the short-lived Civil Rights Congress Bail Fund, so successful for a few short years in guaranteeing bail for persecuted "reds" and Blacks, was for all intents and purposes being destroyed by government challenges and attacks. Cash, ranging from dollar bills to life savings, would have to be borrowed from friends, relatives and sympathizers in order to secure our release.

While the top leadership of the Philadelphia Communist Party sat in prison, a significant conflict regarding strategy erupted in the party around the inordinate amount of bail being demanded. "Get them out in a hurry! No bail is too high," clamored William Patterson, the National Executive Director of the Civil Rights Congress. He was seconded by Arnold Johnson, a member of the National Committee of the Communist Party and its legislative director, and Frank Donner, a New York attorney with previous Smith Act experience. "They are needed to lead a defense of the Party." But, fortuitously, none from within the group we referred to as "mass organization workers" was among those arrested in Philadelphia.

Jack Zucker, Executive Director of the Philadelphia Civil Rights Congress, was working with another longtime communist leader of the Jewish Peoples' Fraternal Order, Sol Rotenberg. They wanted to link attempts to reduce bail to an all-out effort to secure proper legal representation for the defendants, and, according to Zucker, to tie those two issues to the "defense of civil liberties and constitutional rights." Rotenberg and Zucker decided to resist pressures from the national offices to secure our speedy release.

It was Rotenberg's brilliant idea that the best tactic to employ would be to *delay* the posting of *any* bail for the immediate release of any of the defendants. Instead, he proposed that our wives "set about doing the leg work" that would be required, in an attempt to get Philadelphia's legal community, in particular the Philadelphia Bar Association, involved in providing us with counsel that would be able to secure our release on reasonable bail.

In the meantime, as lunches were being delivered back in our cells at Holmesburg, the trustee continued to put Philadelphia's three daily newspapers on the tray he passed through the window of my barred door. I, in turn, continued to select stories and read them aloud. This became an early afternoon ritual during our quarantine period that was subsequently extended to song. But that is another story I promise to tell a bit later on.

Much more than newspapers, what we all craved was news from home. On August 6, 1953, one week after my arrest, my wife Pauline wrote to me, "It's very early in the morning. I'm due to go out again...the conference [on bail] last night was serious and level-headed....The wives got together afterward to discuss which lawyers we are to visit today. We plan to see the most prominent lawyers in the city...."

What Pauline had written was confirmed by Vi Katz, my co-defendant Chick's wife. When I interviewed her during October 1990, she told me, "At the beginning, the raising of bail and securing of counsel did not go well....Things started to straighten away when it was insisted that the job was not for the left or left attorneys, but that it was America's problem, not ours alone." Saul Waldbaum and Harry Levitan, two prominent civil liberties lawyers previously identified with left-wing issues, agreed that "an outstanding lawyer who could not be intimidated by the court or frightened by the press" should be found to take the case.[1] Waldbaum recalled, "I told them to go to the bar association. I felt that the Philadelphia Bar Association as I knew its traditions...might very well do something."[2] Pressure from the national offices of the Communist Party and the Civil Rights Congress to "get them out on bail immediately" continued to be resisted by the local leaders left to secure our release. They believed that an attempt should be made to turn the Philadelphia Smith Act trial into as broad a defense of civil liberties as possible instead of a defense of and platform for party principles. The defendants' wives, who were deeply involved in the discussions and planning, concurred. In their few brief visits, they listened to our questions and kept us apprised. And as they tirelessly threw themselves into the tedious task of "reaching out," our wives also reached us with their confidence in, and commitment to, the strategy and tactics being employed.

When the nine of us finally met, during our first yard-exercise time after an extended "quarantine" period in our cells, the process was well under way and, with little reservation, we found ourselves in agreement. We also decided that we would determine the order of our own releases. Whatever questions remained among us could be put aside until we were all out of prison on bail—whenever that might be. The process proceeded with no further pressure from the national offices of either the Civil Rights Congress or the Communist Party.

The guard I saw the most was young, tall and blond. Thinking him an "Aryan type," I was consequently surprised at his lack of open hostility. After about two weeks I asked him when we would be allowed to go into one of the yards outside. He said we had to complete quarantine. When I asked when that would be, he said he would check. The next day, for the first time, the nine of us were taken from our cells into an adjoining yard and left alone. Hardly a moment had passed when three or four small black handballs came sailing over the stone walls from elsewhere into our yard. Word had apparently reached other prisoners that the communists were outside. For that brief instant I felt both welcomed and appreciated. I beat Joe Kuzma in a couple of games of handball, and learned from him how he kept moving his chair in his cell as he chased the few rays of sun shining through the skylight.

On the way back to the cells, pleased and somewhat taken with the probability that my intervention resulted in the day's yard time, I asked the guard how come we were alone. "When will we have a recreation period in the yard with other prisoners?" I don't know if he was threatening or just warning me when he answered, "Let well enough be. There are some very patriotic cons here who wouldn't think twice about using a 'shiv' on you." I was pleased to be at the cell door with no time left for bravura.

As the door slammed shut, the guard offered me an alternative diversion: a job. In addition to yard time the next day, my co-defendents and I were given the opportunity to pick off the ends of bushels of green beans and break each bean in half. The task kept the nine of us sitting on stools outside our cell doors for several hours. We compared notes of visits and letters from our wives.

At the same time that I received the letter from Pauline, Chick Katz heard from his wife Vi: "I am out of the house every morning by 8:30...seeing the best, the cream of Philadelphia lawyers. Our onslaught on the bar association precedes us, and the top Philadelphia lawyers know they are dealing with wives who are proud of their husbands who have done nothing wrong and want them OUT...the bail fight is beginning, and there's a long pull ahead."

Vi Katz remembered three of those visits when I interviewed her in October 1990: "One was to the sumptuous offices of a big shot in Philly's Board of Education. I can't remember his name, I had no appointment. I just popped in. His secretary was curt and rude, but let him know that I was there and was surprised when he came out of his office to greet me. Of course, he had all kinds of reasons why he shouldn't take the case....I had an appointment with a well-known politician and city solicitor who said he had begun to think he was slipping because he hadn't been contacted earlier. You know, he wasn't interested....And, I saw one lecherous old S.O.B. who professed sympathy for our situation, and when he escorted me to the elevator, startled me by suddenly planting a wet and mushy kiss full on my lips."

On occasion, our breakfasts included a couple of tablespoons of peanut butter. Everybody knew that I had a passion for peanut butter. Soon the trustee who brought me things from the commissary also brought the globs of peanut butter sent by my colleagues and co-defendants, enough to make the many sandwiches I carefully stacked for final bedtime snacks or "bad times" ahead. The trustee—young, Black and gay—began stopping at my cell door a bit more frequently to chat. Bars always separated us. He had been thoughtful, sensitive to my naiveté about prison life, certainly helpful and had not even requested, let alone demanded, anything in return. On one visit he asked quietly, "Do you love me?" Somewhat surprised by the question, but not in the least at a loss for words, I responded affirmatively, and launched into a long lecture about my love for all mankind and the connection that love had with my commitment to socialism and my prison predicament. I recall he was a good listener. He had nothing more to say!

Every night, sometime after "lights out," sensuous whisperings that evolved into comprehensible love talk could be heard from the cells of the gay prisoners at the rear of our corridor. Jamie, at his cell door's barred window, was flirting with the others. And each night the same jealous lover's voice would also be heard, at first a repeating plaintive plea but eventually angry, screaming and demanding, "Jamie, get away from that door!" Expecting the same performance as lights went out on still another night, Chick Katz, a one-time fruit huckster, shouted at the top of his lungs, "Sherm, gay avec fun der tir." (A literal Yiddish translation of what we had been anticipating—"Get away from that door.") I recall how funny we all found that to be and what comic relief it provided at the time. In retrospect, and with eyes much older and wiser, I see the sadness more than the humor.

From prison, Chick wrote to his three children: "I am proud to write from here because I am fighting for what is best...You may have a little trouble understanding how people can be put in jail for doing what is best...I believe it is wrong for rich men to get richer off the blood of poor men! I believe it is wrong for so many young American boys to have to die in Korea or some other place so that men who own the factories that make guns and planes and tanks can get rich. These same men are rich enough to tell many of the people who run the government what to do. So they arrest people like your Daddy. That is the reason I am not ashamed to write to my darling children from prison....Be a help and comfort to your mother until I get home....You all know how much I love you and miss you. Save up lots of hugs and kisses for me."

The Chancellor of the Philadelphia Bar Association, Bernard Segal, was well aware of our inability to procure counsel of our choosing. By the time Ben Weiss' wife, Helen, visited him on August 7, and asked him in writing two days later to intervene, Segal had already been advised that one law firm, after initially accepting, had returned a retainer. In addition, he knew of the great number of attorneys who were unwilling to represent us even at the bail proceedings. Segal had heard the concerns of the bar association's Civil Rights Committee Chairman, James Brittain, who had also been visited by Helen Weiss and my wife, and who had been asked personally to take the case. In addition, Chancellor Segal had reason to believe that some Philadelphia lawyers, like Robert N.C. Nix and Bernard Cohn, would serve if sanctioned by the bar association.[3] In fact, a very interested Tom McBride, one of the city's best-known criminal defense lawyers, was already Segal's top candidate for the job. McBride was not, however, in the best of health and would need support for what promised to be a long and arduous trial.[4]

At the request of Chancellor Segal, James Brittain convened a meeting of the bar association's Committee on Civil Rights.[5] According to a formal statement issued immediately thereafter, in addition to members of the committee, those present included the Chancellor, Vice Chancellor C. Brewster Rhodes and Walter E. Allesandroni, Chairman of the bar association's Board of Governors. The statement noted the inability of the defendants to obtain counsel, and that "the defendants urged in court that if they were released on bail they would be in a position to secure counsel...and make proper provisions for their defense." The statement also indicated that the highly respected Thomas D. McBride, Chairman of the bar's Committee on Criminal Justice and Law Enforcement, and by all accounts "one of Philadelphia's two leading criminal defense attorneys," would be willing to appear at the bail-reduction hearing. The statement went on to say, "Should it develop any time in the future that any of the defendants are unable to secure counsel, the committee will meet promptly to review the situation." The statement ended with the complete text of a bar association resolution affirming a right to counsel for unpopular defendants.

By August 10th, various imperatives seemed to be coming together. Our arraignment had already been postponed several times because we could not meet the bail demands and, consequently, could not help in the selection of counsel. The direction taken by our wives to visit the city's most prominent attorneys in an unrelenting search for competent counsel had not as yet overcome the fear of Philadelphia's lawyers. The resultant discomfort of the court, as well as the embarrassment of the Philadelphia branch of the ACLU and the Philadelphia Bar Association, culminated in a special bail-reduction hearing before Judge Alan Grim on August 12th. We were represented by Tom McBride, together with a former Philadelphia City Solicitor, Joseph Sharfsin, and a prominent member of the Society of Friends, William Woolston. In 1951, Woolston had been appointed as a Special Assistant District Attorney to head the grand jury probe of graft and corruption in Philadelphia. At the conclusion of the hearing, Judge Grim reduced the required bail to $25,000 each for five of the defendants and to $10,000 each for me and the remaining three. Even those significantly reduced amounts were staggering in 1953, when $60 was considered to be a decent weekly wage, when full-time Communist Party workers in Philadelphia earned $35 to $40 a week, and when 15 cents could purchase two rides on the Philadelphia Rapid Transit system or a gallon of gasoline.

On August 12th, Pauline wrote, "I received your letter and glowed....I've done nothing in comparison with what must be done. What was done [bail reduction] was due to the fact that the wives worked together, shirking at nothing and tirelessly responding to the need of the moment." On that same day, Vi Katz wrote to Chick: "Where does an ordinary working person get $10,000? Yesterday, three Philadelphia contractors were released on $1,000. But they only robbed the city of $250,000...building defective playgrounds. Possible injuries to children and robbing citizens of our city are considered minor crimes. Bondsmen fall all over themselves in their rush to post bail on thieves and human leeches, but it has been impossible to find one [bondsman] in this city to post bail for decent people being framed on phony political charges."

Unlike today's prevalent practice, we could not be released by posting one-tenth of the bail demand in cash. Back then the full amount had to be produced. But with the court-directed reduction came another concession. Philadelphia's Civil Rights Congress Bail Fund, still in existence although lacking in funds, had established a precedent in a couple of cases whereby the courts accepted property in lieu of cash for bail. The court now agreed that property would be accepted at its assessed value for tax purposes, less any outstanding encumbrances or mortgages. Most people I knew who "owned" their houses had mortgages in excess of the assessed value. For example, my house in the Strawberry Mansion section was worth about $5000, but it was assessed for tax purposes at only $2800. Because my mortgage was more than $3500, the house could not be offered for bail purposes. The court's ruling did, however, make it possible for a few more people to offer very tangible support. Subsequently, as each defendant was released, one or more homes went into his "making bail."

Besides acting as ombudsman for the defendants to the guards, I sang. Ever since I was an adolescent, there was always someone to encourage me to sing. One newspaper account of my arrest made reference to an alleged alias, Lee Sherman. It was never an alias. It was part of a dream that I shared with teenage peers—if I got to sing professionally, Lee Sherman was to be my stage name—and it was a piece of useless information the FBI dug up that helped them to create for me the image of a mysterious, dangerous, alias-using subversive.

While reading the newspapers aloud for the other defendants, I found myself fascinated by the wonderful acoustics in the prison corridor, and I tried a song. As anticipated, there were requests for another and, as the days passed, a lunchtime followed by my reading and singing became the routine. On one particular day, however, my "vast" reservoir of folksongs, worksongs, popular blues and ballads was being emptied. My repertoire had been tapped that day, not only by requests from my codefendants, but from inmates at both far ends of the corridor, who shouted out the names of songs they wanted sung. I was, of course, obliging. In fact, I was delighted! Taking advantage of the resounding resonance of prison walls, my voice grew with each request, and I became oblivious of all but its sound.

Suddenly, the tall, blond guard's back was at the barred window of my cell door, and he shouted, "If whoever that is doesn't turn it off, I'll shut the door." It was a solid iron door to which he referred, and his threat ended my lengthy recital. I learned later from my colleagues how neither his earlier demands to "tone it down," nor their warnings that he was slowly moving up the corridor for a confrontation, were heard by me as I was carried away by the mellifluous tones of my last encore.

Shortly after the hearing that did result in a modest reduction in bail, Tom Nabried was the first of the defendants to be released. A child of former slaves, Tom was born in Georgia at the turn of the century. He started school in Augusta and, after moving to Philadelphia at an early age, attended night sessions of a grade school. He joined the Industrial Workers of the World in 1919, became a building trades laborer and helped organize the Lathers' Union in 1928. After joining the Communist Party, Tom visited the Soviet Union in 1933, where he attended the Lenin Institute. He also played a role in the beginnings of Philadelphia's Butcher Workers' and Longshoremen's Unions. When we were arrested, Tom lived in the Northern Liberties section of Philadelphia with his wife, Gladys.

Tom was tall, very dark and handsome. Always immaculately dressed, he was the epitome of a proud, dignified and deeply respected community and party leader. His appearance was matched by a soft-spoken eloquence. Once, during a heated party meeting, a local leader was charged with "white chauvinism" for having employed a Black female domestic worker. Tom silenced the accusers by asking, "Would you now deny Negro women just about their sole source of legitimate income?" The quiet, informed power of his bearing immediately engaged and captured his audiences, whether at a small club meeting or in a classroom, at a street-corner demonstration or in a large auditorium. But Tom was his absolute best in personal discussions. We all loved him.

For the rest of us left in prison, there was precious little to occupy our time. Except for those green beans we cracked, there was nothing but voracious reading of whatever old magazines or religious tracts still remained on the traveling library cart a trustee pushed through the corridor once each week. I did manage to find on that jailhouse "Parnassus on Wheels" a copy of Fulton Oursler's huge representation of The Old Testament, *The Greatest Story Ever Told*. While it was not exactly something I would have otherwise considered reading, I devoured its pages.

Walter Lowenfels, on the other hand, wrote all day long. Even in prison he remained a columnist and one of the editors of the communist newspaper, *The Worker*. Each day his requests for paper, for carbon, for pencils and erasers were received with less and less amusement. Late one afternoon an agitated prison guard came to my cell door complaining, "Say something to that old man, will you! The crazy nut now wants a typewriter. The next thing you know he'll be asking for scissors."

Several days after Tom Nabried's release, Walter Lowenfels followed him. Both had been diagnosed as having coronary insufficiencies and the other defendants had agreed that they should be the first to leave prison. On his first day at home, Walter wrote:

> My first night out. I wandered through the house
> touching things, making as if free
> at my side eight whispering voices
> saying: Remember me, Remember me!
> I drink a cup of coffee, draw up plans
> to help set my eight companions free,
> one hundred and sixty million other voices
> whispering: Remember me, Remember me![6]

Later that week, Dave Davis, the oldest among those of us who remained, was our third man out.

On August 14th, two days after the bail-reduction hearing and coinciding with Tom's release, the bail fund's director, Jack Zucker, was subpoenaed to appear before the McCarthy committee in an obvious attempt to further hinder the fund's effectiveness. To this day, my image of the newspaper account remains sharp. Zucker, confronting a verbal attack by the erstwhile senator from Wisconsin with the little finger of his right hand pointing up and out at McCarthy, defiantly shouted, "Mr. Senator, I want you to know that I have more patriotism in this little pinky than you have in your entire body."

On the same day, Sadie Alexander, Vice President of the ACLU, wrote to Bernard Segal commending the bar for implementing its resolution and supplying counsel for the Smith Act defendants. Chancellor Segal responded on August 18th:

> Despite the fact that members of the board of governors of the
> association are pretty well dispersed by summer vacations, I
> thought that the situation so clearly called for our intervention I
> assumed the authority to do so. We are fortunate in having a
> Committee on Civil Rights which readily cooperated in the
> course of action I recommended. It seems to me that nothing
> could be more fundamental than the two principles we have
> been espousing. First, that these defendants like any others are
> entitled to counsel of their own choosing, and the fixing of rea-
> sonable bail so that they may proceed to interview and engage
> such counsel, and second that any attorney representing them
> must be protected against any unfair relating in the public mind
> of their representation with an assumed agreement with the
> social, political or economic view of their clients. You may be
> sure we shall remain vigilant to protect the constitutional rights
> of defendants in the city of Philadelphia and be sure that the
> bar lives up to its highest traditions in this respect."[7]

Walter Lowenfels wrote to me on August 18th: "I continue trying to get counsel...have an appointment today and another tomorrow. Several have already said 'No' over the phone. One of those was Judge Bard who suggested I call the chancellor of the bar association, which I did. Found him away on vacation, was referred to the chairman of the Civil Liberties Committee, Brittain. Mr. Brittain said he would call a meeting of the committee but that I should continue trying to find counsel, which I am doing. The *Bulletin* [editorialized] about excessive bail...the *Philadelphia Tribune* had an editorial saying that Smith Act people had a right to counsel."

At about this time Chancellor Segal received another letter from Helen Weiss, thanking him for his efforts. The letter spoke of the extreme difficulties that the wives of the defendants were encountering in trying to raise bail. "In visiting bondsmen we were subjected to insults, both political and personal....We consulted with [the bail] attorneys and asked to have the case appealed to the circuit court. [They] were hesitant and said that an opinion from you would be of great value. We find ourselves in a position of having not enough bail, our men remaining in jail, an arraignment set for the 24th of August, and their inability to secure counsel on their behalf. We were referred to Mr. Brittain, whom we shall be happy to see, but since the original conversations were with you, any suggestion or help that you could offer would be greatly appreciated."[8]

As our wives continued their pressure, the bar association's Committee on Civil Rights deliberated about our inability to obtain counsel to represent us beyond our release on bail. According to the committee chairman's report, "There was considerable difference of opinion on the part of committee members as to just what action should be taken...."[9]

The arraignment, scheduled for August 24th, was postponed for the fifth time. We had been to court for each of those postponed arraignments. We had been there for the bail reduction hearing. We had voraciously read all of the newspaper accounts and heard reports when our wives made their occasional monitored visits. And we had several opportunities to exchange opinions while exercising in the yard. Our sense of where things stood during those last few days in August 1953, a sense with which we were delighted, was that Tom McBride, Philadelphia's leading criminal and constitutional rights attorney, wanted to defend us. But because of the enormous amount of time and work he believed would be required and because of his precarious health, he was taking steps to guarantee assurances from the Philadelphia legal community that he would not be left out on the proverbial limb. The assurances he wanted were not to be found in bar association resolutions, but in the provision of sufficient legal assistance throughout a long trial. McBride also made it clear that he expected to be paid for his services. We were aware that he commanded top fees. We knew that a defense led by Tom McBride would be highly expensive.

On August 29th, three weeks after my 29th birthday, bail was posted for my release from prison. The $10,000 assurance to the court that I would appear for trial was in the form of four houses. Three friends and neighbors, and my wife's uncle, gave the court the deeds to their homes to guarantee my presence. That evening, for the first time in over a month, I had dinner with my family. My mother, ready to help, was there; so were Pauline and my two young sons, Marc and Gary; and my mother-in-law, Jenny, once more a tower of strength and unquestioning support, came in from Arizona. I had been anticipating my absolute favorite dish, a steaming spicy bowl of my wife's delicious chili. But in deference to my mother, who kept a kosher kitchen, Pauline had decided to serve flounder. Over some belated birthday cake, I brought out the many birthday cards I had received behind bars. We shared thoughts, feelings and experiences. Afterwards, while Pauline's mother remained with our sons, we drove my mother home and Pauline and I went to the movies to see Alan Ladd in *Shane*. I remember feeling "free." Freedom, however, includes a sense of some measure of control, of being able to make decisions, choosing from among viable alternatives. The troubling and crucial question of how we would be represented by counsel remained unresolved and unclear.

Chapter 4

INDICTED CO-CONSPIRATORS

On August 17th, while still in prison awaiting a resolution of the bail situation, I was finally indicted, together with my co-defendants, for conspiring to violate the Alien Registration Act of 1940, commonly referred to as the Smith Act. The indictment charged:

> the defendants unlawfully, willingly and knowingly did conspire
> with each other (and with certain other named persons and
> with others unknown) to commit offenses against the United
> States prohibited by Section 2 of the Smith Act,...in violation of
> Section 3 of the said Smith Act...and in violation of U.S.C., Title
> 18, Section 371 (1948 Ed.)...advocating and teaching the duty
> and necessity of overthrowing the Government of the United
> States by force and violence...as speedily as circumstances
> would permit; and by helping to organize, as the Communist
> Party of the United States of America, a society...with the intent
> of causing the aforesaid....

What were we charged with specifically? Before the listing of any alleged overt acts of criminal behavior, and in more than 600 words, the indictment labors to spell out nine counts against us. Aside from the first charge—not actually advocating and teaching, but "*conspiring* to advocate and teach" and "helping to organize the Communist Party"—the indictment charged in a second count that "as part of said conspiracy," the co-conspirators, "knowing the purposes of the Communist Party, would become members, officers and functionaries and assume responsibility for carrying out its policies and activities."

And what were those policies and activities? Count three states that while "concentrating on persons employed in key basic industries," we would "recruit and encourage recruitment of new members." That the U.S. Government really had thought control in mind, and that that was the intent of the indictment, becomes even more obvious with the fourth, fifth and sixth counts. These charges implied that there was something especially sinister going on when we "would publish, circulate, and cause to be published and circulated, books, articles, magazines;...would write, and cause to be written, articles and directives;...would cause to be conducted schools and classes...to indoctrinate recruits and members in the principles of Marxism and Leninism"—all in furtherance of the "said conspiracy." Count seven charged us with having "detailed plans to go underground in the event of an emergency" so as to "continue in all respects...the conspiracy."

Perhaps the way in which the names of the defendants are listed at the top of the first page of the indictment is meant to explain what is found in the eighth count which charged that all of us had "false names in order to conceal our identities." The list follows:

JOSEPH KUZMA, also known as Joe Kuzma
ROBERT KLONSKY, also known as Robert Kirby [a pen name]
SAM GOBELOFF, also known as Joseph Roberts [his legal name]
BENJAMIN WEISS, also known as Ben Weiss
DAVID DUBENSKY, also known as David Davis [his legal name]
THOMAS NABRIED
IRVIN KATZ, also known as Irving Katz
WALTER LOWENFELS, also known as William Lerner [a pen name]
SHERMAN MARION LABOVITZ, also known as Sherman Labovitz [My original middle name was Marvin, not Marion. In 1942, a clerk in Warren County, Pennsylvania, made the error on a duplicate birth certificate I needed in order to enlist in the Air Force.]

The final count in the indictment alleged that we "would do other and further things to conceal the existence of said conspiracy."

The formal indictment is supplemented with a description of 28 alleged overt acts, occurring between June 20, 1946 and April 11, 1953, that were meant to demonstrate the specific extent and manner in which our behavior was criminal. The particular overt acts of "criminal behavior" attributed to me were that I "did attend and participate in" five Communist Party meetings, two Communist Party conferences, one Communist Party convention, one Communist Party class, one forum and one picnic; and that I "did formulate and cause to be published and circulated copies of a letter and a plan of work for the recruitment of Communist Party members and Communist Party building."

The list, which is longer than that of any of my co-defendants, demonstrates the disparity between those alleged acts and what people generally believed that avowed Communist Party leaders were being tried for—attempting to overthrow the United States Government by force and violence. Not only was there no evidence for such a charge, there were not even any alleged overt acts that suggested preparations or plans for the use of force and violence. Most important, in spite of the Smith Act, *leadership and activities in the Communist Party of the United States had never been forbidden by law.*

Had I and my co-defendants attempted to overthrow the government, or had we participated in some conspiracy to do so, surely the prosecution would have included this in their list of overt acts. Surely they would have shown some plans for taking over institutions, even a building or two.

Certainly they would have demonstrated our use of weapons, or our collection and stashing of them until that time when "circumstances would permit" their use. At least they might have shown that we had stolen or planned to steal secret government documents.

But the alleged overt acts claimed nothing that violated law. We wrote letters, sent out press releases, talked at meetings, and played softball at picnics. We were active leaders of a legal political party, the Communist Party of the United States of America.

So what was so dangerous? The government's case depended upon linking those overt acts to "dangerous" and "subversive" teachings and doctrines. And in an effort to prove that link, the government needed to parade "experts," their well-paid professional informers. They testified as to their version of the true meaning of the Marxist-Leninist position on the use of force and violence, a position that my co-defendants and I have argued is no different from that stated in the American Declaration of Independence and in Abraham Lincoln's First Inaugural Address.[1] The Marxist position categorically holds that there is a *right* to revolution only under *certain* circumstances. This is fundamentally different from *advocating* revolution under *any* circumstances. Two conditions must exist at the same time: the ruling government is unable or unwilling to carry out the will of the majority, and when force and violence to accomplish revolution has the support of and represents the will of the majority. In other words, according to Marx and Lenin, revolution is justified only when a tyrannical government does not abide by the will of its people unless force is used, and where the majority of the people support force against that tyranny.

Abraham Lincoln told the House of Representatives on July 12, 1848: "Any people anywhere being inclined and having the power, have the right to rise up and shake off the existing government, and form a new one that suits them better. This is a most valuable, a most sacred right—a right which we hope and believe is to liberate the world." And on March 4, 1861, in his First Inaugural Address, Lincoln stated: "This country with its institutions, belongs to the people who inhabit it....Whenever they shall grow weary of the existing government, they can exercise their constitutional right of amending it, or their revolutionary right to dismember and overthrow it."

The Declaration of Independence proclaims: "We hold these truths to be self-evident, that all men are created equal, that they are endowed by their Creator with certain inalienable rights, that among these are Life, Liberty and the Pursuit of Happiness....that whenever any form of government becomes destructive of those ends, it is the Right of the People to alter or abolish it, and to institute new Government...it is their right, it is their duty to throw off such Government, and to provide new Guards for their future security."

But this was neither Thomas Jefferson's 1776, nor Abe Lincoln's 1861; it was 1953. It was a time when almost anything could be done to "combat communism" in the United States, even if this was clearly in violation of our constitutional rights to free speech, thought and assembly.

Chapter 5

HOW I GOT THERE

There are a half-dozen or so incidents that remain very vivid in my memory about my early years. However, I can't imagine that anyone other than members of my immediate family would be interested in details about my being thrown into a snow-covered ravine, on the lookout for "wildcats" every time I passed the trap-door my mother was afraid I would open, almost drowned in a vat of red tannery dye, stepped on by a horse named "Chuck," or stomach-pumped for eating rat poison I thought was peanut butter. Well that's how it was in 1928, when together with my next older brother, "Dood," and our parents, I left the town in which I was born, Sheffield, Pennsylvania, to join my other brothers, uncles, aunts and cousins in Philadelphia.

As with most children, my attitudes, basic values and ideas about life were born in the family circle and were intruded upon by everyday circumstances, the media, schools and playmates. From those earliest days on, I knew of my membership in a particular group, my difference and my identity. I lived in a Jewish home which was kept kosher. We observed the Jewish holidays, at home and in the synagogue, and my family life emphasized unity and stressed togetherness.

The first 25 years of my parents' life in America were spent in Warren and Sheffield, two small working-class towns in northwest Pennsylvania where Jews were scarce. Early on they developed a command of English, discarding the Roumanian they spoke in "the old country." However, their use of "mamalushen" (Yiddish) continued, but sparingly and only to communicate those things I was not meant to understand. Perhaps I learned more than my parents appreciated at the time. Much later, I expanded a little upon using a language I grew to love.

My father's four sisters, two brothers and their families all lived in Philadelphia. Not only did I become acquainted with uncles, aunts and cousins, I got to know my oldest brother, Harry, and his wife, Peg. They already had a son and soon, in addition to my nephew, Arthur, I had a couple of nieces. My father's younger brother, Uncle Calman, and my Aunt Ann lived in a big house on North Sixth Street that exited into a large shop where they operated a business bottling "soda water." The entrance to that bottling plant was in the very heart of Marshall Street where, on any given day, you would find scores of Jewish merchants, peddlers and pushcarts. There, thousands of shoppers with their wicker baskets would seek and barter for the myriads of available sundries. Stand after stand was filled with fresh fruits and vegetables, and there were separate stores for freshly caught fish, for newly and properly killed poultry ready to be plucked, for rabbi-inspected beef, and for the scores of cheeses and other dairy products. On this one bustling ethnic street could be found salamis, pastramis, bolognas, spiced and corned beef, lox, smoked salmon and sable and white fish, long-forgotten eastern European delicacies like belaribitza, chabak, kabchanka and many different styles of herring, and my two favorite treats, messlinnas and halvah. It was a "lebediga velt" (lively world) and we all enjoyed eating kosher hot dogs and corned beef sandwiches and drinking "Calman's Beverages." Being Jewish in Aunt Ann's kitchen was so much fun!

I grew up on the streets of West Kensington, then a German and Irish working-class community, but now infamous for its poverty, misery and drug trafficking. We did not live on Fifth Street, where several Jewish merchants and their families could be found. We lived on streets either east or west of the storekeepers. I was readily accepted by my Jewish companions on frequent visits to "their" street. However, in order to win acceptance by those on my street, I had to be better than they at the games we played. I rapidly became an excellent street ball player and brawler.

One afternoon, on my way home from Fairhill grade school, I was stopped by a gang of several older boys who demanded to know, "What are you?" This was my very first lesson in the significance of ethnic identification. After answering that I was an American, I was thrown to the street. I can't say that I knew instinctively what they really wanted to hear, but somehow I did know that by telling them my parents came from Roumania, they would not be appeased. And once again, they threw me to the street. After the second assault, I told them what they wanted to hear, their "justification" for the beating I was about to receive. Ready to ward off their blows and fight back, I announced, "I am a Jew." Before two passing teachers intervened, they hurt me. They took the three pennies I had. They humiliated me. But however determined, they never succeeded in their efforts to make me "kiss the ass" of their leader.

One day I fought with the grocer's son, who had ventured onto Lawrence Street. Louie Klein was a year or two older than I and as dismal at games and sports as I was good. He mistakenly thought he had an advantage because he was bigger. But something did take place that fixed that particular fight forever in my mind. A group of unemployed adults who lived on our block were hanging out on the street corner that afternoon during the Great Depression. As Louie and I fought, a circle formed around us. Poor Louie was all alone and my neighbors were urging, "C'mon Sherm, kill the Jew. Kill the Jew bastard!" I don't remember how the fight ended; it was probably stopped by the lady who used to put the sprinkler on the fire hydrant on hot days. I don't remember the names of those encircling supporters, only some of their faces. I do, however, remember Louie, his older brother Jake, their parents and all the questions I had about why they joined a synagogue that was different from the one I knew—the one attended by the Metzmans, Beckers, Henkins, Resnicks and Schaffs.

Ironically, it was Miss Silverman, my lovely Jewish second-grade teacher at the Fairhill school, who confused me one day. She would not permit me to show off my ability to sing, and she was not impressed with how quickly I had learned the season's new songs. Instead, she sternly admonished, "Jewish boys do not sing Christmas carols!" Somewhat later, in fifth grade, an older "spinster" teacher, Miss Johnson, taught me another lesson about being Jewish. On my first report card that semester I was graded E-E-9—excellent behavior, excellent effort, and on a scale of one to nine, tops in achievement. For the second report period, however, I was stunned by a P-F-6—poor behavior, fair effort and failing. On the final report card, Miss Johnson returned to the initial grading. The lesson I learned was to expect to be penalized for being absent from school when choosing to observe the Jewish holidays.

A couple of two-story row houses were the setting for an Orthodox synagogue about six blocks from where I lived. It serviced and was supported by working-class, first-generation, immigrant Jews. The first floors were broken through to provide space for meetings and prayer. The rooms on one second floor were used for the Cheder (Hebrew school). The other second-floor rooms were occupied by the Shamas (caretaker). Our Shamas was also the Hebrew teacher. In addition to looking after the facilities, he gathered together the minyan (a quorum of 10 men required for prayers) three times each day: at sunrise and immediately before and again just after the sun set. This congregation could not afford both a Shamas and a Rabbi for their synagogue. Therefore, presiding over prayer services was shared. I received my first Hebrew training in that setting. After public school hours three times a week, I learned, by rote, to read the language of the prayer books. And for the eleven months of mourning that followed the death of my father, I recited the Kaddish (prayer for the dead) at every sunrise and sunset and at each evening service.

While at Fairhill, I competed with Irwin Schneider for excellent grades. He was a playmate and one of my best friends. He was also a nephew of the Kahls, owners of the neighborhood German bakery. Irwin lived with his grandparents about one block away from the bakery. Almost all of our contacts were at school, at my house or at the bakery. Eventually I became afraid of his grandparents. It all started when one day we broke our pattern of meetings and I went to his grandparents' home to find Irwin. What I found was a portrait of Adolf Hitler hanging in their dining room! Things began to change between us and soon I learned that during each summer vacation, Irwin visited his parents, who lived in Germany. I became concerned with being in his presence and our relationship soured. After we moved out of the old neighborhood in 1935, I didn't see Irwin Schneider again until we returned to high school in September 1937. By that time, he was wearing a swastika armband! We avoided one another for a few weeks and then I never saw him again. After World War II, I learned that in 1938, Irwin returned to his parents and remained in Germany. My childhood chum became a Luftwaffe officer and died on the Eastern front during Hitler's invasion of the Soviet Union.

I moved from West Kensington to Mayfair in 1935, and to a new school in Tacony for eighth-grade classes. At Disston I found that two of my teachers, Miss Potts and Miss Sullivan, were very much like my fifth-grade teacher, Miss Johnson—filled with strange notions about Jews. They were unfriendly, unsettled and unnerved by my presence. During my first week at the new school, Miss Potts falsely accused me of dropping an eraser on the floor one morning so that I could look up the skirt of a girl who was walking near my desk, noting that "you are all alike." While possible, it seemed very unlikely that Miss Potts was making reference to my gender. Deep inside, I've always known that she thought of me in the very same way as did Miss Sullivan, who believed me to be "a dark-skinned Jewish boy from way down in South Philly who doesn't know any better than to talk in class."

During the autumn of 1935, my Jewish life was in transformation. Bar Mitzvah training had something to do with it. It also probably represented some family aspirations for greater identification with other sections of the Jewish community and "a step upward." We found Congregation Adath Jeshurun, a large, stately, conservative synagogue with a middle- and upper-middle-class congregation. For a relatively short period of time, Adath Jeshurun, Rabbi Max Klein and a few teachers—Abram Piwosky, Harry Warsaw and Harry Leopold—became significant figures in the awakening of another piece of my Jewish consciousness. Up until that time, it had been defined by tradition, religion and my personal experiences with anti-Semitism. But I was becoming increasingly aware of the hatred and antagonism toward my people that was growing throughout the world and the devastating toll that fascism was taking. At Adath Jeshurun, I learned about a nationalist movement that was responding to anti-Semitism. Zionism, with its 40-year history of organization and settlements in Palestine, felt protective to me. It was filled with pageantry, and it made me feel proud. I found that being Jewish, while threatening, was also very beautiful.

My earlier Orthodox experiences did not prepare me socially for the later ones at Adath Jeshurun. The new temple was beautiful and its religious services could be quite moving. I still remember and occasionally even sing the Ki Mitzion—the prayer that is recited when the Ark is opened and the Torah is removed. It had been gloriously set to an aria from Gounod's opera, *Faust*. The cantor and choir in the loft were always magnificent. But while my old Shamas had succeeded in making me a "wiz" at reading Hebrew, in all other respects I was literally out of my class. Everyone I met seemed so accomplished, so sophisticated, so rich. In hand-me-down pants and jackets, I still lived in a row house among West Kensington's mill workers and walked to Hebrew school three times each week because we did not own a car. The stylishly dressed Adath Jeshurun congregants all seemed to come from the larger single homes of wealthy East Oak Lane, suburban Cheltenham, Elkins Park and Melrose Park. They drove their children to services in Buicks, Lincolns, Cadillacs and Packards. During the summer months, I frequented the city-run swimming pools and played ball on the streets. They were members of one of the two Jewish country clubs and played tennis on carefully manicured grass courts. However, there was something even more significant in my sense of not really being a part of Adath Jeshurun. Only I "belonged"; no other member of my immediate household ever became involved at that synagogue.

About this time, my Jewish consciousness and identification were given a new direction. I became aware that a very tiny body of immigrant Jews in America were providing an inordinate number of members, supporters and leaders to groups and organizations that were committed to social reform. They were actively engaged in struggles to bring about radical change. As I moved into my mid-teens, this new dimension became congruent with my own growing awareness of the problems of the world around me that needed fixing.

For the most part, by 1935, my childhood had disappeared. One year earlier my father had suddenly died of pneumonia. I had four living brothers who were older than I by nine to 22 years. All but the eldest, who by then had his own family, lived with my mother and me when we moved into a two-bedroom apartment above a store. Mom was determined to keep us together as a family, and she succeeded. My brother Abe was almost 23 years old at the time. Seven mornings a week, between 2:00 and 5:00 a.m., Abe delivered newspapers on the small route that had been left to my mother when "Pop" died. At the same time, Abe used the storefront to begin a business selling furniture and appliances. Bill, who had worked his way through college as a part-time candy clerk and soda jerker, was by then 25. With a full-time position managing a store for the same candy company, Bill was also Abe's "silent" partner. "Dood" was 20 and bent upon becoming a concert pianist. Eight to 10 hours each day, he practiced in a living room that was also my bedroom, into which I rolled my fold-up cot each night. I was 11 years old, had "skipped" three grades in grammar school and was placed in the eighth and final grade of junior high. Now everyone was older than I. Rapidly, I worked at developing a persona that appeared more mature. By the end of the first year in the new apartment, I became Abe's helper, delivering the morning newspapers on weekends and assisting around his store.

These were not only the years of the Great Depression, they were also the years of reactions and responses to that international economic and social catastrophe. And these were the years in which I matured and became aware of unemployment and poverty and workers who chained themselves to their machines; of the search for scapegoats, the lynchings of Black people and the rise of anti-Semitism in the United States. I began to see that, in many nations, conditions were even worse. Rulers responded to their economic crises with even greater restrictions and more brutal forms of repression. Fascism had become an international phenomenon, and I could not understand why my country remained unconcerned as fascists tested their strength. By then I knew of the Spanish Civil War and of the U.S. blockade, of Nazi Germany's assault on my people and the world's silence. I was frightened by the Nuremberg edicts that prohibited or restricted Jewish activities; by Kristallnacht with its smashing, looting and burning of the properties, homes and synagogues of Jews; and by reports of concentration camps and slave labor. These all weighed heavily on me, and the course of those events had an enormous impact upon my life. I looked about for answers, and, with the help of significant others, I found what I thought would be the solution.

I was only 15 when Dood married and brought his new wife to live with us in our small apartment. The atmosphere was charged. The new bridegroom was literally a "starving musician." While his bride was a registered nurse who helped with their share of the household expenses and was accepted into our household, there was still some resentment at her presence. Tillie wasn't pretty in the usual sense, nor was she endowed with other attributes that an adolescent male might have appreciated. In fact, she was to become ill and die in just a few years. To me, however, she was always radiant; she changed the course of my life. There was an ethereal quality about Tillie that set her apart from everything and everyone I knew.

Turmoil and tumult were the orders of the day. Values were being challenged, and leaders were screaming their solutions. My sister-in-law had answers too, and on many an afternoon I raced home from high school to her bedside. There I would listen enraptured while she expounded on the theatre, on music, on philosophy, on poverty, on war, on fascism, on socialism—calmly, quietly and oh so lucidly.

On one fall afternoon I rushed home to tell my confidante of an appointment to discuss my application to the seminary in Cincinnati. Tillie listened, then asked, "Why do you want to be a rabbi?" It was all so simple. It needed no real thought. Quickly I blurted out, "Because it's as good a way as any to earn a living." To which her simple "Oh?" cut like a rapier. I never did keep that appointment, nor was it ever necessary for my brother's wife to pursue the subject. Our afternoon discussions continued, but somehow they took on a new kind of meaning.

Soon I found that communists had been involved with all of the activities and proposals that seemed right to me: unemployed councils and tenants' leagues, marches and demonstrations, moves to "organize the unorganized," coalitions to stop fascism, support for Loyalist Spain and an end to the blockade, and activities to end "Jim Crow" laws and "legal" lynchings. Frequently alone in their advocacy, they were never praised, seldom credited and often attacked. Sensing injustice in those attacks, I looked more seriously at what those communist critics of American capitalism offered in the way of ideological solutions to our nation's inability to deal fairly and equitably with its social problems.

There were several factors that made the Young Communist League and the Communist Party the natural places for me to turn. Undoubtedly the influences of my sister-in-law and my brother were foremost, for it was they who introduced me to party periodicals and literature. On the pages of those publications, particularly those of the *Daily Worker*, I found that the Communist Party was in constant battle. During those days of the Great Depression, the party not only attacked a sick and corrupt economic system for its privileged few and impoverished masses, but it was also proposing that it be replaced by a long-term alternative, socialism. And it also appeared to me that unlike other proponents, it was Communist Party members who were socialism's most down-to-earth advocates. They were actively engaged with everyday problems, in the forefront of struggles to provide immediate amelioration for victims of the economic catastrophe and to reform the social condition.

All of these things made an enormous impression on a teenager with a responsive mind eager to change the world. In and of themselves, they probably would have been sufficient to draw me into the Young Communist League. But without any question, it was the Communist Party's persistent attention to prejudice, to discrimination, to oppressed minorities and, especially, to cancerous white supremacy and anti-Semitism that came together with my own limited experiences but very strong emotions about being Jewish. Not only did I find myself in strong agreement with what the communists were saying and doing, I found that many of the advocates whose accounts I was reading were Jews. They were among the top leaders of the party and frequently were candidates in national elections for public offices. Exhilarating, and most persuasive of its truth, was the ethnic composition of a list of Communist Party candidates for President and Vice President of the United States and for New York's U.S. Senator. Respectively, those candidates were the party's national chairman, William Z. Foster; its African-American vice-chairman, James W. Ford; and its Jewish, New York state chairman, Israel Amter. To someone like myself, scarcely beyond adolescence, that was really practicing what one preaches. And as I grew a bit older, many of the Jewish communists I came to know wore their ethnicity on their sleeves. They helped me to a better understanding of, and an even greater pride in, the long history of my people's struggle for liberation. As a result, holidays like Passover, Purim and Chanukah took on new meaning for me. Finally, this awakening that was taking place within me, these realizations about the significance of strength in unity and in struggle, was happening at a momentous time. Fascism was growing worldwide; Adolf Hitler was a looming menace; and the communists were organizing marches and demonstrations that called upon all people to join in a "Popular Front" and in a "United Front Against Fascism." It all made such eminently good sense!

Chapter 6

IN THE ARMY

By the time I graduated from high school, I was certain that socialism was a desirable alternative to capitalism. Not long afterward, I was just as convinced that the Communist Party was the vehicle to bring socialism to the United States.

Capitalism, the so-called free enterprise system, did not seem to work very well. It was not an efficient system; it planned for nothing but profits. While it created great wealth for a select few, it produced abject poverty for far too many. History had demonstrated to me that the periodic crises of capitalism could be temporarily overcome only by the blood transfusions of war. When it was young and vigorous, capitalism survived its frequent crises and bounced back, but that, I thought, could not continue. The frantic search for new world markets to exploit would eventually lead to more and more deadly conflicts. Still, the leaders of capitalist societies and the governments that represented their interests would resist any efforts to change the destructive system they controlled. If that system were threatened, I was certain that they would resort to any means in order to maintain their power—even if that meant eliminating all democratic forms and processes and replacing them with a despotic and brutal government of rule by terror.

While this was most certainly a very grim picture, I was convinced of another way. Just as capitalism was an improvement over the serfdom of feudalism, on the horizon a vastly superior system was rising, and given the opportunity, the American people would freely and democratically choose that alternative. This was a system within which the major instruments for production and wealth need not only be cooperatively operated, as they were under capitalism, but they could and should also be socially owned. Private ownership, exploitation and profits did not have to be the determinants for production. They could be replaced by production that was planned for need and use. In that way, production would keep pace with consumption, thereby eliminating overproduction; as a result, periodic depressions, unemployment, poverty and the need for wars would be eliminated.

I was convinced it could work in the United States if only the people were willing. Had not a nation as backward as Russia put the socialist dream into practice, accomplishing such amazing feats in so short a period of time? I could only imagine the achievements under socialism that were possible for a nation with a democratic history and traditions, a nation as great as the United States.

What would it take to get to socialism? I also thought I knew the answer to that question; it would take organization and struggle. Millions of Americans would have to be involved in attempts to improve living standards for all. Millions more would have to be moved to demand the full extension of democracy and freedom for all our citizens. The mobilization of these millions would take the form of specific and timely struggles for better wages and working conditions, for decent housing and health insurance, and against "Jim Crow," anti-Semitism and war. In this process of involving so many people in attempts to better their lives and achieve their potentials, many thousands of them would come to realize, I was convinced, that capitalism was no longer viable, that only under socialism could their aspirations be met. This delicious, delectable, perfectly desirable dream and the possibilities for my contributing to its fulfillment led me into the Young Communist League, and following my discharge from the Air Force after World War II, into the Communist Party where I rapidly moved into leadership positions.

It was early June in 1942, six months after Japan bombed Pearl Harbor, when I volunteered for service in the United States Air Force. During World War II, the manner in which young communists were treated in the armed services varied greatly. Sometimes it seemed to be determined by the needs, at other times the ideological position, of particular commanding officers. There appeared to be no clear and prevailing policy. In some places, known communist leaders found that they were placed under surveillance and restricted to performing menial, low-security types of tasks. In other arenas, young American communists became both noncommissioned and commissioned officers right on the battlefield.

Problems developed after I completed months of training as a radio operator/mechanic at Truax Field, Wisconsin, and was selected for further schooling in radar. At the time, radar was a relatively new science that called for tight security regulations, and candidates were thoroughly investigated by Air Force Intelligence. My career as a Communist Party leader did not really take shape until after I returned from military service at the end of the war. However, I can speculate from several experiences during the war years that I must have failed the security check because of my earlier, relatively minor leadership activity in the Young Communist League, because of my support for Soviet-American friendship and because of my opposition to socially segregated units in the armed forces. I never did get to radar school. Neither did I get to use my earlier training. Instead, I was shipped to Chanute Field, Illinois, where I became a "casual" and was given kitchen police and guard duty to perform.

While at Chanute Field, I was instrumental in organizing a Friday night forum under the auspices of the information and education office. Since many of the soldiers at the field were transients and had little else to do on a Friday night, the forum was a welcome diversion for some of them. One Friday evening, I had arranged for a University of Illinois economics professor to speak about "Problems Facing American Workers on the Home Front." His presentation suggested that it was not all "peaches and cream" for those at home working in defense plants. This provoked a very lively and critical question and discussion period that I attempted to moderate. As more negative feelings than I anticipated were being expressed, and as I was looking for a way to end the meeting, I was fortuitously rescued when I recognized a request to speak from a soldier sitting at the rear of the now somewhat raucous auditorium. He was a tall and lumbering fellow, but as he stood, he looked stooped and pained. His deep and resonant voice added to an already formed Abe Lincoln caricature. The soldier held out his long arms, looked at the palms of his hands, and as he lifted them ever so slowly he drawled, "These callouses come from working every day in the fields and in shops. The problem with you folks is that most of you have never done what it takes to earn them." As I took advantage of the hush that followed his comments to thank the guest professor and adjourn the meeting, I made certain not to lose sight of that last soldier to speak—that "articulate, elegant farmer-orator from the State of Illinois." He was just as eager, and as we shook hands he said, "Hi, I'm Morty Lippman from the Bronx. I'm an actor. My friends call me Johnny."

John Randolph and I became friends. And a trip up to Chicago on a subsequent weekend is noteworthy because on at least a half-dozen occasions—on the train, on the streets of the city, at a restaurant and in front of a "left-wing" office building—we both noted the presence of a "tail." In any event, a constantly reappearing Air Force sergeant seemed to be spending that weekend in Chicago with us.

Incidentally, a short time thereafter, a *Chicago Tribune* editorial asked, "What's going on?" The editorial complained of "Marxist propaganda" at a regular Chanute Field forum. While never referred to, the editorial was acted upon. Rather quickly, I was returned to more kitchen police and guard duty and subsequently summoned to the field's Office of Intelligence. As I recall that "interview," it was conducted in a large, sunny room, and I sat at the middle of a long conference table. At the end to my left sat a lieutenant colonel and facing him at the other end sat a captain. The chairs opposite me were occupied by an assortment of officers. A stenotypist sat on my immediate right and recorded all questions and responses. And, oh yes, my "tail" from the Chicago trip appeared embarrassed and nonplussed when he realized I recognized him as he inadvertently entered the room and then hastily exited.

My inquisitors were not the least bit overtly hostile. In fact, they appeared downright friendly. In retrospect, they were disarmingly friendly. I was young, perhaps naive, and quite willing to openly express my views about fascism and socialism, about William Z. Foster, Earl Browder and Jacques Du Clos, and about "the nature of World War II." And since my parents had been born in Roumania, the questioners were even interested in my feelings about the Soviet Army's offensive that had, at that moment, reached the Roumanian border. There was only one "64-dollar" question that revealed their misinformation. I was asked if I had ever been the Educational and Cultural Director of the Young Communist League for eastern Pennsylvania, Delaware and southern New Jersey. I never held that position and so stated. I had held the title of educational and cultural director for a small club of the League in North Philadelphia, but not for the entire district to which they referred. That question was the last one asked of me before the colonel said I could make any final statement I wanted. I had no statement to make, but instead asked why I had been singled out for the interview. The colonel told the stenotypist to "strike that question from the record," and then said to me "off the record," "Please be assured that you were not selected for any special reason. All of this is purely routine."

Shortly after that interview with Air Force Intelligence, I received my shipping orders. This time I was one of a few enlisted men together with a group of Signal Corps officers sent to Scott Field, Illinois, for training in radio range. Several more months of "high-tech" training found me with a former editorial writer for the *Milwaukee CIO News* as the only two graduates not shipped into action abroad. Already very experienced in what to expect as a "casual," I quickly made myself available to my squadron's information and education officer. The lieutenant was an experienced supply officer with little interest in "these propaganda responsibilities." He was delighted to be able to turn over whatever could be done to an interested and willing GI. The squadron commander was a young captain but an old army regular who had no problem with the assignment and, in fact, encouraged me.

I doubt whether the top brass of Air Force Command had any notion or cared about what their Office of Information and Education was all about. No doubt, Air Force Intelligence did. Scott Field's Office of Information and Education had all kinds of what today would be called ultra-liberal literature and materials about national, religious, racial and cultural groups, and about the evils of fascism. It had pamphlets that presented all of our allies, especially the Soviet Union, as friends. And they were interested in the dissemination and discussion of these materials. I was most obliging. With the squadron commander's approval, a barracks was converted into a dayroom/library filled with the available pamphlets, books and newspapers. After securing a huge bulletin board, I used it daily to post news headlines and other appropriate materials. The information and education office supplied huge maps of Europe, Asia and the Far East upon which the war fronts were superimposed. I moved them daily to designate the conduct and progress of the war.

Heady with success, I prevailed upon the commanding officer to have each of the 30 to 40 barracks appoint a discussion leader. Regular weekly discussions were to be held with the leaders around topics suggested by the materials from the I & E office. In turn, the leaders would conduct similar discussions in their respective barracks.

One day the commanding officer called me into his office. "Private," he asked, "were you ever arrested in civilian life? Did you ever have any trouble with the law? I don't mean traffic tickets or stuff like that. Anything serious?" When I assured him that I had not, he jumped up and said, "I don't know what the hell's going on, but I got a call from S2 [Air Force Intelligence] and they wanted to know what you were doing. When I told them, they almost blew off the phone and said, 'That private can't be doing that!'" The C.O. paused for a moment, stared at me and then added, "No damned 90-day wonder is going to tell me what to do. You're doing a great job, so keep at it. But if anybody comes into the day room and asks, you tell them you're cleaning up the place! Got it?"

A few days later my C.O., accompanied by several other officers, walked into that day room. As I snapped to attention he barked, "Soldier, what are you doing here?" "Cleaning up, sir." "O.K.," he said with a wink as they all left.

Within a week I was shipped to Texas and given a scooter to deliver Western Union telegrams for the balance of my Air Force career. During the first 12 of the 18 months I spent at the San Antonio Aviation Cadet Center, I made several attempts to be reclassified by volunteering for infantry service and glider pilot training, only to be informed that I had too many Air Force specialties in flight, radio operation, radio mechanics and radio range to be spared for other service.

While on furlough in Philadelphia early in 1943, I met a beautiful activist with whom I would share the dream for the rest of my life. I fell in love and following an eventful on-again, off-again, many-miles-separated courtship, on May 21, 1945, Pauline joined me in San Antonio. Two days later we were wed.

Chapter 7

VICTORY AND AFTER

December 7, 1945 was the fourth anniversary of the Japanese attack on Pearl Harbor. It was my mother's 65th birthday and it was the day I left San Antonio, Texas, honorably discharged from the United States Air Force. Pauline and I ran down to Nuevo Laredo, Mexico, that day, then hurried north to Chicago to hold the canopy for my brother's wedding in his room for the day at the Palmer House. After the ceremony we made our way home to Philadelphia, bent on rejoining the movement we staunchly believed would usher in the better world. As the new year began, we were firmly planted on 31st Street, bordering beautiful Fairmount Park, in an almost entirely Jewish section of the west side of the city's 28th Ward known as Strawberry Mansion. The overwhelming majority of those who lived to the east of that community were African Americans, and it was there that the 28th Ward Communist Party concentrated its activities and recruiting efforts.

During those post-World War II years and into the early 1950s, communists placed enormous importance on what was referred to as "The Negro Question." Predating the civil rights movement, at virtually every meeting, conference and convention I attended, it was a major agenda item. The party held innumerable theoretical discussions and organized classes about "The Negro Nation," "The Black Belt," "The Right to Self-Determination," and "The National and Colonial Question." I participated in just about all of them; some I helped teach. At all times, there was a focus on "Black-White Unity," "Jim Crow and White Chauvinism" and a special emphasis on the need to support and participate in the economic, political and social "liberation struggle" in which those who were later to be called Black and still later African Americans were involved. Almost as a precursor to the subsequent struggle against "white racism," in 1949 and 1950 the party waged its own war against the "dangers of white chauvinism," not only as it was then being manifested in the general society and in the labor movement, but also within the ranks of the party itself. During those years, a tremendous amount of my time and energy was devoted to those discussions and the activities they generated. While today I can better understand and deplore the amount of patronizing, breast-beating and victimization that took place during those years, I can nevertheless look back with considerable pride at the measure of that early involvement in the struggles against racism and for civil rights.

The 28th Ward Communist Party Club under my stewardship took on the "last-hired, first-fired" issue that involved one of the dozens of the mini-market American Stores located on street corners throughout Philadelphia. Near the end of World War II, faced with a labor shortage that conscription for the armed forces created on the home front, the American Stores for the first time hired a Black man to manage one of its stores located in the primarily Black east side of the 28th Ward. When the war ended and previously employed white veterans returned home, the Black manager was fired. The Communist Party Club organized to save his job. Hundreds of leaflets were mimeographed and handed out in a door-to-door canvassing of residents. We engaged individuals in discussion and enlisted them in planning and organizing several street-corner meetings at which I exhorted others to picket, protest and boycott. We put together a petition campaign and, with the help of others, I led a community delegation to the city offices of the parent company. The issue was unwinnable in an atmosphere that guaranteed returning veterans priority and preference for jobs. However, the residual good will that the campaign left in the community resulted in increased subscriptions for the party-supported newspapers, the *Daily Worker* and the *Sunday Worker*, as well as a dozen recruits to form a new 28th Ward East Communist Party Club.

Following the war, an inordinate number of Blacks were defendants in what many believed to be "frame-up" rape trials. They appeared to be mirrors of the infamous 1930s case of the "Scottsboro Boys," in which nine young Blacks between the ages of 13 and 21 were accused of raping two white women (one of whom repudiated the rape charge). Tried without counsel and convicted by an all-white jury, one was sentenced to life in prison and eight received the death penalty. Years of left-led protest, in this country and throughout the world, saved the lives of the Scottsboro Boys, but five of them served lengthy sentences and the last left prison almost 20 years after his arrest.

In the late 1940s and early 1950s, we were to witness the executions of the "Martinsville Seven" in Virginia as well as the execution of Willie McGee in Mississippi. I was deeply involved in activity aimed at preventing those atrocities. Protesting the probability that these would turn out to be "legal lynchings," Communist Party activists all over the country spoke on street corners and at rallies in their defense, wrote and distributed leaflets, collected petitions and coordinated fundraising for their legal defense. While we helped organize significant national and international protest and pleas for government intervention, we did not save their lives. However, in still another case involving "The Trenton Six," a four-year-long battle against a concerted attempt by authorities in New Jersey to execute young Black men we believed were falsely accused of murder, the work that I and others gave to their defense was much more rewarding. These victims were not executed; instead, two were sentenced to prison for life and the remaining four were freed.

These were also years of considerable intra-party conflict and factionalism and a struggle against "white chauvinism" which was often blurred by a myopic and vindictive need to purge and cleanse. There were two occasions when I received veiled threats of expulsion. The first was at a leadership training school. In a class being taught by Harry Haywood, chairman of the party's National Negro Commission, we were discussing his book, *Negro Liberation*. Haywood held that all of the conditions for nationhood existed in a contiguous belt of counties running through several southern states, that this was a Negro nation with the right to self-determination. I was fascinated; I had many questions and I was persistent about seeking answers. The white director of the program accused me of being "much too critical, personal, pressing and insensitive," and added that I "could be brought up on charges." I remember feeling totally humiliated. And instead of questioning how my struggle to better understand a concept with which I wanted to identify could be so misinterpreted, I began self-critically looking for what was wrong with my classroom behavior.

The second incident took place after I disagreed with what I thought were some poor fundraising ideas suggested by a Black leader of the Civil Rights Congress. I had relegated the suggestions to a back burner despite his many efforts to convince me to act on them. I was not present when the issue was discussed at a party district staff meeting. However, on one Saturday morning, I was formally "put on record." Some of the district staff considered the issue an example of my failure to help build and support Black leadership and warned that there would be consequences at a subsequent meeting of the district committee. Expelled from the party? It was a devastating thought! My wife sat with me in the kitchen most of that day and we felt as if our entire belief-system was in question; our world was falling apart. There was a big party that night in the home of a Black comrade. Unable to face it, I remained at home. Pauline went instead, "to save face and to hold my head high in pride." In a room apart from the gathering, she burst into tears—the effort was too great.

Others have described incidents that were just as foolish, inappropriate and insensitive—like the one involving a very active wife and mother, Rose. Already in disfavor for not being sufficiently arduous about helping the party's Black city chairman and his family relocate into her white but changing community, Rose was charged with white chauvinism and expelled from the party because she insisted that she did not know why "her pet dog barked only at Blacks."

During the decade that followed the end of World War II, the American Communist Party also directed a considerable amount of its energy and resources toward trying to build an anti-fascist peace coalition. Much of my activity was rooted in an ideological conviction that American capitalism was bent on world domination. The twin evils of domestic fascism and nuclear war seemed imminent to most of us. We had no doubts about the Truman Doctrine and the Marshall Plan being aggressive attempts to overthrow legitimate governments moving toward socialism. The newspapers we sold by canvassing communities door to door, and the leaflets we distributed by the thousands, continually condemned U.S. foreign policy. We opposed American intervention in the national elections of France, Greece and Italy. We were against the formation of NATO and we fought armed support for Chiang Kai-shek and the Koumintang in China. We linked our nation's increasingly repressive domestic atmosphere with our government's aggressive foreign policy. At meeting after meeting, we exhorted those of our members who were active in trade unions and in community, fraternal and religious organizations to work in those groups in ways that would help forge coalitions to oppose our country's domestic and foreign policies.

When I was discharged from the Air Force in December 1945, workers on the home front were demanding increases in their take-home pay envelopes. The cost of living had increased substantially during the war and most workers had been tied to pre-war agreements and no-strike pledges for the duration. The year 1946 was marked by huge strikes for higher wages that took place in almost every major industry of the nation. Some of the very first Communist Party-encouraged activities in which I participated were in support of the massive picket lines and demonstrations that enunciated the demands of those on strike at the Westinghouse and General Electric plants in Southwest Philadelphia. I was present at the Westinghouse site. The mounted police, mobilized to use their billy-clubs on the arms, legs, backs and heads of protesting workers and supporters, were unable to break up that demonstration. Their horses, while not injured, had been hobbled by hundreds of marbles rolled into their paths and under their hoofs. The local Communist Party Club collected food and clothing for the strikers and urged members to organize others to meet them on the picket lines and at the demonstrations.

Many of the strikes that took place during that first post-war year were successful. Big industry reacted with a campaign that succeeded in getting Congress to pass legislation to curb the strength of trade unions. During the next months, we in the party attempted to halt the passage of labor-restrictive laws by pointing out the dangers inherent in the many proposals. In 1947, the Taft-Hartley Act was passed and in some 30 states, additional labor control laws were enacted. Taft-Hartley set the labor movement back to pre-Depression days; it abolished the closed shop, outlawed mass picketing, condemned secondary boycotts, re-established the use of injunctions, instituted a 60-day "cooling off" period before strikes and denied unions their right to use their funds for political purposes. When the law passed, the Communist Party pressed the major unions to resist compliance. Initially, some trade union leaders, such as John L. Lewis of the United Mine Workers, urged noncompliance. However, the leadership of the largest unions acquiesced to the provisions of the Taft-Hartley Act. The Communist Party saw this "crippling" of the American labor movement as the first big step in what we feared was Wall Street capitalism's drive toward domestic fascism and another war.

Early in 1948, not far from Philadelphia in the city of York, the Progressive Party was formed around former Vice President Henry Wallace. At the time, Wallace was an advocate of peaceful collaboration between the United States and the Soviet Union. The next months produced feverish activity as the Communist Party mobilized its membership to make certain that the Progressives got on the ballot in virtually every state. When this newly formed third party held its national convention during the summer of that year, Philadelphia was its site and post-war Communist Party activity was at its peak. When the convention ended with a huge meeting that all but filled Connie Mack Stadium, home of the Philadelphia Athletics and the Philadelphia Phillies, the Progressive Party had adopted a platform calling for "peace, freedom and abundance."

I was now a full-time Communist Party functionary; my major assignment was the circulation of the party press, the *Daily & Sunday Worker*. On the eve of the closing session at the grand old ball park, scores of Communist Party activists were strategically placed and poised. They were ready to distribute 20,000 copies of that Sunday's *Worker*. I was bringing them, hot off the press, from a location on East 13th Street in Manhattan, some 90 miles away. I had pressured Bart, one of my star newspaper salespersons, to lend his services and his old one-ton, open-stake truck for the job. Bart and I had no trouble getting to New York City, but he did feel put upon and he was unhappy. He did not feel any better when, in order to finish in time to make the return trip to Philadelphia, we had to help the laborers load the truck. Once loaded, unless Bart pressed hard on the pedal of his dilapidated vehicle, we would most certainly disappoint the folks at Connie Mack Stadium. We left 13th Street and Bart went flying further into downtown Manhattan. Gliding into the Holland Tunnel, he crossed the lanes three times to race past those who would delay our spreading the word. At the end of the tunnel we were stopped and Bart was given a ticket for failing to stay in his lane. Because of what we were carrying, I was certain that the police would delay us at best, or even hold us and confiscate our cargo. They never looked nor seemed to care. We did make it back to Philadelphia that evening and 20,000 *Sunday Workers* were sold and distributed. And Bart? To the best of my knowledge, he was never reimbursed for gas, tolls or the fine and, I suspect, he's still angry!

The next months were filled with nonstop electioneering activities in Philadelphia. The District Committee of the Communist Party added another assignment to my press circulation responsibilities. I was the party's city representative in the 24th Ward, where a special effort was being made to organize the anticipated huge support for the Wallace ticket. With Communist Party responsibilities, Progressive Party concerns, trade union and neighborhood block activities, and with meetings and planning sessions too numerous to count, it was a busy time meant to turn out the largest possible vote for Henry Wallace.

I don't believe the Communist Party's analysis was ever clear as to why the very significant amount of support for the Progressive ticket within community organizations and labor unions, as well as the energy we spent during that year, was not reflected at the polls on election day. Henry Wallace received only a little over one million votes. Some in the Progressive Party valiantly remained for a couple more rounds, trying to build a viable third political party. Others, however, saw those efforts, including the 1948 campaign, as failures. Eventually, most concluded that socialist-minded political activists needed to function where the "masses" could be found—in other words, within the mainstream Democratic Party. Consequently they turned, I believe in error, toward gaining a foothold within that party in order to try to influence its platform and program. They've been trying ever since.

Those of us in Communist Party leadership sincerely believed that the representatives of American capitalism were absolutely paranoid in their fear of a world rapidly turning toward and embracing socialism. As the months rolled by and one international crisis after another unfolded, each was viewed with increasing alarm. We believed our government would use any means to prevent the rise of socialism. Therefore, when the United States became involved directly in the post-war elections of France and Italy, and when it interfered in the peoples' struggles inside Greece and Turkey, we attempted to rally opposition. In the late 1940s, when our government supported the attempts of England and France to suppress the many independence movements in the Mideast, Asia and Africa, we communists joined in support of those movements for liberation. When American conservatives charged that the ousting of the rightwing Koumintang from mainland China was a direct result of treason and betrayal, we joined with those who called for recognizing the legitimacy of the Chinese Revolution.

All these crises took place during those years that the Communist Party of the United States was facing bitter government prosecution, or as we believed, persecution. Nevertheless, when the "Korean Conflict" (it was never called a war) broke out, we communists were open and unequivocal in our opposition. We warned of the danger that the fighting in Korea could escalate into a third world war and a possible nuclear holocaust. We demonstrated for a cease fire and an end to hostilities. We called for the recognition of the People's Republic of China and its seating in the United Nations so as to facilitate peace negotiations.

The more we opposed the foreign policy of our government, the greater its attack upon us, providing the rationale for two distinct categories of members and leaders to develop. First, there were those of us who freely spoke of and advocated socialism. We were identifiable communists openly engaged in defending the Communist Party while at the same time promulgating its very unpopular program. We tended to be among either its youngest or its most senior members. Most of us had significantly little to lose financially. Except for some participation in groups that were ideologically identified as being a part of the "left," we were uninvolved in the life of other organizations.

The second group consisted of equally committed party members who, because of their business or professional status, needed to be protected from the harm that exposure would incur. Undoubtedly, the influential positions they held in community, ethnic, labor and professional organizations would have been compromised or endangered if they were thought to be communists. We believed that this group provided the necessary inroads to the larger mass organizations upon whom support for economic and social change depended. Some of the people from this second group were attached to one of several clubs in the "business and professional section" of the Communist Party. Where possible, these clubs consisted of members with similar interests: teachers, lawyers, health professionals and government employees. Where this was not possible, others maintained varying degrees of anonymity while attached to party clubs in or near their respective communities.

In regard to party morale, the problems posed by this obvious dichotomy in membership were never fully addressed or understood by the Communist Party leadership. We even had our own descriptive terms for the split. Some of us were the "inner party workers," and those in the second group were referred to as "mass organization workers." Many of the latter bristled at what they considered the "insensitivity" of inner party workers. They felt that their need for special protection and support, required for the very important work they were doing as key forces in the broader community, was never really appreciated. As a result they had little sympathy for those party members who, in turn, resented them as "closet communists." Nor did most of them ever come to accept the extent to which those of us who were open communists felt isolated in our communities, restrained from turning toward those other "comrades" for fear that we might expose them in a "selfish" search to satisfy our own needs for comfort and support.

The fight for peace and the struggle against nuclear proliferation were crucial to the life of the Communist Party during those years. International conferences and organizations resulted, in turn, in national conferences and organizations. These frequently translated into a myriad of community movements, petition campaigns, mass picnics and demonstrations. In retrospect, it is certainly possible that many of these activities, particularly those with the greatest amount of international support, were inspired by members whose paramount interest was the continued success of the Soviet Union. In that respect, and with 20/20 hindsight, those activities might be seen today as more self-serving than virtuous. There is no doubt in my mind, however, that no one I knew as a member or leader of the American Communist Party ever believed that those activities were anything but truly patriotic and in the best interests of the overwhelming majority of the American people. As I reflect back upon what a very small number of communists in the United States actually accomplished during those troubling times, I am pleasantly surprised by the positive significance of so many of those activities.

By far, however, our most pressing and time-consuming concerns centered around issues like the solidification of membership, the protection of a cadre of leadership and the endless demand for funds. While dues were collected and were meant to pay for some of those activities and the meager sustenance wages of full-time functionaries, they were supplemented by funds from regular club social events. Long before the height of the Smith Act prosecutions, the need for defense funds had become almost intolerable. Years of deportation and denaturalization proceedings, contempt of Congress citations, perjury trials, and sedition and espionage cases had made fundraising almost a full-time occupation for some of us. Raising money became increasingly more difficult as the repressive atmosphere became more intense and as the danger of domestic fascism became more credible. Normal activity was further hindered by expectations of immediate and even greater mass arrests. I recall sitting through a matinee and two evening performances, naively hiding inside a Philadelphia movie theatre with a visiting woman party leader from Washington, D.C. An early morning telephone message attributed to O. John Rogge, a former government official and noted attorney, told us that on that day the FBI had scheduled a roundup of all communist leaders throughout the nation.

Although the tip was inaccurate, something similar was anticipated a few years later when some of those convicted at the first Smith Act trial in New York jumped bail. Purportedly, they went "underground" to be in a position to provide national leadership when the "sweep" took place. There were no more "bail-jumpers," but expecting arrests, a number of communists elsewhere became "unavailable." In order to secure a cadre, they left their homes and functioned in a quasi-clandestine fashion. Others of us maintained our regular living patterns. I don't know how successful they were in other parts of the country, but in Philadelphia, being "unavailable" meant little. Everyone so designated had an occasional rendezvous with family members or attended some sort of special meeting. Having always functioned in the open, most of us were novices at concealment. At the time of the arrests in Philadelphia, Joe Roberts, Bob Klonsky, Joe Kuzma and Chick Katz, the four so-called unavailables, were every bit as available to the FBI as the rest of us.

Chapter 8

THE CITY OF BROTHERLY LOVE

As part of a major effort to justify new foreign and domestic policy emanating from the paranoia of a "world-wide communist conspiracy," the United States Government would find the Smith Act useful. Bureaucrats imposing federal loyalty oaths, the Senate Internal Security Sub-Committee, the House Committee on Un-American Activities, other Congressional investigations and their counterparts in every state throughout our nation were busily engaged in harassing tens of thousands as they enlarged upon the myth of a "menacing threat" to our internal security. If people could be brought before star-chamber committees because of peace and civil rights activities, or for past associations or long-abandoned views, and then lose their jobs or be cited for contempt of Congress and possibly even sent off to jail as the consequence, how could known Communist Party leaders *not* be rounded up and imprisoned?

The arrests and convictions of the first group of 11 national leaders of the Communist Party, at Foley Square in New York City in 1948, were confirmed by the United States Supreme Court on June 4, 1951. Between that confirmation and our arrests at the end of July 1953, there were eight more groups of three to 16 communists indicted under the Smith Act, a second group in New York and then, in rapid succession, in California, Baltimore, Pittsburgh, Honolulu, Detroit, St. Louis and Seattle. By the time of the arrests in Philadelphia, a total of 77 "conspirators," leaders of the Communist Party, had already been convicted. Forty-nine of them were awaiting the outcome of appeals to the higher courts, and each of the remaining 28 were serving out sentences of five years. They may have attended different meetings, conferences, conventions or schools, and they may have circulated different articles and letters to recruit new members, but the charges against them were identical to those leveled against the nine of us in Philadelphia: "conspiring to teach and advocate the necessity for overthrowing the government of the United States by force and violence as soon as circumstances would permit." In the three years that followed, still another 55 communist leaders would be similarly indicted in Cleveland, Connecticut, Denver, Puerto Rico and Boston.

Despite the small size of the American Communist Party, there was a growing frenzy to wipe it out. The "Cold War" had turned hot. Thirty-five thousand Americans were in the process of losing their lives fighting the

"Reds" in Korea. In addition to this concern in the Far East, the Soviets had found the way to make atomic weapons and many Americans feared their intentions. Major re-armament was at the top of our government's agenda, and "brinkmanship" became the "art" of foreign policy. As defined by Secretary of State John Foster Dulles, brinkmanship meant the ability to get to the *verge* of war without actually getting *into* war, based on the idea that "if you are scared to go to the brink, you are lost."

Aside from the organized political and ideological left, there was little opposition to those first arrests, trials, convictions and imprisonment of Communist Party leaders. A Gallup Poll of 1953 reported that two-thirds of those asked said they opposed allowing communists their right even to make public speeches.[1]

In Philadelphia, the mood of the general public seemed equally hostile. A questionnaire circulated there by the American Civil Liberties Union found overwhelming support for denying the right to vote to those refusing to serve in the armed forces; for permitting police censorship of books and movies; for allowing local government bans on the printing and selling of communist literature; for government loyalty oaths and non-communist affidavits; and, as in the Gallup Poll, for denying communists permission to speak publicly.[2]

"The air was inundated with McCarthyism...such that anyone who expressed anything but total disapproval of communists and communism would be considered a communist sympathizer....I myself was regarded with suspicion," Judge Joseph S. Lord III told me in an interview 36 years later. "I never did think you could get a fair trial, and I don't think you did. The air was filled with hobgoblins, and no jury could find in favor [of the defendants] in that atmosphere. The distinction between the charge and the fact that the defendants were communists was too great to overcome by most people."[3]

"It was McCarthyism at its absolute worst," said David Cohen, a Philadelphia councilman, when he was interviewed in 1989. "Fortunately, we haven't had or seen anything like it since. You could not get a fair trial. No such thing but an already determined verdict. It would look fair, but the atmosphere was such that a fair trial was impossible."[4]

Benjamin H. Read, a former Undersecretary of State in President Carter's Administration, who had been a member of our defense team, remembered the atmosphere at the time of our trial: "Utterly appalling in its madness."[5]

In general, the leaders of the major associations of the legal profession were no less affected by the anti-communist hysteria. In fact, for a period of time, it even appeared as if they were in the vanguard of the movement to deny communists their privileges under the Constitution. Resolutions were passed supporting loyalty oaths for the profession with recommendations that advocates of Marxism be expelled from the practice of law. In September 1950, the American Bar Association adopted a resolution that all attorneys be required to file affidavits declaring whether they were, or had ever been, members of the Communist Party. In February 1951, the ABA went one step further and urged that all communists and advocates of Marxism be expelled from legal practice. In 1953, there were operationalized proposals for investigations of attorneys who used their Fifth Amendment rights as protection against incrimination when they were questioned about possible communist affiliations. And there were the professional censures and the initiation of proceedings that led to the disbarment of some of the attorneys who had been cited for contempt of court following the first trial of communists under the Smith Act.[6]

Taken together, all of these factors were too much to overcome for most attorneys faced with deciding whether they could afford to defend Communist Party members. When these concerns mixed with the fear lawyers had of losing other clients or the fear that a hostile community would "paint them with the same brush" used on those they were being asked to defend, the selection of counsel of one's choice became nearly impossible for many an accused communist.[7] "It was not possible to get a fair trial in that atmosphere," recalled John Rogers Carroll, the youngest of our attorneys. "When my mother learned I was going to defend you—she was a typical Irish Catholic, you know—she said to me, 'You can't be with them and not of them' [the communists]. Her attitude reflected what most families of lawyers felt at the time. In fact, what lawyers themselves felt."[8]

In such an atmosphere it should not be surprising that even the national leadership of the American Civil Liberties Union had been so thoroughly intimidated that they, too, were reluctant to become overly involved in protecting the civil liberties of avowed communists. Consequently, despite some public disclaimers by the leadership of a couple of its local chapters, the ACLU, in the main, followed a policy of not participating in the day-to-day Smith Act trial proceedings. Instead, it filed occasional *amicus curae* briefs on constitutional issues and seemed particularly careful about publicly proclaiming its opposition to communism.[9]

In fact, FBI documents obtained in 1977 and 1984 through the Freedom of Information Act reveal that at least as early as November 8, 1939, and continuing to at least as late as October 8, 1964, there was direct and personal correspondence between J. Edgar Hoover and the chief counsel and spokesperson for the national offices of the American Civil Liberties Union, Morris Ernst, in which Ernst supplied names and information, as well as his personal services, to his "cherished friend," the Director of the Federal Bureau of Investigation, J. Edgar Hoover, so as "to aid in the traditions which you have established."[10]

"It was a scary period," Spencer Coxe, the past Executive Director of the Philadelphia branch of the ACLU, told me. "I wouldn't have taken a bet on your chances. The way in which the national ACLU office behaved was a disgrace....Although they had been pressed by us, they never made a statement about the loyalty oaths and all the other stuff during the McCarthy period. They were namby pamby, so afraid of being tarred with the communist brush. They never mounted a campaign against the McCarthy hysteria around the national security program."

"We here in Philadelphia were champing at the bit," Coxe continued. "We couldn't even get the national office to put out a pamphlet describing the rights of individuals when confronted by the FBI. They stalled and stalled, and we finally put one out ourselves.[11] The national ACLU took a most unfortunate, restricted view about the civil liberties of communists. And it's a view we did not share here."[12]

Other prominent jurists and lawyers agreed. When I interviewed Edmund B. Spaeth, one of our attorneys and later a justice of the Superior Court of Pennsylvania, he thought seriously for a moment, then observed that Philadelphians were not at the time "quite as paranoid about communism as others seemed to be in other parts of the country."[13]

Another of our attorneys who was to emerge as a leading civil libertarian activist and a fiery member of City Council, Henry W. Sawyer III, recollected that "while it was a period of hysteria throughout the nation, Philadelphia, however, was much more calm and complacent during the period than other places." He cited as examples the lack of disciplinary actions or firings at the University of Pennsylvania despite pressure to do so; the fact that there had been no bar association censorship of attorneys in Philadelphia, contrary to the national pattern; and his own candidacy and election to City Council shortly after his involvement with the Philadelphia Smith Act trial. I asked him if he thought that we might be found innocent at the time. "I really hoped so. I believed it possible but not likely....The jury, after all, was drawn from the same population that was constantly being told of a communist menace and had to have a strong mindset of guilt."[14]

On balance, the political and religious peculiarities rooted in Philadelphia's history and social institutions contributed to what would become the unique—and precedent-setting—defense of the Bill of Rights in that city. McCarthyism's relentless drive toward greater and greater restrictions upon the individual freedoms guaranteed by our Constitution, toward conformity in thought and passive acceptance of the status quo, was in contradiction with political developments in Philadelphia. Reformists there had been flexing their muscles for a few years and were growing stronger. For more than a century, the city had been controlled by Republican Party machine politics. And for almost 50 years, the city's citizens, seemingly proud of it, carried the famed muckraker Lincoln Steffens' label of "corrupt and contented." Not even the ravages of the Great Depression could break the hold of the party of the elephant. During the late 1930s, Republican city leaders refused $19 million of federal assistance rather than be beholden to President Franklin Delano Roosevelt. Some years after the end of World War II, the Republicans remained in control and while the city was still "corrupt," its citizens were no longer "contented."

During the late 1940s, a group of "Young Turks" emerged. Many of them were Depression-era college graduates, and they crossed party lines. Some of these young intellectuals were rebellious members of "old Philadelphia" families bent on reforming the city. One such "old Philadelphia aristocrat,"

Walter Phillips, succeeded in finding and recruiting allies for the reform movement. From among the families of other Philadelphia social and financial leaders emerged an Ingersol and a Hopkinson. Even though the Americans for Democratic Action was under national attack by McCarthyism, its Philadelphia branch was flourishing. It had been founded by the former owner of the Academy of Music and the President of the Academy of Fine Arts, John F. Lewis, and his wife. ADA became a part of Philadelphia's political reform. Albeit there were, indeed, other players. Fabled ethnic-minority business successes such as John B. Kelly, Jack McCloskey, Frederick Mann and Albert M. Greenfield joined in the campaign, and the "movement" made the Democratic Party its home. By 1952, Joseph Sill Clark, himself an old Philadelphia aristocrat, teamed with an adopted aristocrat, Richardson Dilworth. They were elected mayor and district attorney, respectively. Except for a brief period in 1881, it was the first time since before the Civil War that the Republicans were not in full control of Philadelphia. Clark, who subsequently went to the United States Senate, was succeeded in the mayor's chair by Dilworth. At the apex of McCarthyism, as if in defiance, a kind of paradoxical Philadelphia progressive reaction was underway.

Many of those progressive political developments during the early 1950s seemed rooted in the historical influence and impact of Philadelphia's Society of Friends. Whenever the Cradle of Liberty rocks promisingly, it manifests some of the best of those qualities attributed to Quaker thought: conscience and courtesy; modesty and moderation; kindness and care; caution and calm; and above all, during those years, temperance and tolerance. Quaker tolerance and support for dissent were important not only to the development of independent political reform, but to the manner in which some significant Philadelphians reacted to various aspects of McCarthyism. This was particularly the case when the defense of the city's Communist Party leadership was about to emerge.

Not the least among the aforementioned imperatives was a sense among some legal professionals of a need, at first among individuals and soon after formally by their organizations, to defend another heralded institution. Being challenged was the 200-year-old tradition of "the Philadelphia lawyer," the tradition begun by Andrew Hamilton which came to the defense of Peter Zenger and free speech. In 1735, Zenger was on trial. The New York printer had been charged with "seditious libel" because of material he had published that was critical of the royal governor. The New York lawyers defending Zenger had already been disbarred by that very same governor. Andrew Hamilton was secretly brought to New York from Philadelphia by Zenger's supporters. Amid considerable furor, Hamilton proceeded to win Zenger's acquittal and plant the seeds for a tradition that gave birth to a popular notion: To secure an acquittal, you need to bring in a Philadelphia lawyer. Thus, 218 years later in Philadelphia, even communists were to have their choice of counsel.

Cutting across those concerns were several of Philadelphia's Main Line aristocrats. These were the ultimate "Philadelphia gentlemen"—deeply conservative, from "old money" families, and forever lawyers. Outraged at some of the excesses of the period, they were so obviously secure in their social position that they could afford to be civil libertarians.

A maverick among them, who was eventually to become one of our attorneys, told me in an interview that "Philadelphia rode through the [McCarthy] era quite a bit better than any other region that I know. We had our share of lawyers who took the Fifth Amendment or were called before committees, but to my knowledge there was not a hint that they should be disciplined or thrown out of the bar association. That did happen in Pittsburgh and Boston and New York. I would say that the aristocrat and the Quaker influence was part of that."[15]

And according to Spencer Coxe, "Philadelphia is a kind of laid-back city...relatively tolerant in regard to radical politics...We don't get hysterical. That was clearly seen with the road shows, the visits by the [House] Un-American Activities Committee and the Senate Internal Security Sub-Committee. The hysteria and the frenzy that accompanied their visits elsewhere was missing. Their shows flopped in Philadelphia. There was much less publicity. The conservative press paid very little attention compared to the type of headlines in other cities....Fully one-third of ACLU's board at that time were Quakers, an equal number of liberal Jews and an equal number of the aristocracy."[16]

The significance of some of these phenomena seemed to have rubbed off on sections of Philadelphia's Communist Party leadership. Some of them had histories of labor union and community organization activities and placed a premium upon finding commonalities, developing ties and looking for coalition opportunities. During the early McCarthy years, two or three of them had set about "consciously developing relationships, building bridges and otherwise individually visiting, talking and acquainting liberals and Quaker leaders—particularly some attorneys—of their stake in the attacks that were taking place."[17]

Philadelphia had already had its small share of "unpopular" political defendants by the early 1950s. Perjury trials in regard to loyalty oaths, denaturalization and deportation proceedings against alleged subversives, arrests for "disturbing the peace" and "inciting to riot" of circulators of the Stockholm Peace Petition had taken place and had been making headlines for several years. These events had served as the background for the conscious and concerted efforts by leaders of the left to reach out. And out of this emphasis on defending civil liberties, a dozen or so of them participated in a series of informal meetings and discussions with local, and occasionally with national, Communist Party leaders.

As executive directors of the Civil Rights Congress and Progressive Party in densely populated Greater Philadelphia, Jack Zucker and "Hank" Beitscher called upon their past experiences and affiliations to advocate the wisdom of working with broader labor and community forces. They empha-sized the special ways that those forces reflected Philadelphia's civil liber-tarian and lawyerly traditions and the city's tolerance for different thoughts and ideas.

Shortly after Zucker's arrival, the Civil Rights Congress in Philadelphia turned its attention toward developing a board of directors congruent with this "reaching out" concept. In particular, the Civil Rights Congress began to establish relationships with groups from sections of the African-American, Jewish and Quaker communities. The Congress involved religious and com-munity leaders such as Rabbi Elias Charry, Reverend Kenneth Forbes, Lucy Carner, Elizabeth Frazier, Helen Philips and Reverend W.C. Williamson with their board of directors. According to Jack Zucker, the net result was the gen-eration of "organization and activity that was considerably different from other CRCs throughout the nation."

In 1950 and early 1951, following the harassment and arrests of sup-porters of the Stockholm Peace Appeal initiative who had been circulating petitions to "ban the bomb," a series of meetings was arranged. They were designed for "each side to better understand the other," and took place to discuss world peace, civil rights and civil liberties, "very seldom around the defense of the Communist Party and never for the purpose of getting any kind of commitment." More than a dozen such meetings took place, gener-ally over lunch, involving Clarence Pickett, Stephen Cary, Mildred Olmsted, Lucy Carner, Sadie Alexander, Elizabeth Frazier and Spencer Coxe. Sadie Alexander was a member of the Philadelphia African-American social elite, an advocate of quality education, an officer in the American Civil Liberties Union and the wife of a prominent judge. Pickett and Cary were national leaders of the American Friends Service Committee; Carner, Frazier and Olmsted were long-time women's rights and peace activists; and Spencer Coxe was the Executive Director of the ACLU.

These unofficial representatives of the Quaker and African-American communities met with Philadelphia communist leaders Ed Strong, Joe Roberts and Jack Zucker, and on occasion with national communist leaders Albert Blumberg, Arnold Johnson and Eugene Dennis. There were no strings attached, according to Zucker: "It was always understood that these discus-sions were to be just that, informal talks about issues of the time and not for the purpose of getting them to do things."[18]

Still, by the time of the Philadelphia Smith Act Trial it seemed that these meetings had had a profound effect; at least some of the participants were convinced that they, too, had a significant stake in what was happening to First Amendment rights during those peak years of McCarthyism.

Consternation over the growing attacks on civil liberties had been devel-oping among some of the legal minds in Philadelphia's chapter of the American Civil Liberties Union as early as the "peace arrests" in 1950. During September and October of 1952, Executive Director Spencer Coxe exchanged letters with no less than nine prominent Philadelphia attorneys affiliated with the ACLU regarding the "need to establish policy for a legal committee to handle civil liberties cases."[19] At about the same time, Coxe helped draft a letter for the Vice President of the ACLU, which was sent to the Civil Rights Committee Chair, Tom McBride. The letter referred to activities in Maryland and New York concerning possible resolutions on legal defense of unpopular causes. William Rahill, the ACLU's Vice President, called upon Tom McBride to bring those activities to the attention of his committee "with a view of the committee's recommending a resolution of similar character for adoption by the Philadelphia Bar Association."[20]

These were not just the natural outcomes of positions taken by an overly zealous local executive director prodding his lay leadership. Communication in regard to a possible resolution traveled in both directions. Still another vice president of the organization, Sadie Alexander, received a letter from Coxe thanking her for calling his attention to a *New York Times* report of similar actions underway within the New York Bar Association.[21]

During the winter and spring of 1953, the Philadelphia Bar Association's Committee on Civil Rights was, in fact, meeting. Its chairman, James Brittain, submitted a report that was printed in *The Legal Intelligencer* on May 28th. The report set forth the considerations and the conclusions of the committee and offered the following resolution, which was unanimously approved at the general membership meeting on June 2nd:

> Resolved, that the Philadelphia Bar Association recognizes that the right of counsel requires public acceptance of the correlative right of a lawyer to represent and defend, in accordance with the standards of the bar, any client without having imputed to him his client's reputation, views or character.
>
> Resolved further, that the association will support any lawyer against criticism or attack in connection with such representation when, in its judgment, he has acted in accordance with the standards of the bar.
>
> Resolved further, that the association will strive to educate the profession and the public on the rights and duties of a lawyer in representing any client regardless of the unpopularity of either the client or his cause.

The Philadelphia ACLU leadership started composing a letter immediately following that quarterly membership meeting, which it sent to Bernard Segal on July 3, 1953. The letter, signed for the board of directors by Earl Harrison, lauded the bar association's chancellor for the June 2nd resolution, "especially during the difficult period through which we are now passing....As you know, some of our courts, including the Supreme Court of the United States, have noted with apprehension that many lawyers, because of the state of public opinion, have manifested apparent reluctance to represent persons or organizations because of the nature of the charges or accusations involved....We could not let this occasion pass without expressing this word of high commendation to the lawyers of this city for their timely pronouncements upon a principle fundamental to the civil liberties of all the people of this nation."[22]

These developments represented a coming together of a movement, if not necessarily in coalition, then certainly pointing in the same direction. Several years of national attacks on the civil liberties of political dissidents led to conscious efforts on the part of Philadelphia's ideological left to pique the latent concerns of sections of that city's Quaker community. These efforts, in combination with a long-revered if seemingly dormant legal tradition and a more receptive political atmosphere, produced the bar association resolution almost as if they knew we would be arrested the next month.

During the month of August 1953, while my co-defendants and I were in prison awaiting bail reduction and release, and our wives, colleagues and friends unsuccessfully sought counsel to represent us, Spencer Coxe of the ACLU was among those pressed. "I was relatively new with the ACLU at the time, and a few of the defendants' wives came and requested counsel." Coxe told me that as a result, the ACLU board of directors met and decided that "they did not have their own counsel to provide....The trial would be of such scope that it would be beyond the capacity of the ACLU to provide counsel on the scale that would be needed....The organized bar in Philadelphia had the responsibility and duty to provide counsel and that they had laid it on Tom McBride to do so....We made strenuous efforts to get the Philadelphia Bar Association itself to designate lawyers to represent them, because we thought the cause of civil liberties would be better served if the organized bar was made to take its responsibility for the defense of unpopular people. This would be a greater service on our part than finding lawyers ourselves to do it....We therefore declined the requests of these communists to represent them, and, instead, we met with the bar association to persuade them to put together a defense team."[23,24]

While most people were cowed by the frightening atmosphere, there were significant others who defied intimidation. The couple who lived next door to me, with their concentration camp-scarred parents, made courtroom appearances to demonstrate their concern for me. Some neighbors sent birthday cards and notes of care to me in prison.

And then there were the denizens of Bobby's. Bobby's was around the corner, next door to my friend Al's watch repair shop on 31st Street, across from Frank the barber, another friend. It was a sort of den of iniquity—no one really wanted to admit to shooting pool in the basement or playing poker in the back rooms. Occasionally, everyone was in the front—to buy one of the biggest ice cream cones or to drink the best ice cream soda in Strawberry Mansion, of course!

My son Marc, by now, was a tough six-year-old, knew his way around and regularly made it to Bobby's, pretending not to know or care about the back rooms. And as he ambled up to the counter stool on this particular day, I was at Holmesburg Prison—not as a visitor. The newspapers all had my "smirking" photo, connecting me to their "violent overthrow" stories on the front pages. I was big news.

Well, Al told me he was there that day and so did Frank, and they were eating ice cream, you can bet, when Marc ambled up to the counter. "I don't know what was going to happen," Al told me. It seems that a regular at the poker tables was at the counter for a soda. He wasn't a nice guy. Al and Frank didn't like him, and they painted me a picture of a real adult bully, a brute, a "bullvan."

Marc never got to the stool, Al told me. Right in front of him stood this 250-pound, menacing-looking hulk, and the confrontation went like this:

Hulk: Whatcha doin' here, kid?

Marc: Gettin' some ice cream.

Hulk (even more menacing): Yeh, what's your name?

Marc (softly): Marc.

Hulk: Dontcha have a last name?

Marc: Yep, Labovitz.

Hulk (even louder): How do yuh spell that?

Marc (spelling): L-A-B-O-V-I-T-Z.

Hulk (pausing): Is'at so?—Your father's name Sherman?

Marc (very wary and whispering): Uh-huh.

The big guy abruptly turned to Bobby, behind the counter with scoop in hand. "Give the kid an ice cream cone on me," he bellowed and returned to his cards in the back room.

A GATHERING DEFENSE

It was the last week in August 1953.

We had gathered at the Weisses' for our first out-of-prison meeting. We sat around a large picnic-like table in a room that served as a meeting and dining area. We were discussing plans for our defense, the inability to retain or commit counsel, the funds required to conduct an adequate defense, the virtual certainty of conviction and lengthy prison sentences in the face of the existing anti-communist hysteria, and the lack of money available for living expenses.

I suppose it was recognition of the enormity of the situation that for the first time abruptly and totally engulfed me. What welled up inside me was an inability to fathom just what was going on and a sudden sensing that I could not take anything more in. It was completely overwhelming. It wasn't the usual kind of fear that one can generally muster the wherewithal to overcome. It wasn't the sense of inadequacy or lack of effectiveness that a closer look at one's progress and accomplishment frequently ameliorates. For me it was a sudden sense of total impotence—of lacking even the least bit of control over my own life. For a second or two I actually "blacked out" until something magical grabbed hold and returned me to the reality of the discussion going around that table. Perhaps it was the sudden sense of strength that one experiences when identifying and joining with others in a common cause and struggle, however seemingly futile.

Meanwhile, what communists used to call "solidarity" was coalescing among the ranks of Philadelphia's most prestigious law firms—on our behalf! Chancellor Segal had again been in contact with Judge Allan K. Grim, who had the case at that time. According to the report of the Civil Rights Committee, Segal discussed the lack of counsel with Grim, and subsequently, "with the aid of the vice chancellor and the chairman of the board of governors," arranged for a meeting of a large number of leaders of the bar, which was held in the chancellor's office. The meeting "was able to arrange to have Thomas D. McBride, Esq. head a group of lawyers who would undertake to represent generally such of the defendants as might wish him to do so." McBride was "assured that he would be given every assistance in assembling an adequate group of defense counsel."[1]

Segal set about contacting all the major law firms in the city, asking each to provide a young lawyer for the team. Interviewed later, almost everyone on the team said he had volunteered readily, in part to work with the highly respected McBride. On September 14, 1953, the nine of us were finally arraigned in federal court. Simultaneously, the bar association announced that its Committee on Criminal Justice and Law Enforcement Chairman, Tom McBride, had undertaken to be chief counsel and would head a group of defense lawyers. In court, Judge Grim commended McBride and the bar association and observed, "Now the case can be argued and tried as expeditiously as we are able...."[2]

On December 17, 1953, Bernard Segal, retiring from his post as chancellor, presented the lawyers to the court for appointment. The team was young, but impressive—and its members would go on to become some of the most influential civil liberties attorneys, trial lawyers and jurists in the country. Without reservation and with no hesitation, each of the attorneys I interviewed said that his defense of nine communist leaders during the height of the McCarthy hysteria was a highlight in a successful career.

Chief Counsel Tom McBride was 54 years old and already the most renowned and respected attorney for the defense in Philadelphia when he took on the Smith Act case. Segal later described him as "without doubt the stand-out lawyer, as good as any Philadelphia ever produced." John Carroll, one of the other attorneys, called him a "walking modern Andrew Hamilton." Tom was tall, thin and stoop-shouldered. What was left of his dark hair was graying rapidly. His squared-off chin framed a rather large face within which sat a pair of twinkling eyes and a nose upon which hung a pair of reading glasses. He reminded many of us of the great character actor, Barry Fitzgerald.

By the time it had become evident that Tom McBride would be our chief counsel, several things were patently clear as to procedure. He would consult and seek consensus, be open to suggestions and welcome assistance from the defendants and others. The trial would be a vigorous and forthright defense of civil liberties and the defendants' constitutional rights. It would not be an exposition of the Communist Party's program. If this was unacceptable, McBride was not interested in participating.

The defendants were not novices, and we had done our homework. From researching some cases in which he had been counsel, from "comrades" who were lawyers and from other sources we probably learned more about Tom McBride than he knew about us. He was without peer and had unquestionable integrity. And if that were insufficient, we were also aware of the close relationship he enjoyed with another attorney, Lou McCabe.

McCabe and several other defense lawyers were cited for contempt of court by Judge Harold Medina as a result of their vigorous participation in the first New York Smith Act trial. We were also informed that McCabe was McBride's "Irish crony and drinking partner" whom he held in high regard and with whom he regularly consulted.

At the time of the Philadelphia Smith Act arrests, McBride had already won an important victory for civil liberties. In 1951, during the course of a loyalty oath perjury trial, *United States v. Winston*, McBride, citing the constitutional right of his client to confront accusations, demanded that the Federal Bureau of Investigation reveal the source of its accusing testimony. Claiming that to do so would endanger national security, the FBI refused. Federal Court Judge George Welsh, in a most unusual move for the time, granted McBride's motion to dismiss the case.[3] At the time of my incarceration, Tom McBride was serving as the chairperson of the ACLU Committee for Civil Rights, and it was he who brought the issue to the bar association's Committee on Civil Rights, of which he was also a member. In addition, McBride was chair of the bar association's Committee on Criminal Justice and Law Enforcement, a member of its board of governors and, subsequently, he was to become the association's chancellor. With his position regarding how the trial should proceed clearly defined, McBride enlisted Joseph S. Lord III as his co-counsel.

If Tom McBride was the conductor, then Joseph S. Lord III was the concertmaster. Tall, straight as a ramrod, athletic-looking, prematurely bald and always immaculately attired, Lord was an established and successful partner in the firm of Richter, Lord and Farage when McBride sought him out personally to become his adjutant for our defense. Lord's presence was a daily factor in all arguments, motions and presentations before the court. He also figured prominently in the appeals process. Not only was Lord most active in our defense, but he became an ardent advocate of our decency as individuals. When I first interviewed Joe Lord, so many years later, it was an emeritus Chief Judge of the U.S. District Courts who warmly and nostalgically reminded me of my visit, during the trial, to the hospital room of his wife. I was carrying flowers. "I can even tell you their colors," he mused.

At the time of our arrests, Dave Davis was the business agent of Local 155 of the United Electrical, Radio and Machine Workers' Union. The union's attorney was Dave Cohen. When the defense team started to shape up, Cohen was the logical choice to represent Davis. Only 41 years old, he was nevertheless about 10 years older than most of the staff with whom he would be working. Of medium height and slightly stooped, he was soft-spoken and, at least outwardly, calm. But Dave Cohen was employed by a labor union and not by one of Philadelphia's elite law firms; he was neither an aristocrat nor an Anglo-Saxon; and his "yiches" (pedigree) came out of the Eastern European immigrant experience. It shouldn't be surprising that from the outset, the defendants were very comfortable with Dave and pleased with his presence on the case. At first he seemed ill at ease, but it did not take long before his experience and adversarial skills were recognized and welcomed by all.

To the extent that the rest of the defendants had one personal attorney at the trial, mine was William S. Woolston. He collected the materials, watched for all references and prepared the briefs relating to me. Woolston was a respected Quaker lay leader and an already well-established attorney who headed the 1951 grand jury probe of police graft and corruption in Philadelphia. Bill had represented us in place of Tom McBride at the first bail-reduction hearing and remained as part of the defense team. Except for McBride, Lord and Cohen, Woolston was older than the rest of the relatively young staff. Following the trial, he continued as an ACLU attorney, represented other victims of McCarthyism and was involved with civil liberties issues prior to his premature death at age 56 in 1964.

During the course of the long trial that developed, inquiries came from various places throughout the country. Leaders of other local bar associations wanted information about our unique team and defense. Joseph N. DuBarry IV, part of a family that long represented revered Philadelphia institutions such as the University of Pennsylvania, was the attorney designated to respond and provide helpful suggestions. DuBarry also was involved in researching the testimony of prosecution witnesses at previous Congressional hearings and court appearances.

The firm of Saul, Biddle and Saul selected Robert W. Sayre for the team. One of the firm's young litigation attorneys, he had the tedious task of examining each day's transcript and organizing the material on file cards so that it could be used efficiently by Tom McBride and Joe Lord at the following court session.

When Chancellor Segal's own firm—Schnader, Harrison, Segal and Lewis—searched for a likely candidate, "I volunteered," recalled still another young litigation lawyer, Charles Hileman. "I thought it would be a great experience, and I believed the defendants deserved a fair trial. While I thought the Smith Act unconstitutional and an abomination, I probably would have volunteered just to be able to work with Tom McBride." During the early days of the trial, Hileman conceived of an intricate instrument for the indexing of testimony and exhibits as they related to the charges in the indictment.

The youngest of the attorneys to join us was the clean-cut, boyish-looking John Rogers Carroll. He was just out of law school and was working out of Tom McBride's office. McBride became Carroll's very demanding mentor. Almost daily, he had the exacting task of preparing the written briefs that were called for with regularity by a frequently impatient Judge Ganey. Carroll also had a major hand in the preparation of materials for a possible appeal.

Benjamin H. Reed was loaned to the McBride defense team by the firm of Duane, Morris and Heckscher. Read always reminded me of the Jimmy Stewart character in *Mr. Smith Goes to Washington*. He was at least 6 feet 4 inches tall, very lean, handsome and sad-looking. Read was a marvelous researcher, and his diligent analysis of previous testimony of the prosecution's professional informers proved to be invaluable and among the highlights of the trial.

Henry Sawyer III came to the defense team from the firm of Drinker, Biddle and Reath. He had been an attorney with the Marshall Plan and was known as a civil libertarian. In his mid-thirties, he, too, was tall and very trim, and he wore pinched ties and collars inside tweed suits. When combined with flaming red hair, a pock-marked flushed face and a "no nonsense" work ethic that placed him wherever there was action, they all worked to make Henry Sawyer an imposing figure throughout the trial. He clearly had the ears of McBride and Lord, and the three of them huddled frequently. Sawyer was also responsible for preparing the cross-examination of a premier prosecution witness, Louis Budenz.

When Harold Evans of MacCoy, Evans and Lewis selected Edmund B. Spaeth, he made it clear to everyone that "I was not to be penalized." Spaeth acknowledged that the trial was of "personal interest and exciting, a real highlight. Glad I had a chance to do it." It was Spaeth, in the first days of the trial, who worked out the duty roster spelling out each attorney's responsibilities. Spaeth indicated that the decision by the Philadelphia Bar Association to get engaged in the Smith Act case probably established a precedent for its subsequent involvement with civil rights, Vietnam and other public issues.

I will always remember being admonished by the future Judge Spaeth late one afternoon in 1954. Court had adjourned, and he and I had gone to the Free Library, on the beautiful Benjamin Franklin Parkway, to find what we might about one of the government's paid professional witnesses, Louis Budenz. After an hour or more of leafing through old newspapers, I let him know that I had a meeting to attend. He, in turn, let me know in no uncertain terms that he felt I should be more concerned with my defense than with Communist Party meetings. I compromised; I was late for that meeting.

On September 16th, the nine Smith Act defendants issued a press release: "We are pleased to announce that we have retained Mr. McBride who will henceforth serve as chief counsel for eight of the defendants. David Davis will be represented by...Mr. David Cohen. Commendation is due the Philadelphia Bar Association and the countless others who assisted in winning this important victory for democracy....We wish therefore, at this time, to publicly express our deepest gratitude, both as individuals and co-defendants, to all persons and organizations, regardless of their political belief, who contributed...to the common effort to preserve our American democratic heritage, restore the Bill of Rights and re-establish constitutional rights of free speech and free association."[4]

On September 17th, in a letter to the national officers of the American Civil Liberties Union apprising them of the retention of Tom McBride as chief counsel, Spencer Coxe wrote: "Philadelphia ACLU can also take some credit for all this, since we acted very swiftly after the arrest of the alleged communists in urging the bar association to help procure counsel. We assisted the bar association Committee on Criminal Justice in drawing up a list of possible counsel...."[5] On January 25, 1954, each member of the defense team of lawyers received a special commendation from the bar association's new chancellor, C. Brewster Rhoads.[6]

McBride's entrance into the case and the campaign for additional attorneys marked a first in the annals of Smith Act trials; the Philadelphia Bar Association had assumed open and direct responsibility for guaranteeing and providing counsel. However, it was also clearly understood that the team McBride would eventually lead would be retained directly by the defendants under the usual arrangements that existed between lawyers and clients. To that end, the defendants contracted to pay $65,000 for the services rendered during the trial in the lower court. While the fee was a huge amount of money in the mid-1950s, in retrospect it was fair and certainly considerate of our circumstances. John Carroll was reminiscing about the attorneys from the other major law firms when he told me, "None of them ever, though offered, accepted any of the $65,000 that the defendants raised and paid for the trial."

By the time the entire group of lawyers was put together and all had cleared their desks and calendars, J. Cullen Ganey had replaced Alan Grim as trial judge. The judge thanked the team for offering their services to assist Tom McBride and set March 8, 1954 as the date to commence.[7]

As our trial date drew near, a couple of stories floated among the defendants that brought our own wishful thinking together with where things really seemed to be. Both anecdotes involved leading Philadelphia lawyers. One of those attorneys, Henry Drinker, an older, conservative gentleman from the Main Line, was the head of a most prestigious law firm. Of course, he was present at the fateful meeting in Chancellor Segal's office to discuss how to implement supplying Tom McBride with a "group" of young attorneys. The meeting, we were told, was long, filled with differences of opinion and fraught with tension, but it hastened to a successful conclusion when Henry Drinker, seemingly exasperated and with no more patience, stormed toward the door, shouting as he slammed it behind him, "I'll send one of my best."

So many years later, during one of my interviews with Henry Sawyer, I told him the story I remembered about his ex-boss, Henry Drinker, and that meeting in Chancellor Segal's office. Sawyer smiled and noted that "Mr. Drinker also said, 'We will do this whether or not anyone else does.'"

The second story had to do with a major public figure, Walter E. Allesandroni. As a leader in the bar association, a member of its board of governors, an active politician and Commander of the Veterans of Foreign Wars, Allesandroni was caught up in the spirit of the time. His anti-communism was legendary and made regular newspaper headlines. A couple of the defendants ran across him in the corridors of the federal courthouse one morning, and after some banter he is alleged to have said, "You were lucky you got McBride. I was determined you'd get an attorney even if I had to defend you, and you know what kind of defense that would have been."

Meetings between the lawyers and the defendants were not always easy. But as time went on, ease and respect increased. I remember one such meeting when all of the defendants and attorneys exchanged views on whether the defendants were to testify or not. I was all charged up that day. I had already spent a couple of days being briefed, preparing what was to be my testimony at the trial, and I was ready. Now, it seemed, we were not to testify.

The thing that stands out from that meeting was the extent to which, by that time, everyone seemed to be listening, and whatever early misgivings I had about the sincerity of my attorneys had all but vanished. Any lingering doubts about their genuineness or trustworthiness disappeared that afternoon. One of the younger attorneys, McBride's protégé John Carroll, may have sensed from my eyes some ambivalence about being prepared and wanting to exercise my right to be heard, while at the same time recognizing the apparent wisdom in sacrificing that desire. He began to push me to break with several of my more resistant colleagues. He immediately realized his insensitivity and nodded when Tom McBride softly admonished, "There is no need to press—it's important to them. He'll work it out with the others." We did, of course, work it out.

Among ourselves, the other defendants and I were not unanimously enthusiastic about the course events were taking. On the one hand, we were to be represented by the finest young lawyers from the most prestigious law firms in the city. On the other hand, how could we trust ourselves to be in the hands of the "scions of steel magnates and other capitalist giants," as, indeed, some were.

There was a party position borne out of lengthy experience with political trials. This position held that it was impossible to present a real defense of the Communist Party because the cards would always be stacked against left-wing political dissidents and juries were never selected that would bring in verdicts other than guilty. Therefore, at best, trials should be seen only for the opportunities they provided to expose the corrupt criminal justice system and to disseminate socialist ideals and the Communist Party's program for their attainment. But again, "on the other hand," there had been nothing in the results of the previous Smith Act trials to suggest that such tactics were producing new respect for socialism, let alone support for Communist Party members or sympathizers. Of even greater significance, the tremendous breakthrough represented in the broader community's involvement in the bail-reduction and counsel-selection processes found most of the defendants ready to accept the proposition that the Philadelphia Smith Act trial should proceed around the defense of the Bill of Rights. Some of us also began to think that, whatever the improbability, there was at least a possibility that in this particular Smith Act case we might even win. Not one of us was interested in martyrdom.

There was surprisingly little disagreement among us regarding either the wisdom involved in going this route or in any break with party principles. While all of us, to the best of my recollection, agreed with the decision and were so inclined from the outset, Joe Kuzma had the most questions and was, perhaps, the least enthusiastic. And from the very beginning, it was

Ben Weiss, whose wife Helen emerged as a leader among our wives, who put forth the most supportive and convincing arguments for the course we were to follow thereafter. Except for some minimal questioning, about the direction in which we were going, there was no pressure to do otherwise from the national offices of the Communist Party. In deference to past principle and with some sensitivity to our pride, there was one compromise. It was to arrive at an agreement with Tom McBride, who told the court that he had agreed "in a perfectly amicable manner to withdraw so that [Joe] Kuzma might act as his own counsel."[8]

Although there were two or three among the defendants with higher Communist Party authority, Joe was the natural choice for several reasons: He did have some reservations about what was unfolding; he did not fit the stereotype of a communist leader—of the nine defendants, Joe was the only one neither Jewish nor African-American; and, fortuitously, it was his name that headed the list at the top of our indictment in the case of *United States v. Kuzma, et al.*

Joe would sit at the counsel table and speak for the political ideologies we were being tried for exercising in a democracy. "I am a communist," he said in his opening statement. "This is probably your first opportunity to see and hear a communist. This is so because we communists have in many ways been deprived of our rights to be heard in spite of our desires and efforts to speak to the people....Marxism-Leninism has nothing in common with the advocacy of force and violence. We believe that it is possible for socialism to be achieved through peaceful means."

Before he was half through, the U.S. attorney would interrupt him a dozen times with objections to his sweeping denial of the charges and to his references to a "thought-control trial." Finally, the judge stopped Kuzma, studied the balance of his prepared statement and, after deleting sections, admonished that "an autobiography is not pertinent."

Tom McBride, in his own opening statement, declared that Joe Kuzma had a perfect right to read the statement exactly as it was written. In fact, McBride told the court, the "issue [is] freedom of speech and assembly."

An open letter, signed by each of us, which was released and circulated on the previous September 16th, had presaged Joe's dramatic speech by obliquely letting our plans be known.

"In the coming days and weeks," we wrote, "we intend to speak out in the most positive and forthright manner in the courtroom as well as before the bar of public opinion, not alone to prove our innocence but to help expose the true conspirators against the best interests of the Nation and its people.

"We know that once learning the true character of this political frameup under the infamous Smith Act, additional thousands will come forward ready to contribute their time, energy and great sums of money, necessary in our common struggle to help save the Bill of Rights and contribute to the defeat of the war plans of American Big Business."

The daily newspapers reminded us the next day that in spite of our line-up of first-string lawyers, the general political climate still menaced our chances of getting a fair trial. Philadelphia's "free press" responded to our open letter with the headline: "9 PHILA. REDS THREATEN TO MAKE TRIAL A CIRCUS—U.S. SET TO CRACK DOWN—Suspects' Letter Tells of Plans." The article in the *Philadelphia Inquirer* went on to distort our appeal for support and funds: "Nine Philadelphia Communist leaders indicted on charges of advocating overthrow of the Government by force warned yesterday they would make a circus of their trial in the Federal courts." This constituted "a threat to create a series of incidents," making the case a "farce and a travesty of justice."

There was no court session when we met the next day. Weary and angry, we discussed how impossible it would be to get a fair trial. We debated our responsibility for meeting the expectations of our membership for still another statement of the party's position. We also talked about how we had only just begun the development of a relationship with our attorneys and that the undertaking in which we were engaged was an ongoing process. At that meeting, we were coming to grips with our need to change the traditional communist strategy in the courtroom of presenting the party position to one of defending our civil liberties and our constitutional rights.

Knowing well the struggles we would encounter in such a climate in the months that were to follow, we decided not to respond to the inflammatory *Philadelphia Inquirer* article. After a long, soul-searching meeting on the following day, we decided on immediate self-defense tactics: a Sunday picnic with our families and friends.

Chapter 10

RIG A JURY AND PARADE THE INFORMERS

"It is March 1, 1954," wrote Walter Lowenfels from his retreat in South Jersey. "In two weeks the Eisenhower Administration plans to have me and eight friends in court in Philadelphia. We are to be put on trial under a federal statute known as the Smith Act—i.e. for 'subversive thoughts.' Meanwhile I just look out of the doors. The thermometer, which was in the 20s for months, now registers 58 degrees. The rose vines are sprouting. At their side, green swords are cutting up from the earth—the beginning of an invasion of jonquils. Looking at our small patch of earth, I am quite aware that I must get used to spending this spring in court. Our lawyer asked me the other day, 'Can I use what you just said?'

"I am now giving him permission in black and white, as follows: When the administration of justice gets down to arresting a poet for 'conspiring to advocate and teach the overthrow of the government by force and violence' they are scraping the bottom of the barrel!"[1]

The prosecution had not charged us with conspiring to overthrow the U.S. Government by force and violence. They hadn't even charged us with advocating its overthrow. We were indicted for *conspiring to teach to advocate an overthrow*. But when it was time, on the 21st day of March 1954, to select a jury, it became clear that they would not even be asked to pass judgment on evidence about that allegation. The selected jurors were going to be asked to judge our views regarding social and economic change and, on that basis alone, decide whether we should be imprisoned.

In all of the previous Smith Act trials, the defense challenged the constitutionality of the jury selection process in the federal courts. Their goal was to demonstrate the exclusivity of the panels from which potential jurors were selected and to show that this discrimination favored white Anglo-Saxons and middle-class suburbanites. These jury challenges delayed the beginnings of every trial for weeks. The first indication that things in Philadelphia would be different came when the defendants agreed with our attorneys' recommendation to forego a jury challenge so as not to appear to be "using delaying tactics." In retrospect, some of us took the view of our attorney, Ben Read. "We may have made an error. [A jury challenge] probably wouldn't have made a difference [except to] maybe increase the possibility of a couple of acquittals."

The old Federal Court House, facing south on east Chestnut Street, was an imposing structure. In order to enter its marble-floored reception area, one had to climb three wide sets of six concrete steps. For the next five and a half months, I did exactly that and entered one of several elevators that took me up to the second floor and Judge J. Cullen Ganey's courtroom. On one of those occasions, as I backed onto the elevator to allow others access, I turned my head to see what I had inadvertently trampled. It was Judge Ganey's foot. I was so startled at his appearance that I failed to offer an apology. He was much larger in all respects than my courtroom impressions of him. Well over six feet tall, he was barrel-chested and had plenty of grayish-blond hair parted in the middle and a flushed fair complexion. As he withdrew his foot from under mine, he did not need to utter a sound; the anger was in his eyes.

Judge Ganey's courtroom could seat about 100 people comfortably. There was additional seating space along the wall at the rear for another dozen who had reasons to regularly come and go. No one was permitted to stand. A rail separated this section from the front, where ample room existed for all participants in the proceedings. Facing forward on the right was a table sufficiently large to accommodate the chief prosecutor, W. Wilson White, U.S. attorney for the district; and as needed, one or two of his assistants; and, up from Washington, D.C., a few special prosecutors considered experienced in Smith Act cases assigned by the Department of Justice. To the left—Should it have been any other way?—was the defense table at which could always be found McBride, Lord, Cohen and Kuzma; and on most days, two of the other enlisted attorneys who answered to the duty roster that had been set up by Edmund Spaeth. Behind this table, directly in front of the rail, sat the rest of the defendants. Everyone faced a perched Judge Ganey, with an elevated witness stand to his left and the sidebar to his right. Two court stenographers were in front of him at our level. The mahogany walls of the courtroom were covered with portraits of erstwhile federal judges, and the Stars and Stripes hung prominently behind the witness stand.

When the headlines were hot, Courtroom 3 generally had its audience of a half dozen or so from the media, at least eight of the unindicted, others from both teams, some supporters, the curious, the vindictive, family members and, of course, each and every day, our wives.

Jury selection started on March 21, 1954. It was a slow and tedious process. The defense and the prosecution had each been given 15 peremptory challenges to be used if Judge Ganey was not satisfied from the lawyers' interrogations that a prospective juror should be dismissed for cause. Neither side wanted to use those challenges indiscriminately, and Judge Ganey dismissed few for cause. It was not unusual, consequently, that there would be 45 minutes of questions and answers before it was determined whether any one prospective juror would serve.

One candidate who believed that "socialism is against the Constitution" added that she would be able to divorce herself from that belief when judging the defendants. Our chief attorney suggested that "the ability to divorce yourself from your beliefs would be a magical feat." The judge admonished, "The vast majority of the American people would say that capitalism is a heritage of our constitutional system. We can't go into the rationations of one's mind." Our attorney responded, "If we can't get an impartial trial, the Constitution guarantees that a defendant cannot be tried at all. Just doing the best we can is not good enough." Since the judge refused to dismiss for cause, the defense used one of its peremptory challenges.

The government attorneys had tried to hold onto this would-be juror, but they used their peremptory challenges to exclude a Black school teacher who was a member of the NAACP and the Fellowship Commission, which she described as being for "better human relations"; a Jewish housewife from my own community who was brought to this country at the age of six months after "being born in Russia"; and a life-insurance salesman who indicated that he had been an active trade unionist.

Another prospective juror identified herself as a Quaker, a clerk of a Friends meeting, a graduate of Swarthmore College and a writer. She was briefed by the judge, and after some preliminary questions by the U.S. attorney, was asked if she was familiar with the Smith Act. She asked for the "essence of it" to be restated so that she "would understand it better." After repeating a brief description of those portions of the Act involved in the trial, the interrogator asked the prospective juror if she would "have any prejudice against finding a verdict of guilty." She replied, "I would not hesitate if the evidence were such that it did prove it, but it would have to be proved...." She then asked the prosecuting attorney, "When a person is teaching in a college classroom, for instance, and brings up communism and the various types of governments and ways of life different from our own, is that in violation of the Smith Act?" The U.S. attorney replied, "No indeed, it is not. I don't think I should go much further into it." The court went into recess.

When the session resumed, the interview continued with a few brief questions from the defense attorney about the prospective juror's three sons and her husband's business and trade union connections. The defense then indicated that it had no further questions. The U.S. attorney, however, did. "Have you formed any opinion concerning the Communist Party in the United States?" To which the prospective juror replied, "Well, it would not be my way of life, if that is what you mean. I don't approve of it as my way of life, but there are many people that differ from the way I feel on a great many subjects." A little later, when asked if the charges had been made clear to her, the candidate responded, "It is a conspiracy...to teach and advocate the overthrow by force and violence." The U.S. attorney then wanted to know if in regard to that particular charge, the would-be juror had "any opinion...one way or another" about the Communist Party. She answered, "I don't believe I do." Then, as to whether she could be objective, she said, "I think that my ancestors that came here and founded Pennsylvania came for religious and political reasons from the other country, and they would be called heretics, too, and I think each person has a point of view which might be different from the other, and it has to be proved definitely by evidence of the charges that are put against them." Seemingly surprised by the response, the U.S. attorney asked, "Well, is it your feeling that these defendants would be tried for their views?" The woman answered, "I think they will be tried for their actions and their views, don't you?"

The prosecuting attorney wasn't doing too well, it appeared, so the judge took over the questioning. Acknowledging the candidate's strong personal aversion and opposition to "communist ideology," the judge wanted to know if her views would "concede to another the right to profess the diametrically opposite point of view," and the would-be juror answered, "I think I would take it from an objective point of view on evidence and not the way I feel personally." The judge pressed further, "Do you think you could do that freely without any real, continual compulsion on your part so to believe?" She responded, "I think so, because that is what Friends try to do in the world—feel that there are many, many peoples, and you try to understand them, not through accepting their point of view, but you can accept or reject according to the way you feel."

The judge had no more questions, and he did not seem particularly receptive to any further questions or comments.

"The government exercises its peremptory challenge, Your Honor," the U.S. attorney announced. And the prospective juror was excused.

The entire exhausting process finally ended with the seating of 12 jurors and four alternates on April 6th. Of the nine women, seven described themselves as housewives, one was a secretary and one was a retired teacher and the jury's only African American. Among the seven men selected were two metal workers, an accountant and four retired business executives. Now that a "jury of our peers" was picked, the trial could commence.

Remember—we were charged with conspiring to teach to advocate a violent overthrow. Remember—the overt acts attributed to us that were meant to demonstrate such a conspiracy were hardly of a violent nature. They consisted entirely of conferences, conventions, meetings and picnics, none of which contained even a hint of force or violence. How would the government proceed?

On April 8, 1954, U.S. Attorney W. Wilson White opened the case for the prosecution and told the judge and jury that my eight co-defendants and I held "highest authority" in the national leadership of the Communist Party, which we "helped reorganize" in 1945 as a "militant machine" for destruction of the U.S. Government by force, and that we were instrumental in discrediting the former party general secretary, Earl Browder, and "his policy of overthrow by democratic means."

"We will show that Marxist teachings and communist principles are that socialism is inevitable...by violent and forceful seizure under leadership of the Communist Party...at the time of national crisis, unrest or disorder." This was pretty tough stuff, and I suppose at least a few in the very crowded courtroom were waiting with baited breath for Mr. White to begin to tell how he "would prove that the nine defendants were prepared to lead the so-called proletariat in the forceful seizure of power." I also suppose that they were a bit disappointed when the U.S. attorney announced just what it was that the prosecution would "show" about each of the defendants. It was exactly what we had already stipulated—party membership and leadership. "We will show that Labovitz was a leader after its reorganization in 1945, and was circulation manager of the *Daily Worker*." No one listening, however, could say that they were not forewarned: "There is no doubt that the case will take longer than the usual criminal trial...we will do a considerable amount of reading from communist literature."

The United States attorney had set the stage, this time in Philadelphia, for the manner in which federal government prosecutors went about proving their cases against all other indicted party leaders. They would follow the pattern established in previous Smith Act prosecutions. The first step was to fan the prevalent hysteria by taking time to identify and prove that the defendants were members of the Communist Party despite the fact that we had already told the court that we were the party's Philadelphia leadership. As in the other trials, to build its case, the government would next proceed to read aloud long passages from Marx, Engels, Lenin and others and ask a parade of ex-communist "experts" to interpret those statements. These self-professed authorities would then finger defendants in an attempt to put them into party leadership positions and place them at meetings while purporting some alleged oblique reference to Marxist-Leninist literature.

Their Herculean task was to demonstrate, first of all, that the important historical writings contained doctrines that advocated forcible overthrow and that those doctrines applied to the government of the United States. Books and pamphlets written as early as the mid-nineteenth century and as late as 1936, with particular emphasis on the period between 1905 and 1920, were introduced in evidence. Entire cases rested on doctrine and ideology; books were being put on trial. The prosecutors then contended that any individual who was a leader or member in an organization that endorsed or accepted that ideology and doctrine, the principles of Marxism-Leninism, was by the very act of leadership conspiring to take part in, or was helping in the organization of a group that advocated violent overthrow of the Government of the United States. Is it any wonder then that the day-to-day conduct of such a trial would consume almost six months?

Paul Crouch was the first of ten government witnesses. It would take 423 pages of transcript and almost three weeks of testimony before the government called its next witness. When Crouch took the stand on April 12th, I was reminded of a farmland scarecrow. Peering over small, round, metal-framed glasses, noticeably balding despite thin wisps of mottled gray hair, the pale Paul Crouch was very tall, very gaunt and painfully thin. I had never seen him before the trial, but I knew of him as an employee of the

Department of Justice and as a paid professional witness who had testified in many previous cases against communists. For the most part, the testimony of Crouch was a recitation of his alleged activities as a member of the Communist Party from 1928 until 1942.

Crouch told the court about how he was reading works by Karl Marx, Frederick Engels and Ludwig Feuerbach at the age of 10, and by 12 had mastered *Das Kapital*; how he learned numerous languages, including Esperanto, and corresponded with kings and potentates. In 1925, he was court-martialed from the Army, he told us, after informing his commanding officer in Hawaii of his "definitely communist" views. After serving 26 months of a 40-year sentence in Alcatraz, he claimed, and with only eight months experience as a supply clerk private, he joined the Communist Party in 1927, was sent on a national speaking tour and, in 1928, visited Russia. Crouch said that there he rode with and even reviewed the Soviet cavalry while discussing strategy with Marshal Tukhachevsky, Vice Commissar of Military Affairs. He was made an honorary colonel, led a cavalry charge, lectured at the Lenin Institute and the Frunze Military Academy (Russia's West Point, we were told), and made speeches over Radio Russia "in Esperanto." While in the Soviet Union, this 25-year-old, self-proclaimed leading American communist, according to his sworn testimony, met with every world communist leader, including Italy's Togliatti, England's Pollet, Germany's Goetwalls, France's Thorez and Lenin's widow, Krupskaya.

Paul Crouch gave all of his fanciful testimony in previous trials and Congressional hearings, always having it especially tailored for the occasion, and this case would be no exception. At our trial, Crouch testified that he returned to the United States with secret plans for "communist infiltration" of America's armed forces and that he discussed those plans at meetings, in 1928 and 1929, where one of my co-defendants, Dave Davis, was present. In considerable detail, Crouch called this task of infiltration his "most important activity" as a member of the Communist Party. This testimony contradicted what he said at an earlier trial involving the Farmers' Union, where it was much more expedient to claim that his most important work was his position on the Agricultural Commission of the Communist Party's Central Committee. On no less than 29 occasions in his testimony, Crouch named Dave Davis, either as the person who helped arrange his trip to Moscow or as a participant in some high-level meeting of the Communist Party.[2]

Crouch did not know me, and except for Dave Davis, he did not identify any other of my co-defendants. His entire testimony related to a period that began in 1925 and ended in 1942, many years before the conspiracy for which we were being tried had allegedly begun, when a "totally disillusioned" Paul Crouch left the party.

Pages and pages of the testimony of this witness went into building his own "credibility" as he dropped the names of numerous international dignitaries with whom he ostensibly attended meetings, conferences and classes. All of this testimony was concerned with purported events some 13 years before the passage of the Smith Act, 18 years before our indictment stated any conspiracy took place and 26 years before the charges that led to our trial.

After more than 40 pages of such testimony, Crouch was shown the government's first exhibit. It was a pamphlet entitled *The Struggle Against Imperialist War and the Tasks of the Communists.* He identified the pamphlet as "the document that was drawn up in the Commission on which I served and which was presided over by [Louis] Barbe in 1928." This piece of evidence turned out to be a resolution of the sixth Congress of the Communist International, which the government's special prosecutor proceeded to read aloud. Word for word, this 17-page document went into the record. Before he finished his testimony and over every overruled objection of defense counsel, Crouch's "expertise" permitted the presiding judge to receive into evidence 21 similar books, pamphlets, reports and resolutions as "going to the aims, ends and objectives of the Communist Party of the United States." The jury heard about each of these documents. Many were presented in the theatrical baritones of several selected special prosecutors. Page after page of the official transcript, consequently, read like the collected works of Marx, Engels, Lenin and Stalin.

On page 203 of the transcript, a collection of articles written by Lenin between 1905 and 1917, entitled *The Revolution of 1905*, was introduced over defense counsel's objection, and Paul Crouch was asked by the U.S. attorney, "What use did you make of that book?" After another overruled objection, Crouch responded, "It was presented to the students as a basic classic authority from which quotations were made which they were obliged to read, study and master."

After overruling additional objections, the court allowed Chief Prosecutor White to ask if national party leaders used the Lenin book other than in schools. Crouch said that leaders of the party directed state and district officers "to organize sales, circulation and study groups based on it and other classics." "For how long?" he was asked. "Until I left all leading positions in 1942," Crouch responded. There was an objection to the book being accepted in evidence. Judge Ganey, sensing the need for more reasons, stepped in to assist the prosecutors. Ganey wanted to know from Crouch how something written in 1905 was "made applicable" to a later time. The experienced professional witness got the message: "Lenin would draw a basic conclusion from a situation existing then and party leaders using that book would apply it to the situation that they were considering...." Crouch's response was exactly what Judge Ganey wanted, and despite objections and arguments by Lord and McBride, the judge reacted: "This book is not offered for its truth; it's the fact that it was taught...to prospective students." "Prior to 1942?" asked McBride, arguing that it was before the dates that the indictment said our "conspiracy" was alleged to have begun. "Yes, yes—this is all subject to—this theory must continue on down [to a later date]. Portions can be read to give some idea of its ends and aims as of that time. *We are not here concerned with the truth of 1905—all we are concerned about is what he and others in the party taught at the time in those schools* [my emphasis]."

"Would it bind these defendants?" interjected McBride. "Well, certainly it would bind these defendants," said the judge. "If that document was taught and persisted down to within the period of the indictment. It is certainly competent; I haven't any doubt about that—not at all." Judge Ganey then received and admitted *The Revolution of 1905* as evidence in our case. Page after page was read to the jury.

Much of what went on with the government's first witness was aimed at the issue of "force and violence" in the literature. The prosecution had Crouch testifying that during the 1930s, he taught about the need to "infiltrate the armed forces of non-communist nations for purposes of insurrection when they would be weakened from participation in imperialist wars." He continued, "I taught that during an imperialist war in which the United States might be engaged, that this country would be much weaker than at other times and that it would offer the possibility of turning the imperialist war into a civil war and at an opportune time during the course of the war, of utilizing the war to organize the armed insurrection for the overthrow of the American government." His testimony was neither anything that my co-defendants and I advocated, taught, planned for or believed, nor, for that matter, was it anything that the government contended in our indictment.

Tall in the saddle and led on by the prosecutors, the "cavalry colonel" hurdled into telling how he taught his concepts, his analyses of imperialist wars and their relationship to the question of just and unjust wars: "the imperialist wars were the unjust wars...a just war was a war in which the Soviet Union would be involved." Having set the stage with Crouch's convoluted testimony, it was time for the prosecution to introduce into evidence the October 1939 issue of a magazine called *The Communist*. Describing it as "the official organ of the Communist Party," they called specific attention to the first article in that issue: "Declaration by the National Committee of the Communist Party, U.S.A." Of course, the article was about just and unjust wars.

From the very beginning of our trial, it was clear that the impressive composition and credentials of our defense team would create an atmosphere in the courtroom that militated against the avenging spirit and vindictiveness present in earlier Smith Act proceedings. However, it also became evident during this part of Paul Crouch's testimony that a calmer and more polite Judge Ganey was no guarantee that this trial would be fair and impartial. Perhaps tiring of what was turning into the introduction of an endless stream of books, periodicals and pamphlets, and apparently aware that this latest piece of reading being offered by the prosecuting attorneys contradicted their own case, the judge intervened. On page 24 of the transcript, we find Judge Ganey turning to the witness:

Judge: Let me ask you, Mr. Crouch, what did you teach out of
           this article? Here, you look at it. You show me what
           you could teach as a *principle* [my emphasis] of the
           Communist Party...an end...an aim or an objective....

Crouch:　I would read this—
Judge:　Let me see where.
Crouch:　On page 901 [of *The Communist* of October 1939].
Judge:　Did you read this [indicating the section]?
Crouch:　Yes, Your Honor.

Judge Ganey then said, "I don't think this is admissible, Mr. White, I really don't." Turning to the prosecutor while pointing at material he did not want the jurors to hear, he added, "Mr. White, if this could be taught, this at the end of the article, without adverting to it, *it is a matter which would be certainly not favorable to the position you assume* [my emphasis]." The U.S. attorney promptly withdrew his latest offer of "evidence" of advocacy of force and violence. The following excerpts from *The Communist* article were their obvious concern:

> The people must demand that the [U.S.] President's promise
> that this country will not be involved [in war] shall be kept invi-
> olate, and they must be constantly on guard against the power-
> ful forces at work in our land toward such involvement....The
> task of the day in the United States is to overcome the artificial
> divisions among the peace forces...and bring them into a United
> Front against the war-makers...to promote a democratic alliance
> of workers, farmers and middle classes to make sharp
> demands...to preserve civil liberties and living standards against
> reactionary attacks....[In] the struggle for the maintainance of
> national and social security, for jobs, democracy and peace, the
> working class...will begin to advance seriously and on a mass
> scale toward the establishment of a new system, without class-
> es and without exploitation, in which the economy of the coun-
> try is the common property of all and used for the common
> good, that is a socialist system—which alone will abolish forev-
> er exploitation, oppression, unemployment, poverty and war,
> and realize all the best dreams of mankind for a happy world.

Nevertheless, with the help of an intervening court and the high-riding "colonel" jumping through the hoops, by the time Crouch concluded his direct testimony, the persistent prosecution team had managed to introduce 22 books, pamphlets and periodicals into evidence from which long, time-consuming passages were read to the jury.

Chapter 11

THE COLONEL FALLS

The prosecution's witness, Paul Crouch, was the first of the three paid finger-pointers who were trotted out at each of the Smith Act trials throughout the nation. The other two were Louis Budenz and John Lautner, and there was every reason to expect that they would make their appearances in Philadelphia. Concern about the government's use of professional informers and their tainted testimony was beginning to be manifested.

"Some of the government witnesses have made, under oaths...contradictory and mutually exclusive statements....This indicates that these government witnesses have perjured themselves even though they have not been indicted for this offense." On April 17, 1954, five days after Paul Crouch took the stand, a letter to the U.S. Attorney General appeared in the *Philadelphia Afro-American.* Prominent Philadelphians including Franklin I. Sheeder, Executive Secretary of the Board of Christian Education; George Trowbridge, Rector of St. Paul's Church; Rabbi Elias Charry of the Germantown Jewish Center; and Stephen D. Cary, a leader of the American Friends Service Committee, urged the prosecution to refrain from using professional informers in the Smith Act trial in Philadelphia. Joined by other notables—Blanche Nicola, D. Wilmot Gateson, F. Snyder Thomas and Mildred Olmsted—they were "repeating our earnest hope that our city, with its proud tradition of liberty and justice, will be spared the disgrace of having this kind of informer used."[1]

When they were not on duty inside Judge Ganey's courtroom, high on the ladder of priorities for most of the young, bright attorneys was to find ways for McBride and Lord to trip up and expose the paid professional informers. No previous Smith Act defendants had the advantages we had going for us in Philadelphia. Unlike the defense counsel at any other Smith Act trial, our attorneys were given their own small conference room in the federal court house in which to work and prepare. They knew who the prosecution's "expert" witnesses would be and, during court the first couple of months of the trial, members of the defense team could always be found in that room poring over and preparing materials relevant to the probable witness each was assigned. As Robert W. Sayre recalled, "We researched and shared in the analysis and approach to the government witnesses, checking their background and previous testimony and providing the information for cross-examination which we put in card files for McBride and Lord.[2] The team's goal was to discredit what another of the attorneys, Charles C. Hileman III, called "the trained seals, their wandering minstrels, the government's witnesses."[3]

One of the junior team members was Ben Read, an attorney who was subsequently to become an undersecretary of state during the Carter Administration and a member of several international commissions concerned with environmental issues. Read's assignment was Paul Crouch who, as a career informer over several years, was paid to testify more than 40 times at hearings of Congressional investigating committees and the Subversive Activities Control Board, at deportation proceedings and at trials.

Crouch frequently boasted of his "imaginative powers," and many others agreed that he had an active imagination. "I wrote to attorneys all over the country who had defendants in cases where Crouch testified, asking them if they would send me transcripts of his testimony," said Read. "I was amazed at the response. Not just a few, but everyone I wrote to responded and everybody included transcripts together with comments like 'Nail the S.O.B. He lies through his teeth.'"[4] This sentiment was shared by Joe Lord, who called Crouch "one of the most accomplished liars I have ever seen in a courtroom."[5]

Every defense team attorney I interviewed during 1989 and 1990 paid tribute to Ben Read's special contributions. Edmund Spaeth recalled his "laborious examination of the scores of transcripts of Crouch testimony"; Charles Hileman remembered Read's "indexing of every word of more than 40 Crouch appearances"; and Henry Sawyer referred to Read's "meticulous research." These efforts were to result in an enormous pay-off.[6]

Ben Read had been corresponding with the nationally syndicated columnist Joseph Alsop, and on April 16, 1954, a few days after direct examination of Paul Crouch began, an 800-word article written by Alsop and his brother, Stewart, entitled "How Reliable is Testimony by Paul Crouch?" appeared in newspapers throughout the nation.[7] They wrote, "There is no space here to list the instances when Crouch has contradicted himself in his lengthening career as a paid informer." The Alsop brothers noted that a couple of years earlier, a federal judge had thrown out an indictment count because of the unsubstantiated testimony of Crouch. In so doing, the judge observed, "I am amazed that the Justice Department should employ him as a member of its staff."[8]

Tom McBride started a day-long cross-examination of Paul Crouch on April 21, 1954. McBride, in a quiet and deliberate manner, scoffed as he got Crouch to admit to writing letters to imaginary people. He elicited Crouch's definition of the "idealism" to which he had been committed as the idealism of seeing the United States Government destroyed by force and violence. McBride asked Crouch if his language mastery included Russian. Crouch said it did not. Then how did he speak to the cavalry, McBride wondered.

Young Sherman Labovitz poses on
Chuck, a favorite horse, in 1925.

Labovitz as a schoolboy, circa 1930.

Labovitz proudly wearing the uniform of the U.S. Air Force, 1942.

Sherman and Pauline on a date in 1943.

The Labovitz family at the close of the Smith Act trial, summer 1954.
Clockwise from top:
Sherman, Marc, Pauline, and Gary.

Sherman and Pauline today.

Pickets representing the Civil Rights Congress protest deportations in 1946.
Joe Kuzma is standing in front of the first sign. *Temple Urban Archives*

Bob Klonsky (*foreground, holding sign*) and Sherman Labovitz (*behind Klonsky*)
picket the Immigration Service to protest deportations. *Temple Urban Archives*

Demonstrators rally at the Federal Building in Philadelphia to protest the arrest of Communists, October 1948. *Temple Urban Archives*

Pickets march outside the Federal Building in Philadelphia. *Temple Urban Archives*

Members of the 28th Ward Communist Party Club at a May Day rally in 1950.
Temple Urban Archives

Tom Nabried speaks at the 1950 May Day rally. Standing to his left is Helen Weiss, the wife of defendant Ben Weiss.
Temple Urban Archives

Ben Weiss (*left*) joins other ex-servicemen in protesting the Korean War, 1950.
Temple Urban Archives

Communist pickets demand the release of W.E.B. DuBois, 1951.
Temple Urban Archives

Front door of the Communist Party headquarters in Philadelphia, 1953. *Temple Urban Archives*

Joe Kuzma (*left*) and Sherman Labovitz handcuffed together at the time of their arrest, July 1953. *Temple Urban Archives*

Sherman Labovitz (*left*) and Ben Weiss after their arrest in July 1953. *Temple Urban Archives*

Robert Sayre, defense attorney in the trial. *Temple Urban Archives*

Left to right: Sherman Labovitz, Joe Roberts, Bob Klonsky, Chick Katz, Ben Weiss, and Joe Kuzma at their arraignment in 1953. *Temple Urban Archives*

Left to right: Walter Lowenfels, Tom Nabried, and Dave Davis at their 1953 arraignment. *Temple Urban Archives*

Jack Zucker posts bail, August 1953. *Temple Urban Archives*

Dave Davis (*left*) consults with attorney David Cohen, 1953. *Temple Urban Archives*

Handcuffed together in pairs, the defendants head to their arraignment in July 1953. *Temple Urban Archives*

Chief defense attorney Thomas D. McBride, 1954. *Temple Urban Archives*

Defense attorney Joseph Lord III, 1960. *Temple Urban Archives*

Edmund Spaeth, defense counsel, in 1956. *Temple Urban Archives*

Defense attorney John Rogers Carroll, 1997. *Philadelphia Bar Association*

Henry Sawyer III, defense counsel, 1966.
Temple Urban Archives

Charles Hileman, defense counsel, 1997.
Philadelphia Bar Association

Joseph Lord III (*left*), Walter Allesandroni (*center*), and Judge J. Cullen Ganey, the judge in the Smith Act trial, in 1961. *Temple Urban Archives*

"In Esperanto," said an increasingly defensive Crouch.

"And in what language, pray tell, did the Russian cavalry listen?" replied McBride. The surprised prosecutors objected weakly.

More and more, McBride maneuvered Crouch into embellishments and exaggerations about his trip to Moscow, his lecture on military tactics and his friendship with all of the world's communist leaders. Nevertheless, at the end of the day, while Crouch's authenticity was undoubtedly a huge question mark in everyone's mind, his direct testimony concerning Dave Davis remained unchallenged.

The next morning at 6:00 a.m., Joe Lord received a phone call from Tom McBride. McBride had become ill the night before and had just been made ready for surgery. Lord was asked to take over the Crouch cross-examination.

"I guess you could consider me as having been the number two man of the defense team. However, circumstances at times made me number one," Joe Lord told me in modest understatement.[9] The last thing Lord and McBride wanted was any appearance of seeking delays. Even McBride's emergency surgery would not be used as a reason to request any postponement that the prosecution could pounce upon to claim that the defense was stalling; that they were following the pattern of other Smith Act trials. But it was Thursday, and Fridays were often used by the judge and the attorneys for work in their offices. Lord agreed that the usual extended weekend would be sufficient to permit him to complete the cross-examination of Crouch.

At 2 o'clock on Sunday morning, Ben Read's wife was awakened from a sound sleep as he ran from the kitchen table shouting, "I got the lying bastard. I've nailed him."[10] Read had been poring over his indexed materials on Crouch's testimony in more than 40 proceedings. He was specifically searching for any reference to Dave Davis, the only defendant directly damaged by Crouch in our case. Read found what he was looking for on pages 2585 and 2586 of the record in United States v. Bridges. Later that morning, a jubilant Joe Lord, "afraid of a tapped telephone line," decided to tell Tom McBride in person about Read's discovery. McBride listened, smiled knowingly and with a glint in his eye said, "You've got one of two ways to go." The two of them then discussed whether on Monday morning, as cross-examination resumed, it would be better to "hit the prosecutors immediately [with the discovery] or lift Crouch gradually way up to the fifth floor and drop him out of the window."[11] They agreed on the latter.

Joe Lord was at his absolute best, continuing McBride's tactics of getting Crouch to repeat his exaggerations while feeding what seemed like an insatiable ego. Lord then led Crouch into repeated identifications of Dave Davis, asking him, "Are you sure? Are you certain?" Joe Lord took Crouch from 1928 through 1941, and then asked, "Has he changed at all?"

"Surprisingly little," responded Crouch, "very much more like [in] 1928, 1929."

"Are you sure you don't have him mixed up with some other Davises in the party?"

"No."

"Benjamin Davis?" asked Lord, referring to the African-American communist, attorney, former New York City councilman and a defendant at the first Foley Square Smith Act trial.

Crouch answered, "I am sure that no one in this room would ever confuse Ben Davis, Jr. and this other Mr. Davis."

Then, over the prosecution's agitated objection, Joe Lord dropped Ben Read's bombshell: at the trial of longshoremen's union leader Harry Bridges, Crouch had insisted on no less than five occasions that he "did not know" and "never even knew of" David Davis.

Crouch never recovered. And Ben Read passed the details on to the Alsop brothers. Several weeks later they wrote, "Crouch might have spoken with less self-confidence...of his alleged knowledge of Davis had he understood a rather special feature of this case"—the competency of the defense team.[12] Pointing out that the Attorney General of the United States had agreed to investigate Crouch for possible perjury and would determine his suitability for future use, the Alsops added that this was important as a first investigation of "this new group that has come to play a considerable part in American national life...it will be interesting to see the results of this first investigation of one of the tribe of informers and government witnesses who have been flourishing in this country since the middle period of the Truman Administration."[13]

While Attorney General Herbert Brownell stalled, a brazen Crouch threatened to sue both Brownell and the Alsops, suggesting that 31 communists would have to be retried because of allegations against him.[14] On June 7, 1954, Ben Read sent to Joseph Alsop "four 15-page memos" of his research on Crouch and "four copies of the transcript" of the cross-examination "concerning Davis...for whatever use you see fit." On June 11th, in a thank you note, Alsop said that he had sent copies to John Oakes of the *New York Times* and Pete Brandt of the *St. Louis Post-Dispatch*. In another day and age, Paul Crouch would have been jailed for perjury. Suffice it to say, the discredited Crouch never again testified for the government as an expert witness against communists or anyone else. "Ultimately and appropriately," one of the lawyers pointed out, "he died of cancer of the throat."

The humor in the obliteration of Paul Crouch was not lost upon members of the jury. They obviously remembered his testimony about how he had been made an honorary colonel in the 10th Red Cavalry Division while he attended the Lenin Institute. When a subsequent prosecution witness, John Lautner, testified that he, too, attended the Lenin Institute to "learn about street fighting," cross-examining defense attorney Joe Lord asked him about his rank. "They have no rank in the Red Army," Lautner responded, "only political commissars." "What!" exclaimed Lord, accompanied by loud laughter from the jury box. "You didn't know Colonel Crouch?"

Chapter 12

AN "AEſOP" FABLE

The prosecution's case continued down the same track—FBI informers testifying about the meaning of Marxist-Leninist literature—without a detour. Almost none of the so-called evidence had anything to do with me or any of my co-defendants.

Louis Budenz, another ex-Communist Party leader, was the government's second "star" witness to swear to tell the truth, the whole truth and nothing but the truth. I remember being quite surprised when he took the witness stand. Not because he was unexpected; I knew he would certainly make an appearance in Philadelphia. But he just did not fit into any of the physical stereotypes I held for someone who had been a newspaper editor, a professor at Fordham University and a convert to Catholicism. He should not have been short and flabby, lined and balding. When those features came together with a light complexion and a very defined squint, the 62-year-old Louis Budenz looked much more like the image I had of a small-time bureaucrat. For several years prior to the Philadelphia Smith Act trial, Budenz provided himself with a rather comfortable professional informer's livelihood; he wrote, he lectured and he testified—and all of it was against communists.[1] At our trial, Budenz said that he had been a member of the party for a decade, starting in 1935, and had been the editor of its newspaper, *The Daily & Sunday Worker*, between 1941 and 1945.[2]

My co-defendant, Walter Lowenfels, was a correspondent for *The Worker* during those years, and he knew Budenz. During the course of his testimony, Budenz placed Lowenfels at a couple of staff meetings of the newspaper.

Walter Lowenfels sat to my left. The seating assignments were deliberate, made on the advice of David Levinson, who had earned his reputation defending left-wingers in the Twenties and Thirties. Levinson had been sitting in the courtroom on the first day of jury selection. Though I had heard of this attorney's exploits, I knew him only casually and as an eccentric old man with thin hair slicked down by what appeared to be bootblack on an almost bald scalp. At the very first recess that day, an agitated Levinson rushed to the defense table to advise what I'm certain he felt we should have already known. We should seat ourselves so that Walter Lowenfels and I would be closest to the jury, because I was the youngest and "best looking" and Walter was the oldest and unlikeliest of the defendants.

Oblivious to his surroundings, Walter sat reading and writing and translating French poetry. Occasionally, in the torrent of words that marked the trial, the name Lowenfels was dropped, at which time I could be certain of a poke in my left ribs and a query, "Wha'd he say? Wha'd he say?" Such momentary disturbances, even by his former editor, left him undaunted. Walter always returned to his writing pad.

By the time Louis Budenz got to the Philadelphia trial, he was well rehearsed from his many previous presentations at deportation hearings, Congressional hearings and Smith Act trials throughout the country. He had also been very well rewarded. Estimates were that since leaving the party he had received more than $100,000 from lectures and book royalties, in addition to substantial witness fees and a professor's salary. Deferred to, cooed over and protected by both the prosecutors and the court, Budenz proceeded to put at center stage all of the Marxist materials previously introduced by Paul Crouch, plus many more. Budenz claimed that when he joined the Communist Party, a member of its national committee gave him many of those books and pamphlets "to be able to develop my communist consciousness more fully." It was then "urged that these documents...be distributed as widely as possible...and be studied incessantly in order to be guided by [their] teachings...a reference...for the creation and extension of the communist movement."[3]

As with the testimony of Paul Crouch, the performance of Louis Budenz was accompanied by long, time-consuming readings. By the end of his direct testimony, nine additional pieces of literature were introduced, portions read by government attorneys and "analyzed" by their "professional expert."

Budenz insisted that the term Marxism-Leninism had a special meaning that initiates knew well. Marxism-Leninism meant scientific socialism, and scientific socialism taught that socialism could only be reached by destroying the capitalist state and replacing it forcefully and violently with a dictatorship of the proletariat. According to Budenz, the Communist Party was committed to overthrowing the United States Government and its Constitution.[4]

Budenz and the prosecutors took turns reciting entire texts of editorials, articles and resolutions from periodicals, interspersed within page after page of passages from Marx and Lenin. After one such lengthy reading, this time from *The Proletarian Revolution and the Renegade Kautsky,* Judge Ganey, presumably searching for greater clarity, intervened: "What is the dictatorship of the proletariat? What does the party mean by [it] as applicable to the United States? Out of the Communist Party, would there be exceptional ones chosen to be dictators?" And Budenz answered, "It meant the establishment of Soviet rule, similar to that which exists in Soviet Russia, here in the United States, a dictatorship with the state completely crushed...this dictatorship to be led by the Communist Party, the vanguard." This line of questioning by Judge Ganey, continuing over 11 pages of the transcript, permitted Budenz to speak for hours, giving his own special "clarification" to the meaning of dozens of terms in the books and pamphlets.[5]

In a contentious cross-examination of Budenz, defense counsel was able to demonstrate that many parts of the aforementioned books and pamphlets frequently not only disavow advocacy of violence, they also insist that in a situation that calls for revolutionary change, violence may be initiated by those resisting the democratic will of a majority wanting that change. In fact, the government's exhibit number 31 in the trial, "The Constitution of the Communist Party of the United States of America," states in Article IX, Section 2: "Adherence to or participation in the activities of any clique, group, circle, faction or party which conspires or acts to subvert, undermine, weaken or overthrow any or all institutions of American democracy, whereby the majority of the American people can maintain their right to determine their destinies in any degree, shall be punishable by immediate expulsion." The constitution's preamble read: "The purposes of this organization are to promote the best interests and welfare of the working class and the people of the United States, to defend and extend the democracy of our country, to prevent the rise of fascism, and to advance the cause of progress and peace with the ultimate aim of ridding our country of the scourge of economic crises, unemployment, insecurity, poverty and war through the realization of the historic aim of the working class—the establishment of socialism—by the free choice of the majority of the American people."

Since this was potentially disastrous to the government's case, Louis Budenz created a convenient explanation to get around the party's constitution as well as those references in Marx and Lenin that contradicted his interpretation. He labeled them all as examples of "Aesopian" language and credited Lenin as his source. Writing in 1916, in his preface to the pamphlet *Imperialism*, Lenin provided a rationale for what he was doing at the time that gave Budenz his implausible way out. Lenin said that he was writing in the fabled language of Aesop because the conditions in Russia, including government censorship, the outlawing of political parties and an absence of freedom of speech, made it impossible for him to say what he meant and that it was necessary, therefore, to substitute the names of other countries for Czarist Russia and Imperial Japan. Seizing upon this, Budenz developed the argument that communists often spoke in Aesopian language.[6] "Aesopian language is the roundabout, elusive language used for protective purposes or purposes of deceit and infiltration under which illegal or violent objectives can be concealed in legal forms. This grows out of...the fables of Aesop, who, the communists contend, was a slave who used his fables in an elusive way to berate or deride his masters."[7]

It was Budenz, however, who crafted "Aesopianism" as a device. During defense cross-examination, every time Joe Lord showed him passages in Marxist classics that differed in meaning from his "explanations" and asked whether, in fact, those passages were taught, Budenz replied, " Yes and no."

> Lord: "The proletarian movement is the self-conscious independent movement of the immense majority in the interest of the immense majority." Do you recognize that?
>
> Budenz: I recognize the language but I just don't know where from.
>
> Lord: Did the Communist Party teach that?
>
> Budenz: Yes and no.
>
> Lord: ...from Volume IV of Lenin's Selected Works... "in order to obtain the power of the state, class-conscious workers must win the majority to their side." Was that taught and used?
>
> Budenz: Yes and no.[8]

Equipped with the defendants' and defense team's research, and showing considerable understanding of the Marxist writings, Lord continued to take on the Aesopianist, forcing Budenz to equivocate about the meaning and use by American communists of many other examples in the Marxist library.[9]

> Lord: ...and let me ask you once again if he [Lenin] said where the violence comes from?
>
> Budenz: He states in part that the violence comes from the Bourgeoisie [capitalist ruling class]. Yes, they [the Communist Party] contend that.[10]

> Lord: ...did Lenin say all those things [references to violence]?
>
> Budenz: Yes and no.
>
> Lord: You mean yes, he said it and no, he didn't say it?

The U.S. attorney, W. Wilson White, seemed worried about what was happening to his witness: "Your Honor, I object to asking the witness whether Lenin meant what he said." To which Joe Lord responded: "I wouldn't have asked him, sir, if he had not originally tried to tell us what Lenin meant."

The experienced informer was faltering. More and more he asked to see the particular edition of books that Lord was using. He said he wanted to put them into "historical context." When he realized that he had assumed the very argument of the defense—that material can best be understood within its historical context—he retreated. The historical context was needed, he said, so that he could understand the "tactics" within the "particular period" something was written. Whatever the meaning of the "principles," the "substance" always remains the same. For Budenz that meant destroying capitalism, replacing it forcefully and violently.

Budenz agreed that yes, all those things introduced by the defense that contradicted his "interpretive" testimony had been written, and indeed yes, the party taught them; but no, they did not mean what they said. When the witness was confronted with many of his own writings, significantly different from the classics, he had the same difficulties explaining them.

It was precisely this type of convoluted rationale which permitted Budenz to summarily dismiss Article IX, Section 2 of the Communist Party constitution as Aesopian by saying: "This was produced for legal purposes...and this section was clearly to be read to the comrades with the limiting and nullifying provision in mind of the dedication in the first sentence of the constitution." Mr. Budenz, the "expert," had already told the court and jury that scientific socialism and Marxism-Leninism were Aesopian terms that meant the violent overthrow of the United States Government. The first sentence of the party constitution reads: "The Communist Party of the United States is the political party of the working class, basing itself upon the principles of scientific socialism, Marxism-Leninism."

To paraphrase Joe Lord's summary of the episode with Louis Budenz, it was like Alice in Wonderland revisited.

Chapter 13

PERJURY CONTINUE**S**

On May 7, 1954, my son Marc's seventh birthday, the *Philadelphia Inquirer's* headline blared: "SURPRISE RED TESTIFIES FOR U.S. AT TRIAL OF 9; IDENTITY SECRET TILL LAST." The third witness for the prosecution, Herman Thomas, had literally slithered into the courtroom. I had last seen him the morning after June 19, 1953, the day that Julius and Ethel Rosenberg were executed—a day forever fixed in my mind. It was six weeks before my arrest.

Thomas was an inch or so taller than I, and kind of sloppy and fat. I had seen him a few times at larger meetings and knew him to be a luncheonette proprietor from the Allentown/Bethlehem area. Although clearly a member of the party, he hadn't impressed me. There was an affect about him that made me uncomfortable. And while he was unexpected, I was not unduly surprised when he found me sitting on my porch early that morning. At the time, I was the party's literature director, and he wanted copies of the magazines *Political Affairs* and *Masses and Mainstream*, as well as the book *In Battle for Peace* by W.E.B. DuBois.

Lumbering, with his head held low, he was a caricature of despair, bemoaning the executions of the Rosenbergs. Late on the previous afternoon, their stays of execution were reversed by what many believed was a hastily summoned Supreme Court sitting *en banc* that Friday so that their decision would be reached in time for the Rosenbergs to be strapped to Sing Sing's electric chair just before the sunset that ushered in their sabbath.

Seeming grief turned to anger, and he lashed out at the politicians, witnesses and prosecutors, the judge, the attorney general, the Supreme Court justices and the president. Each was responsible and all were murderers. Even though I felt keenly the events of the previous day, he didn't engage me. His concerns for the Rosenbergs and the manner in which he linked their executions with anti-Semitism and anti-communism bothered me. They seemed poorly rehearsed and meant to impress. In any event, I doubt that his visit lasted 10 minutes. He left with the books and magazines he wanted.

Now, well into the second month of our trial, in the middle of the usual parade of "expert" witnesses, joining the "wandering minstrels" was Herman Thomas, the government's "surprise" paid informer for the FBI.

During his direct testimony, Thomas told the court that he joined the Communist Party in 1937 and quit two years later, because leaders of the union to which he belonged discovered his membership and threatened to have him expelled. He said that in 1944, the FBI urged him to rejoin the party.

Thomas testified about the details of numerous meetings that took place as early as 1937, and continued until he walked into the courtroom.[1] He referred continuously to party plans for the infiltration of veterans' organizations and for their indoctrination with the literature of Marx and Lenin.[2] Thomas claimed to know each of the defendants and to have attended, over a period of 17 years, scores of party meetings, conferences and conventions with us. However, he recalled only one occasion, in all those years, when just one of the defendants, Tom Nabried, mentioned the word revolution.[3] Later, Judge Ganey intervened in another attempt to solicit information from him that could help the prosecutors. A long series of questions was directed at him by the judge about discussions and educational meetings Thomas attended with one or more of the defendants. The most damaging information the witness could produce had to do with one meeting in which, he said, Joe Roberts and Chick Katz were participants. Thomas alleged that in their presence still another person "explained that we had gone on from time to time without accomplishing anything and that we must return to our Marxist-Leninist theory." Thomas admitted that in all those years of meetings at which the defendants were present, we never once discussed the use of force or violent overthrow of the government.[4]

Tom McBride's cross-examination of Herman Thomas produced a couple of dramatic episodes. Once McBride asked a married couple, named earlier by the witness as the hosts of a meeting some of the defendants attended in Allentown, to stand up in court. Thomas did not know who they were.

This informer admitted to having filed reports with the FBI for over 10 years, "usually the next day...sometimes the day after...after every time we had a meeting," and sent whatever literature was distributed along. At the time of the trial, he was receiving $275 each month; over the years he had been paid "about $15,000" and had never reported it on income tax returns.[5] Having elicited from the witness how he invited people to meetings and added their names to his reports, gave individuals pamphlets and reported them, got others to read the party newspaper and included them on lists to the FBI, McBride pressed, "You used the word 'provocateur,' Mr. Thomas. What is a provocateur?" ["Agent-provocateur" is a term describing a person, generally paid, who manufactures serious incidents for which others are blamed and held responsible.]

McBride's question went flying way over Thomas' head. "It's someone who is against the party....I never looked it up in the dictionary....The same thing as a Democrat or Republican or anti-communist."[6] McBride then reminded the witness that he had told the judge during the direct examination that he was considered a theoretician and asked, "You're sure you don't know what a provocateur is? Well...did you read [those] Marxist books and discuss them?"

Thomas: That is correct.
McBride: Did you study Marx?
Thomas: I read him.
McBride: What did you read of Marx?
Thomas: Very little.
McBride: What did you read?
Thomas: I don't know; I tried to forget.[7]

And so it went. Thomas was unable to answer any of McBride's questions about anything relating to Marxism-Leninism. Challenged about this, and his inability to remember any details or recall events and places, he was asked to explain his ready memory during direct testimony for the prosecution. Thomas suggested it happened that way because he "had time to collect [his] thoughts" during lengthy arguments that followed McBride's objections to the government's questions.

During the second week of May, McBride demanded that the prosecution produce the hundreds of reports Thomas filed with the FBI and to which he testified. The government, invoking "the threat to the nation's internal security" as its reason, refused. Saying it was a communist plot and a ploy used at every Smith Act trial, they moved to quash the subpoena. An infuriated McBride, demanding an apology, said that he never even consulted the defendants and the move had been his decision alone. He told the court that the defense had every right to see the reports being used against them, and if that was a threat to internal security, then the government should end its prosecution rather than violate the defendants' constitutional rights. The Justice Department was probably concerned that McBride, who won a directed acquittal in an earlier case because of the same issue, might again emerge victorious. After a week of deliberations, U.S. attorney W. Wilson White told Judge Ganey that Attorney General Herbert Brownell instructed him to turn over the files with a stipulation that the judge would screen the papers to be used for anything that would "impair the national security." In the meantime, the prosecution had already stipulated that none of the papers contained the words *force and violence*.

McBride agreed to the arrangement. But he had his own stipulation; decisions were to be made by the judge and not the Justice Department. "I don't agree that the attorney general or anybody else has the right to say he will be the deciding factor as to whether documents are to be produced in answer to a subpoena issued under competent judicial authority."[8]

Sunday, May 23, 1954 was my ninth wedding anniversary; another reason for celebration was that things were looking a little better for the defense. Two days later, the headlines of the *Philadelphia Inquirer* read: "FBI SPY FAILS TO NAME 9 REDS AS ADVOCATES OF U.S. REVOLT."

Herman Thomas, in 11 full days of testimony spanning almost three weeks, no matter how prodded or prompted, was unable to link any of the nine of us to the use of force or violence. He did, however, recall my having signed a recruiting letter and speaking at a party conference. He also remembered "reporting" to me at a picnic attended by "thousands." And, of course, there was the infamous literature transaction on the morning of June 20, 1953! How could that be forgotten?

It turned out to be a very unpleasant spring. My older son Marc, a budding star athlete, was more and more frequently in excruciating pain from a previously undiagnosed congenital kidney defect. There were many emergency hospital visits, cystoscopies and two major surgical procedures. In addition, my wife, Pauline, was found to have a thyroid cancer requiring surgery and long-term radiation treatment. I don't know how we would have survived but for the support of the few wonderful friends, neighbors and comrades who helped, and several sensitive physicians who cared. But during the McCarthy era, it was too frightening for others, who may have cared, to offer help and support. They feared that they might be seen, subpoenaed, hauled before investigating committees, spread across newspaper columns, or fired from jobs. And all the while, the Smith Act trial rolled on.

The prosecution still had to unveil another Justice Department employee and veteran performer who had been regularly traveling the Smith Act circuit. On May 24th, just as expected, the fourth witness, John Lautner, turned up in Philadelphia for his act. Coming after the prosecution's first three unsavory witnesses, his stocky muscular frame, steel-gray wavy hair and ruddy complexion made John Lautner appear as if he would be a very formidable adversary. Nevertheless, his repertoire was just more of the same from another of the government's well-paid and well-traveled informers. When he finished testifying on June 8th, not a single word of his lengthy recital connected any one of the defendants with force or violence.

At first Lautner testified that he had been a member of the Communist Party from 1929 until he was expelled as "an enemy agent" in 1950. Following the pattern previously established by Crouch and Budenz, this new witness, in concert with the government prosecutors, read additional scores of pages of Marxist-Leninist literature into the transcript.[9]

Lautner's testimony described his rapid rise through many leadership positions, culminating in his selection to serve on two important bodies of the Communist Party—its National Education Commission and its National Review Commission. The latter Lautner described as the "disciplinary arm of the Communist Party. In short the judge, jury and police force all rolled into one."[10]

Over strong defense objections, the judge permitted Lautner to tell in some detail what it looked like inside the national offices of the Communist Party on 12th Street in New York City. He declared that he knew each of the national leaders convicted in the first Smith Act trial concluded earlier at Foley Square. His "pedigree" thus established, Lautner returned to 1929, the year he said he joined the party, and told about a full-time leadership training school that he attended. It was at this school, he said, that he was first introduced to *The Communist Manifesto* and *The Program of the Communist International*.[11] Lautner's testimony appeared critical to the government's case since, unlike Paul Crouch and Louis Budenz, he remained a member of the Communist Party after it had been reconstituted in 1945. Throughout the testimony given by the earlier witnesses, Judge Ganey had permitted the introduction of Marxist literature as "going to the aims, ends and objectives" of the Communist Party and "subject to being brought down to the period covered in the indictment by the government." When Lautner was asked by the prosecutor if he used the aforementioned literature after 1945, Judge Ganey again intervened in the questioning. This time he wanted to make certain that he got into some 15 pages of the court record the answers he needed to place things within the period of time covered in the indictment.[12]

Judge: When after 1945?
Witness: Your Honor, in 1946, '47 and '48.
Judge: In use after '48?
Witness: Yes, Your Honor.

But this was not enough; Judge Ganey wanted still more: "About those schools, where were they held? How were students selected? Were there required hours for them to attend? How many teachers?" After the judge managed to get the witness to place himself at classes in 1949, Lautner was returned to the special prosecutor, James Cronin, who began: "Ladies and gentleman, I am now going to read from *The Program of the Communist International....*" There were more defense objections and the judge asked the witness to "summarize" what he taught from the book in question.

Witness: [It had to do with] the basic aims and the basic
          objectives of the Communist Parties as laid down at
          the Sixth World Congress in 1928...those basic aims
          and objectives remained intact.
Judge: What are the basic aims—as you taught them?
Witness: The basic aims as I taught them is [sic] the establish-
          ment of socialism throughout the world by the
          destruction of imperialism and capitalism; by
          destroying and smashing their ready-made states.
          And to establish through the proletarian revolution
          and the dictatorship of the proletariat—socialism.
          There can be no other way in establishing socialism,
          on the basis of the basic program of the Communist
          Parties.[13]

Judge Ganey, obviously satisfied with what he had elicited from the witness Lautner, permitted the special prosecutor to read 16 more pages into the trial record of passages from *The Program of the Communist International*.

There followed a similar exchange concerning a work by party chairman William Z. Foster, entitled *Marxism and American Exceptionalism*. Judge Ganey allowed the witness to link and compare parts of Foster's work with excerpts from both Lenin's *State and Revolution* and Stalin's *Foundations of Leninism*. On this occasion, 14 more pages were read to the jury.[14]

During his lengthy testimony, Lautner placed three of the defendants at the 1945 convention that had dissolved the Communist Political Association and had reconstituted the Communist Party. He testified further that "Eugene Dennis ran the convention [where] in discussion regarding the pre-amble to the [party] constitution a delegate asked, 'Where is the dictator-ship of the proletariat incorporated?' and Dennis got up then and said, 'It is in there, even the blind can see it' and that was it."[15]

Lautner claimed that he taught Marxism-Leninism in many classes and that he used all of the literature previously introduced in the trial. Once more the materials were introduced and, piece by piece, they were identified by the government prosecutors. As Lautner was testifying about a "re-education program" adopted by the party after 1946 and a "national outline" used to facilitate the teaching of classes, Judge Ganey again intervened: "Could you volunteer judgments of your own, or did you have prescribed a set of rigid principles to which you had to adhere?" And Lautner responded, "...there was a school director sitting in my class supervising the teaching, and if I would say anything that would be anti-Marxist or anti-Leninist, that would be the end of my teaching." At this point, the government prosecutor added: "I am going to read to you from—*The Outline on Fundamentals of Marxism for Class Use or Self-Study*, issued by the National Educational Commission." The jury was then treated to another 55 pages of outlined materials on Marxism-Leninism.[16]

And so it went with John Lautner—the same process over and over. A glance at the transcript reveals that approximately one half of Lautner's 290 pages of direct testimony are punctuated by Judge Ganey's helpful interventions and given over to lengthy readings to the jury from the writings of Marx, Lenin and Stalin.

During the course of the government's interminable presentation, its prosecutors introduced 98 exhibits as "evidence"; one was a letter of recruitment and there were several bank deposit applications. In all there were 91 books, pamphlets, periodicals and resolutions. Small wonder that the trial ran on for more than five months!

Henry Sawyer started the cross-examination of John Lautner on June 3rd. In a spirited philosophical debate with the witness, Sawyer quoted from the Marxist classics to show that communists believed that revolution could be accomplished without violence. At one point, he called Lautner's attention to a previous Smith Act trial at which Lautner had testified where he was asked, "Isn't it a fact that you taught that revolution means fundamental change in the class control of society?" At that trial Lautner answered, "I taught that revolution means a fundamental change in relationship of forces to the base of society, to the economic base of society, specifically to our means of production and to the sources of raw materials to that relationship." Sawyer asked, "You didn't say anything about violence there, did you?" The witness, who had already indicated that his problem testimony was a result of "tricky communist paid lawyers," responded, "It was a tricky question." "Do you want to explain why?" asked Sawyer. To which Lautner replied, "That question is also tricky."[17] Not a single word of what Lautner had to say connected any of the defendants with force or violence.

In regard to revolution, this witness acknowledged that Lenin wrote about a set of objective preconditions that were necessary before a revolution could take place. "Capitalism is in crisis. It cannot rule by accepted forms. It must use extracurricular, extraordinary measures to maintain its power. There is a war situation. These are the objective conditions...a crisis...masses of people desperate...and discontented."[18] Lautner further acknowledged that those preconditions came about independent of the will of the party; that they never existed in the United States; and that all of those concepts were accepted Communist Party doctrine.[19]

Lautner had been turned over to Tom McBride who, in a blistering cross-examination, tripped him into admitting that he committed perjury more than once. The transcript shows that he lied in annulling his marriage; he lied on a passport application; he lied when applying for unemployment compensation; and he lied in testimony at previous trials.[20]

Finally, on the issue of force and violence, McBride was asking questions about a Marxist education program that Lautner said he had a major hand in teaching after the 1948 Communist Party Convention. They had an interesting exchange:

McBride: Did you ever teach how to carry out sabotage?
Lautner: No, I didn't teach that.
McBride: Did you ever teach the desirability of knowing where railroad yards and control centers were?
Lautner: I not only taught them, but I told them when to distribute leaflets over there, when to have shopgate meetings over there.
McBride: Did you ever teach the desirability of knowing where the telephone exchanges were so that when you were going to take over, you knew where to grab them?
Lautner: No, I did not.
McBride: Did you teach them where the major food distribution points were?
Lautner: In New York we made a survey of all the teamster sheds there, and picked out concentration points.
McBride: Oh, you mean to throw leaflets; we're talking about violence and force.
Lautner: Teach about throwing bombs over there? No, no, no, leaflets.

And so it went on—Lautner admitting that he never taught, nor was he ever taught, anything concerning the use of weapons or about the tactics of armed uprisings.[21]

SIX MORE SAD EXCUSES

Witness number five, Kenneth Eckert, must have been selected by the government for the sole purpose of adding some additional color to the trial. Eckert, brought in from Michigan, said that he joined the Communist Party in Ohio in 1931. One year later he was sent to Moscow to attend the Lenin Institute, where he claimed to have met my co-defendant, Tom Nabried, whom he saw just once again, at a convention in 1938. Eckert claimed that "the [Lenin] school was maintained by the Communist International" to instruct professional revolutionaries "for the purpose that when we returned home, we would organize the working class into the Communist Party and when a revolutionary situation would develop, we would use our teachings to overthrow the existing government and establish the dictatorship of the proletariat." Eckert also added that the Russians gave him instruction in the use of weapons.[1] The next morning's headlines best describe the atmosphere: "REVOLT TRAINING CITED AT RED TRIAL; WITNESS LINKS DEFENDANT TO MOSCOW SCHOOL; PLANS FOR ARMED REVOLT BY PARTY."

After Eckert's relatively brief stint on the stand, Judge Ganey declared a recess that lasted through the next day. However, there was no need for news editors to fret about their assignments or to be overly concerned with maintaining continuity with the anti-red hysteria. On that day, June 9th, the Third Circuit Court of Appeals was using our courtroom to listen to arguments appealing the results of an earlier Smith Act case in Pittsburgh. On June 10th, the headline in the *Philadelphia Daily News* made reference to "BLOOD AND THUNDER" in Ganey's courtroom.

Although Eckert, when questioned by Judge Ganey, told about his weaponry instruction in Russia, under cross-examination by Joe Lord, he testified that after returning to the United States, he never taught anyone how to use weapons. In addition, he admitted that while he was a member of the Communist Party, he never even saw a weapon and he never heard of the party teaching anything about how to use weapons.[2] At the end of his time on the stand, following a vigorous defense objection to the relevance of Eckert's entire testimony, the judge admitted it, but "only as it pertained to the defendant Nabried...."

Although I never saw Harold Mosher before or after the trial, the sixth government witness left me with a lasting impression for a couple of reasons. As the youngest defendant in the case, I was especially conscious of age, and Harold Mosher was probably even younger than I. However, there was a second and more commanding reason. During and after the trial, I played around a bit with the sound of his name. Mosher could be made to sound like Musser. And Musser is a Yiddish word for the lowest of all low-life—an informer, a stool pigeon, a rat-fink. Mosher the Musser!

During a very short direct examination by the prosecuting attorney, Mosher said that he had joined the Communist Party as an informer for the FBI in April 1947 and remained a member until August 1950.[3] His sole contribution to the government's case was to say that my co-defendant, Joe Roberts, was the State Chairman of the Communist Party in Connecticut when Mosher joined and that Roberts made a speech at a party school that the witness attended to study Marxist literature over a period of nine days.[4]

Mosher was a witness (like all of the others) who understood and conjured up, in some detail, whatever it was that the prosecuting attorneys wanted to hear. But when the time came for cross-examination, Mosher responded with, "Would you rephrase the question?" and "I don't understand." Either his earlier excellent memory failed him or he was just plain evasive.[5]

Mosher said that when he joined the party as an FBI informer, he told his father, who had been a member of the party for 15 years. The following exchange took place between the witness and defense counsel, McBride:

Q. Did he [Mosher's father] know you were acting for the FBI?
A. Repeat the question.
Q. Did you tell him that you were working for the FBI?
A. Yes, sir.
Q. When did you?
A. When did I what?
Q. When did you tell him?
A. When I became a member of the Communist Party, I told him.
Q. Did you harbor any feeling against the Communist Party as the result of any experience your father had with it?
A. Repeat that question, please.
Q. Did you harbor any feeling against the Communist Party as the result of any experience your father had with it?
A. I don't follow. Will you try to rephrase it?
Q. No, I won't rephrase it....If you can't answer it, is it that you do not understand the question?

Mosher's final response was, "I do not understand the question."[6] Later, Mosher's reason for his lack of candor became clear. He had included his father's name in his reports to the FBI.[7]

Mosher also agreed that at the school he attended where Joe Roberts was a speaker, Roberts spoke of Marxism and its application in the light of present-day circumstances and, in the course of his remarks, did not mention force and violence.[8] This was reiterated when, a bit later, the judge intervened in an obvious attempt to make something ominous out of what was taught at the nine-day school. The witness was no more able to deal with Ganey's hints than he had been with McBride's questions. The prosecution, mindful of McBride's earlier success with the subpoena for Herman Thomas' reports to the FBI, stepped in to the rescue. They acknowledged that Mosher never mentioned force and violence in any of his reports to the FBI.[9] This was a particularly significant verification in view of Mosher's own description of his role for the FBI. "Your Honor, I am not familiar with the Communist Party theory as far as the teachings that they advocate because I was not interested in them. I was interested in obtaining information of value, that I thought of value, not of learning the Communist Party principles itself as far as the theory."[10]

Ralph Heltzinger, witness number seven, needed a "good-paying job" when he was discharged from the Marine Corps in 1944, so he "went to the FBI" in Reading, Pennsylvania. After some discussion about "helping my country, [an FBI agent] gave me a membership application" for the Communist Political Association. "I mailed it in and was accepted for membership."[11] Heltzinger claimed his status as an informer for the FBI existed right up to the time he took the witness stand, and as he pointed to "the man with the moustache," he included me among six defendants who attended a meeting at an Elk's Hall in Philadelphia in 1952, and who apparently had nothing to do or say.[12] Heltzinger told the Court that he once heard Tom Nabried make a speech within which there were no references to revolution. In fact, Heltzinger made no mention of force or violence in the course of his entire testimony. He did recall a class he attended in March 1949, where Tom Nabried was supposed to be a teacher and at which Bob Klonsky "organized...passed out the course outline...distributed the literature [and] discussed security."[13] This piece of convenient testimony set the stage for another of the special prosecutors up from Washington, William McCusty, to read 20 more pages of the Marxist classics into the court record. Following those revelations, Heltzinger declared that his sole purpose for joining the Communist Party was to look for violations of the Smith Act. He then promptly retired from the witness stand.[14]

The last three witnesses for the prosecution were Larry Maynard, Tom Carolan and Sam DiMaria. I used to see Maynard and Carolan on the many times that I picked up my wife for lunch, at the headquarters of the National Maritime Workers Union, on the west side of Broad Street just south of Poplar. Pauline was the port agent's secretary during 1946-47, at a time when she was pregnant with our first son, and Maynard and Carolan were both active minor officials and permanent fixtures at the union's "shape-up" hall.

Sam DiMaria worked around the corner on the south side of Poplar Street, just west of 15th, at the offices of Local 155 of the United Electrical Workers. He was one of the local's organizers. My wife had also been employed by that union a few years earlier and, in the late 1940s, we had continued our acquaintanceship with some of its office staff and officials. In addition, one of my co-defendants, Dave Davis, with whom I frequently met, was the leader of that union. Consequently, I had opportunities to see DiMaria many times and to get to know him. He was literally "tall, dark and handsome," with wavy ebony-black hair and a trim, muscular appearance. Popular and charismatic, he enjoyed the reputation of being a skilled and able organizer. Several years before the Smith Act trial, DiMaria's teenage son was arrested after an auto accident and accused of driving a stolen vehicle. The case somehow "mysteriously disappeared," and though I never knew it to be an absolute fact, all of us believed that DiMaria's testimony was the price he had to pay for his son's freedom.

Larry Maynard testified that he had joined the Communist Party in 1935, following his release from the New Jersey State Penitentiary where he served almost seven years after being convicted of burglary, possession of burglar's tools and receiving stolen goods. He remained in the party until October 1951 as a member of the party's Seaman's Club, whose organizer, he said, was my co-defendant Chick Katz. Maynard described 17 meetings that he attended, but in only two of those meetings had there been any reference to revolution, once by Chick Katz and once by another co-defendant, Ben Weiss. Both of these statements were related to what could be found on page nine of one of the government exhibits, *The History of the Communist Party of the Soviet Union.* On both occasions, Maynard quoted my two co-defendants, in almost identical words, as saying that the ruling class would never give up its power peacefully; therefore, the working class had to understand that it was only through its own strength, its own efforts, that they would ever be able to take over from the ruling capitalists.[15]

As Tom McBride finished with Maynard and he was about to leave the witness stand, Judge Ganey intervened. Once again it was clear that the judge was attempting to elicit statements that could damage the defendants.

Judge: At this convention, you talked about how it was said
           that the workers were going to be the gravediggers of
           capitalism. You used that phrase, didn't you?
Maynard: Yes, sir, I did.
Judge: And that they would take over the means of produc-
           tion. Was there any discussion about...ways of
           digging the grave of capitalism and taking over the
           means of production?
Maynard: No, sir, there was no such discussion.
Judge: ...you weren't told how or the means by which the
           taking over was to be accomplished?

Maynard: I don't believe I said [that it was said] that the workers were going to take over the means of production.

Judge: I thought you did. I made this note of it. I may be wrong.

Maynard: That phrase comes from the Marxist classics, that the workers are the gravediggers of capitalism....It was a quotation from one of the classics.[16]

Judge Ganey had not gotten what I'm certain he wanted from Maynard: no arrangements for taking over; no plans for insurrection; no plots for revolution; no bombs, no guns, no force and violence. Just a paraphrase from *The Communist Manifesto,* written in 1848, in which Marx and Engels suggested that as capitalism developed, its ruling class (the "bourgeoisie") was creating a large working class (the "proletariat"); and as in "the history of all hitherto existing societies," those two classes would become engaged in class struggle out of which the working class would emerge victorious. "What the bourgeoisie therefore produces, above all, are its own gravediggers."

Tom Carolan identified himself as having been a member of the Communist Party from 1934 to 1942, and again from 1945 through 1947.[17] After talking about some meetings and a convention, he told about a conversation he had with my co-defendant, Joe Roberts, in 1937. Roberts, he said, told him to use his knowledge of Marxism-Leninism to build the party in shops and unions and to increase the sale of party literature.[18] Carolan's principal contribution to the prosecution's case was his description of how the communists placed subversive literature like *The Grapes of Wrath* and *How Green Was My Valley* into the libraries of merchant ships. Carolan, however, seemed to score a point for the defense when he testified that he had a conversation with Dave Davis in 1945 in which he told Davis about his experiences on a voyage to Russia. In the words of Carolan, Davis "pointed out that there was a more highly developed proletariat in this country than there was in Russia, that they were better organized, and *when the revolutionary situation arose,*[19] and the party attained the leadership of the working class, that the transition to socialism in this country would be less violent than it was in Russia, that it might be even possible to establish the dictatorship of the proletariat without any transitory stage at all* [my emphasis]."

The prosecution's last witness was Samuel DiMaria, who testified that he had been a member of the Communist Party from 1939 to May 1951. He had been a member of the Pennsylvania party's district committee, its highest body, between 1946 and 1949. During that time he had gotten to know all of the defendants except for Joe Roberts. DiMaria told the court that in the spring of 1947, because he was then "sufficiently knowledgeable," he was appointed to the party's education commission in order to establish a program of instruction and discussion of Marxist-Leninist theory, and that he attended many meetings of that commission.[20] DiMaria also testified at length about his involvement with secret party activities and claimed that Dave Davis told him to drop out of all open party activity in December 1947, because of the imminence of arrests.

At one point in his testimony, DiMaria alluded to a party school held in Philadelphia during October 1947. He described it as a five-day, full-time series of morning, afternoon and evening sessions which he was told to attend in order to "receive instruction in the fundamental concepts of Marxian ideology."[21] He testified that Joe Kuzma and William Z. Foster, the party's national chairman, were among the school's instructors, and that Kuzma said "that the basic heart of the revolutionary program of Marx, Engels, Lenin and Stalin lay in the fact that the Communist Party's historic mission was to lead and direct the working class to the dictatorship of the proletariat by violent revolution, and that unless we understood that, the tactical questions facing the Communist Party could not be carried out with any degree of success whatsoever." DiMaria went on to state that Foster spoke in the presence of four of the defendants when he declared that "the only basis upon which the proletariat could ever seize control of the state away from the bourgeoisie was by violent revolution."[22]

Answering Tom McBride during cross-examination, DiMaria could not remember the location of the alleged "intensive" communist school, at which he said he attended some 15 to 20 sessions. When McBride expressed doubt that such a school ever existed, DiMaria proceeded to place it "somewhere between Market Street, South Street, Broad Street and the Schuylkill River."[23] It was a ridiculous assertion for someone who worked daily out of an office near Center City Philadelphia and knew that area contained hundreds of homes, apartment buildings and commercial businesses. When McBride asked DiMaria if he had any of the books or other materials used in the classes, his response was, "I burned them." Neither could DiMaria recall the names of more than two of the 10 to 15 students he said had attended.[24] That which he did "remember" about the "school" contradicted the testimony he gave, under oath, to the House Committee on Un-American Activities.[25] DiMaria's memory regarding the almost identical statements of Kuzma and Foster at that special institute also seems remarkable considering that they are separated in the transcript by five pages of other testimony, and considering further that DiMaria remembered nothing else about the school.

Once again, chief defense attorney Tom McBride demanded FBI records, this time of DiMaria and the alleged school, but he agreed that only the judge needed to see them. After examining the FBI reports, Judge Ganey said that there was an "error" in DiMaria's testimony; that the records indicated that one of the two "students" DiMaria remembered as being there was shown to be in Europe at the time. However, it required prompting by McBride to move the judge to add that there were no references, in any of DiMaria's reports to the FBI, to any school in Philadelphia. The testimony of DiMaria's secretary, called later as a defense witness, placed him at other locations during the times he testified he was in classes.[26] All in all, the testimony of Sam DiMaria concerning a communist training school in Center City Philadelphia during October of 1947 was false in every detail.

As to DiMaria's testimony about his involvement with secret Party activities, other testimony shows that Dave Davis and all of the other defendants functioned openly. Each and every one of them, as well as DiMaria, could be found six months later at the open Communist Party District Convention. And the "secret" and important "underground" activity with which DiMaria said he was engaged, the transcript shows, had to do with the storage of such dangerous weapons as mimeograph machines, stencils and paper.[27]

The cross-examination of Sam DiMaria also produced evidence strongly suggesting that he had stolen 600 dollars of funds entrusted to him. In redirect testimony, the government made absolutely no effort to refute that allegation.

As contradictory and incredible as was his testimony, this last witness for the prosecution acknowledged, like all the others before him, that Lenin's concept of the objective preconditions for revolution, operating independently of the will of the party, was what he was taught and was the accepted Communist Party doctrine.

It was June 18, 1954. Following the testimony of Sam DiMaria, in a move that surprised everyone, the government rested its case. Court was recessed for three weeks.

The research and analysis done by Ben Reed in regard to Paul Crouch had produced an early dramatic highlight in the trial. Similar skills by the other outstanding members of the defense team revealed unsavory character, lies and additional perjury that enabled cross-examination to discredit just about all of the government's paid witnesses. The defense team also was able to demonstrate that these informers were paid handsomely for their anti-communist "expertise," in amounts that ranged from $15,000 for Herman Thomas to $70,000 for Louis Budenz—very healthy sums in 1954.

Chapter 15

A DEFENJE AND THE VERDICT

Our strategy had been to conduct a simple, dignified defense: to make a strong case for the defendants' constitutional rights and at the same time to discredit the prosecution witnesses. We had tried to eliminate delays and postponements, and any cause for the determination of a mistrial. "The trial would not be turned into a circus with loud interruptions," Joe Lord recalled. "We were determined to demonstrate that we were gentlemen and that we represented gentlemen."[1]

A New York attorney with considerable Smith Act trial experience, Frank Donner had been called in as a consultant. Donner helped me prepare the testimony I wanted to present—an accurate and concise statement of my life to date and my Communist Party activities. My co-defendants were similarly briefed, either by Donner or one of the other members of the defense team. Each of us worked at it for many hours, and while I may have been alone with my performance fears, every one of us was ready and eager to take the stand.

We had, in fact, accomplished a major goal. "The prosecution witnesses were hurt and looked bad," said Edmund Spaeth when I interviewed him in 1990, adding that there was the chance that the jury wouldn't like the defendants. In that case, he said, "what we gained from discrediting Crouch and the others would be a washout...[but] we wanted to preserve the constitutional and statute-of-limitations arguments."[2] When the prosecution concluded, the defense attorneys believed that the government had failed to make its case and the record, as it stood, was already as good as it could be. There was no evidence that we had used force and violence. Neither was there any evidence that we advocated force and violence to overthrow the United States Government. It was shown only that we advocated Marxism-Leninism. Consequently there was no need, our attorneys had argued, to prove any constitutional right to freedom of speech by putting defendants on the stand. In addition, we were told that admissibility of statements to show participation in a conspiracy is relatively easy. And since there was very little in the record that fell within the three years permitted by the statute of limitations, there was concern that should a defendant testify, he might be tricked into, or himself make, an otherwise innocent statement that could be compromising.

The defense team recommended that the nine defendants not take the stand, and we did not. Instead, the decision was for the defense to supplement the skillful cross-examination and exposure of the witnesses for the prosecution with the presentation of supporting documents. As to the theories and principles of Marxism and the issue of their relationship to force and violence, that would be left to two real experts. They were neither on trial nor named in the indictment, and they would be called to testify as witnesses for the defense.

The first of those witnesses was Dr. Herbert Aptheker, a noted Marxist historian and author. At the time of the trial he was the managing editor of *Political Affairs*, the official theoretical organ and monthly journal of the American Communist Party. When he was not interrupted and when government attorneys were not objecting to his testimony, Aptheker presented the Communist Party position in regard to numerous theoretical questions previously introduced by the prosecution. He also delivered a point-by-point refutation of Louis Budenz's testimony, particularly as it related to Aesopian language. Aptheker was referred to many of the books introduced into evidence by the government and asked his explanation of such terms as Marxism-Leninism, dialectical and historical materialism, revolution and the dictatorship of the proletariat. "Communists believe the change to a socialist society will be a drawn-out historical process in which there is no room in the theory for advocacy of violence....Revolution is a developing process according to Marxism-Leninism. It is not like a Hollywood production where you can call it on and call it off....I cannot say when or how [socialism] will come to the United States. Yes, capitalism will be replaced by socialism here, as everywhere else in the world; however, there is no blueprint....The overthrow of American capitalism is not on the agenda of the United States Communist Party."[3]

There were many prosecution interruptions, on occasion rude and disdainful. On July 14th, a bristling Tom McBride, upset by the deportment of government attorneys, jumped to his feet and addressed Judge Ganey: "I want to bring to public attention that government counsel has been sitting here, snickering and smirking every time they don't agree with what this witness says." U.S. attorney W. Wilson White broke in: "Well, you've sure made your point." "I certainly did, and I hope I don't have to make it again," McBride retorted.[4]

Just about the entire prosecution two-day cross-examination of Dr. Aptheker was devoted either to an attempt to establish that the managing editor of the party's theoretical journal was not really someone who was inside the inner circles of Communist Party leadership or to an unsuccessful attempt to get him to divulge names of people with whom he associated during his early party activities in 1939. "Who gave you...what materials [and] literature?...To whom did you pay your dues?...What was the name of the club chairman...secretary...treasurer [and] who gave out the assignments?"[5]

When Aptheker's testimony was about to conclude, Judge Ganey, wanting something meatier, engaged him regarding "the party arrogating to itself the right to determine whether a war was just or unjust...." Aptheker responded that there wasn't anything peculiar to communists or Marxism-Leninism in such a position, and he cited Abe Lincoln and Mark Twain and their open opposition to the wars with Mexico and Spain. He went on to say that if the communists concluded, "after democratic discussion," that the nation was engaged in an unjust war, "we would start a propaganda campaign to convince the rest of society to stop the killing." Alluding to one of Aptheker's previous comments concerning the communist belief in the eventual evolution of a society with no class distinctions, a sarcastic Judge Ganey went on to ask Aptheker if that meant that there would be "no involvement [in civil war] with respect to the ultimate accomplishment or attainment of the Communist Party with respect to the classless society?"[6] A few days earlier, at the end of his direct testimony, Aptheker had dealt with that question. Judge Ganey asked, "Is it possible that what your party envisages may be an indulgence in an illusion?" And Dr. Aptheker responded, "Well, Judge, historically, one man's illusion is another's reality."[7]

The appearance of Dr. John Somerville at the Philadelphia trial marked another important first—the first time a non-communist expert witness testified for the defendants in a Smith Act case. He would discuss Marxist theory and present balanced analysis of the trial's major issue—the advocacy of force and violence. His appearance was a conscious move by a broad-based defense team to build upon that breadth and step outside the confines of the Communist Party.

Somerville was an internationally renowned non-communist expert on Marxism-Leninism, the author of *Soviet Philosophy: A Study of Theory and Practice*, a consultant for UNESCO and Professor of Philosophy at Hunter College. His works could be found in scores of reference books and scientific journals worldwide. Dr. Somerville said that he agreed to testify at our trial because "It appeared and appears very clear to me that if ever there comes a time in this country when the citizen who possesses special knowledge relating to some public issue is afraid to come forward and place it at the disposal of a judge and 12 jurors in a courtroom, justice will be dead and the moral meaning of this country will have vanished.

"The question of the actual content of communist doctrine has clearly become one of tremendous importance. Whatever I or anyone else may know about that matter certainly ought to be passed on to others and utilized. It would be difficult to believe that anyone acting responsibly and in good faith could counsel me to do otherwise."[8]

There was considerable irony in the government's position. The prosecution fought to prevent Dr. Somerville from testifying as a witness for the defense, because he had never attended communist schools or meetings and was not a communist. Communists, they claimed, were self-serving, but a non-communist could not provide knowledgeable testimony!

As a non-communist, Somerville testified that neither the principles of Marxism-Leninism nor the policies of the Communist Party advocated the overthrow of the government by force and violence. The Hunter College philosophy professor said that there was no doubt that communists in the United States understood that proletarian revolution was impossible unless there was a revolutionary situation. Such a situation, he added, is one in which the government can no longer rule, has completely broken down, and the majority of the people support a revolution. He went on to say that U.S. communists neither taught nor believed that such a situation existed. However, he was prevented by the prosecution's constant objections, and sustained by the court, from presenting any analysis or explanation of that testimony.

Witness:	To understand the attitude of Marxism-Leninism, we must carefully note...that the principle of revolution advocates a belief in the right of revolution under certain circumstances and is a very different thing from advocating revolution itself under any circumstances. That difference is clear and compelling.
Govt. Counsel:	I move to strike this point out as argument.
Court:	I think that is right. I don't think he can say whether it is clear and compelling at all.
Witness:	It is the difference between saying that I have the right to do something under certain unusual conditions and the belief that I have the right to do that thing irrespective of conditions. For example, most people believe they have the right to strike...
Govt. Counsel:	I object to this part—the examples, Your Honor.
Witness:	I am drawing a comparison between this and the right to self-defense.
Govt. Counsel:	The right to strike?
Witness:	To illustrate the meaning of the doctrine.
Court:	I am going to sustain the objection there.
Defense Counsel:	When you started to read 'the right to strike,' did you mean the right to go on strike applicable to labor unions, or the right to strike another person?
Witness:	I was talking about the right to self-defense.
Govt. Counsel:	That is stricken.
Defense Counsel:	It is stricken because you did not even let him complete it, and nobody understood what he was about to say.

At another point in his testimony, Somerville was attempting to explain with an example:

Witness:	...consider our own American Declaration of Independence.
Govt. Counsel:	I object.
Court:	Strike that out.
Defense Counsel:	Will Your Honor hear me? I think that it's basic to the principle if it can be demonstrated that a quotation from the Declaration of Independence is similar to the position taken in the Marxist classics.
Court:	No, he has been asked as to the totality of Marxism. I think he can do that without bringing in the Declaration of Independence. We will leave that out.
Defense Counsel:	What is the relationship between the theory of the Communist Party of the United States as to the right of revolution and the right of revolution stated in the Declaration of Independence?
Govt. Counsel:	That, of course, is objected to, sir.
Court:	Objection sustained.[9]

The character and intellect of Dr. Aptheker and Dr. Somerville were unimpeachable. They stood in sharp contrast to the discredited prosecution's parade of paid informers.

If the defense team had any lingering questions about the defendants' innocence, these had all but vanished by the time the jury was prepared to hear the final summations. David Cohen, the labor lawyer who joined the defense team as attorney for Dave Davis, and a longtime Philadelphia City Council member, remembered: "There was something about the defendants....Tom McBride believed in the honesty, integrity and innocence of every one of them....He would tell us that the defendants were not communists as the public believed communists to be, and that not one of them was guilty....He was outraged by what the government was doing....McBride thought that the government's case was just plain nonsense....It didn't take long for the entire team of attorneys to see that....The more the lawyers got to know the defendants, the more we believed in them."[10] In a similar vein, Joe Lord observed, "every single counselor became convinced as a result of the government's case that the trial was a horrible abridgment of the right to free speech."[11]

As I wished Joe Lord well on the day of his summation, we could not help noting the similarity in our light gray double-breasted suits. With a bit of a twinkle in his eye, he pointed to a distinctive feature I had never noticed on my hand-me-down jacket as he wondered aloud if the jury would think the less of him because he couldn't afford a suit with hand-stitched lapels.

In a lengthy summation, Lord dealt extensively with two concerns as he analyzed the quality of the witnesses for the prosecution and some questions
raised in the introduction of Marxist literature. Lord stressed how the prosecutors had talked about the content of books they had offered in evidence but had
studiously avoided saying anything in summation about the "liars," the "ex-con-
victs" and the "perjurers" they had brought into the courtroom.[12] He did not
skip a single witness. One by one, he ran down the list, summarizing their performances and the success of the defense in discrediting them—John Lautner
for "his perjury"; Lawrence Maynard for "his criminal record"; Sam DiMaria for
"lying under oath" by placing himself and many of the defendants at a communist training school that the defense demonstrated never existed. And then
there was Herman Thomas, who was able to go through 52 different meetings
in chronological order on direct examination, but who "couldn't remember
anything when tested under cross-examination." "What sort of parade of
pirates have they brought here for you, members of the jury?" Lord asked.

Lord was at his best when his contempt for the government's case turned
him toward witnesses Paul Crouch and Louis Budenz. Invoking characters
from *Alice in Wonderland,* Lord likened Crouch to the Queen of Hearts.
When Alice observed, "One can't believe in impossible things," the Queen
responded, "Why, sometimes I believe in as many as six impossible things
before breakfast." Lord added that the Queen was a "piker compared to
Crouch," who lied under oath constantly and was completely untrustworthy.

When confronted with out-and-out conflict in his testimony, Crouch simply stopped, lost his composure and remained silent, but Louis Budenz was
much more facile, Lord argued. He was "a reed that bends with the breeze,"
a master of double-talk, of "semi-Aesopian" and Aesopian language, conve-
niently using the same words to mean different things at different times and
attributing that quality, when necessary, to others. Lord quoted Humpty
Dumpty as a surrogate for Budenz: "They are my words, and when I use
them they mean what I say they do—nothing more, nothing less—and you
don't know what they mean 'til I tell you what they mean....The question is
which is to be master, that is all."

Turning to some theoretical questions, Lord demonstrated an impressive
understanding of several Marxist perspectives as he talked about the meaning of the terms "revolution" and "dictatorship of the proletariat." He continued with a Marxist view of who would be responsible for the initiation of
violence, should it occur in a revolutionary situation and whether there can
ever be justification for insurrection. Lord then said to the jury, "All we are
asking you to do is weigh what those beliefs are. [You can] say, 'I do not
agree with them,' but they are not unlawful." And he argued that when
Article IX of the Communist Party constitution states that anyone who advocates force and violence will be summarily expelled, it is not sufficient to
"put Humpty Dumpty on the stand to refute it with 'They don't mean it.'"

The stage was set for Tom McBride. "I have never, in all my years, seen such
an unhealthy lot," he said of the prosecution's witnesses, describing them as

"such a succession of men who have something wrong with them—weak, greedy for money, with records or some bias or hatred or with disappointed lives." Throughout history, he told the jury, "whenever men prosecuted and others were found who in order to get paid, gave evidence...generations of jurors have set their seal of condemnation upon such men...as provocateurs, dangerous, evil, whose hearts are corrupt and untrustworthy." McBride concluded these observations with "falsus in uno, falsus in omnibus": if just one lie was found in any informer's testimony, then everything that informer said had to be construed as false and, consequently, discounted.[13]

Here was, by consensus, the best defense attorney in town, a leading authority on constitutional law, a future chancellor of the bar who really believed that the lady with the scales was deeply shamed by what was occurring in the federal courts. "I need not pretend, members of the jury, that this is not the most important case I have ever participated in. I need not pretend for a single instant that this is not the most important case ever tried in this courthouse. It may well be the most important case that will ever be tried in this courthouse," he said to them that day. Speaking of the defendants, McBride went on to say, "The plain and simple issue in this case is whether they have the right to walk the streets as citizens...to remain out of jail...to hold the views they hold without being put in jail." These were views gained from books, he argued. Books that were available to one and all were the evidence in the trial. McBride was appalled at "this primitive notion that you can try books, that you could put people into jail not for reading, not even for writing, but for believing in them. [This] is an idea that I never thought I would ever have to stand on my two feet in a federal court and condemn." McBride went on to characterize the theory of the prosecution: "I will show you that my ideas are better than your ideas by putting your ideas in jail." Indeed, the defendants were communists and were, consequently, very unpopular people, but "civil liberty fights are always conducted on behalf of unpopular people...and it is people who are saying things with which we do not agree that we constantly try to put down....This case in its full aspects is one of the most important civil liberties cases that will ever come to your attention."

Ever quiet and controlled, McBride made his outrage sing. "These men are just as solidly based on the Constitution as any citizen in all the land....When they take their stand upon the Constitution and come into...the greatest temple of justice in all the world and they bring that Constitution in with them...nobody can say they don't believe in the Constitution. It doesn't even matter whether they do or not, and there is no evidence that they don't. They have said they do. They have indicated by their acts as shown in this courtroom that they do. They have been responsive and respectful in this court throughout. There has not been one of them ever even late. There hasn't been one who has shown the slightest disrespect for this court or the jury or anybody else since the case started."

McBride wanted the jury to understand that the prospect, the very thought, that the defendants could be sent to prison "simply because they are communists, is one of the most un-American, the most destructive, the most evil doctrines that can enter the mind of a human being." Returning to his defense of the Bill of Rights, he added, "These men had a perfect right to teach and to advocate just exactly what the record shows that they did teach and advocate....These men believe in the inevitability of socialism and that it will come in accordance with the way that would be decided by the American people....If this were 1970 and we were looking back...we would consider it quite remarkable that in a federal court in the city of Philadelphia men like these were put on trial for their ideas."

After eloquent references to Socrates, Galileo, Zenger and Scopes and the tribulations of their trials, McBride brought his summation toward its close: "Now these defendants have placed upon their shoulders by history the duty to stand trial. History chooses in ways that I can't fathom upon whose shoulders it will place that mantle to stand trial or to be the particular persons involved in a consideration of tremendously important issues, far beyond what the defendants might be, far beyond what the lawyers might be and far beyond who the prosecutors are. This, I sincerely believe, is such a trial."

Five and a half months had passed, more than two million words of testimony had been spoken. The jury deliberated overnight and well into the next afternoon. No previous Smith Act jury had stayed out as long. But when they came out of their chambers, it appeared that only Walter Lowenfels had something positive to show for a spring and summer sitting next to me in the courtroom: he had translated a complete set of sonnets by the great French anarchist poet, Louis Aragon. It was, after all, August 1954—a time for heroic attorneys but not yet for courageous jurors. The Philadelphia Smith Act jury returned its verdict: *guilty.*

Chapter 16

JENTENCING AND FREEDOM

Have you ever experienced the exhilaration and camaraderie that comes from shared identification with ideas, with beliefs, with a dream? Have you ever been filled with the sense of strength that arises from commitment to a view of the universe, a "cause" that you know to be moral and just, even when the numbers of your supporters are small? I was high on the beauty of those feelings during the hours that followed the vindicating summations to the jury by Lord and McBride.

I was also very aware that it was August 13, 1954. Our fate, that of "nine reds," had already been determined and sealed. A most oppressive atmosphere had invaded and taken hold in the City of Brotherly Love. Riding herd in Philadelphia during 1953 and 1954 were the many state legislative investigating committees, McCarthy's Senate Internal Security Sub-Committee and the House Committee on Un-American Activities (HUAC). Two teachers from the Association for Retarded Children, three professors from Jefferson Medical College plus a research assistant who was the wife of one of them, a professor from Temple University, and 32 teachers from the Philadelphia public school system had all been fired from their jobs—the victims of well-publicized, headline-making investigations and interrogations that questioned neither their academic nor their research skills, only their political loyalties.

On September 23, 1953, Barrows Dunham, a distinguished Temple University philosophy professor, was dismissed by the university's board of trustees for having "illegally" invoked the Fifth Amendment before HUAC. In November 1953, the "Un-American" Committee held three days of hearings in Philadelphia where they investigated and challenged the loyalty of the city's public school teachers. Everyone subpoenaed, either for the Philadelphia proceedings or for subsequent ones in Washington, D.C., early in 1954, was also summarily dismissed by Philadelphia's superintendent of schools.

By this time, Senator McCarthy was alleging that there were "spies in the Signal Corps" at nearby Fort Monmouth, New Jersey, and that the Army was "promoting known communists." The senator was also demanding favored status and preferential treatment for his committee's counsel and investigator, David Schine, who had just been drafted for military service. McCarthy had become publicly embroiled with the Army, and it looked like he could take on the entire military establishment. Philadelphia was not the place, nor was it yet a time for forthright behavior on the part of my "jury of peers."

In mid-September 1954, our defense attorneys presented our arguments for a judgment of acquittal or a new trial. They cited 29 reasons, among which were four errors by the trial judge. Judge Ganey received the briefs and retired to deliberate.

Nine months would pass before he ruled on the motions for acquittal or a new trial. I marked those months selling lamps, tables and greeting cards from a new store two of my brothers opened so that I would have a means of supporting my family. Deep down inside my gut was a mostly buried fatalistic feeling that I would inevitably be imprisoned. But there was also an underlying conviction that we would "arise triumphant." I knew that throughout the world, country after country was adopting socialism, and I believed that it was only a matter of time before a majority of the people in my own country would embrace the idea. For those nine months, I was free: to enjoy going to work each day and home each night, to relax and play with the kids, to share with Pauline in all those worries about the health and well-being of our family.

Despite the verdict of the jury, the ever-optimistic Walter Lowenfels saw a half-filled glass. I remember going to his home one afternoon during this period and finding him with the portly folksinger and songwriter Will Hays. Sprawled across the dining room table, they were working over some lyrics. "Isn't this a time, a time to try the souls of men? Isn't this a wonderful time?" Perhaps it was not such a wonderful time, but at least the pendulum seemed to have reached its endpoint and was ready to swing back in the other direction.

McCarthy had indeed taken on the military. Despite efforts by Vice President Richard Nixon to mediate the Army's differences with McCarthy and his Senate Internal Security Sub-Committee about those alleged "spies" and "promotions," the United States Army, pushed to its limits, fought back. The dispute culminated in a series of televised hearings between April and June 1954. McCarthy's unsupported allegations, his grating voice and his crass and rude behavior were viewed and heard by millions. On July 30th, Senator Ralph Flanders introduced a resolution rebuking him, and on December 2, 1954, Joseph McCarthy was censured by the United States Senate by a vote of 67 to 22. At the end of 1954, the man whose name symbolized the worst in an era of witch-hunting had been effectively destroyed. But McCarthyism, while mortally wounded, was sufficiently strong to inflict its dying damage for years to follow.

By early 1955, C. Brewster Rhoads had replaced Bernard Segal as Chancellor of the Philadelphia Bar Association. Tom McBride, chief defense counsel in the Smith Act trial, was the bar association's newly elected vice chancellor. He would become its next chancellor.

On March 14, 1955, as we continued to wait for Judge J. Cullen Ganey to acknowledge his errors and rule on motions for acquittal or new trial, Philadelphia newspapers reported that one of our defense attorneys had come under fire. Henry W. Sawyer III had become a candidate for Philadelphia City Council. A telegram had been sent to the Chairman of the Democratic City Committee, Congressman William J. Green, Jr., criticizing the candidacy. One of the grounds given was that Sawyer had "volunteered his services to the defendants in the Philadelphia Smith Act trial."[1]

Ex-Chancellor Bernard Segal immediately sent out a newspaper release, which he "hurriedly prepared upon having read to me on the telephone the reference in the press to the telegram," and enclosed it in a lengthy letter to Congressman Green.[2] The letter, a masterpiece of understatement, intended to present the "true facts of the situation." Segal was certain that Green would "agree that it was unthinkable" that the Smith Act defendants were in jail in Philadelphia, unable to be arraigned or to have a hearing on fair bail due to their inability to secure counsel.[3] Summarizing the events that led up to the selection of Sawyer and the other attorneys who assisted in our defense, Segal made it clear that his letter to Green had the "enthusiastic support of my successor as chancellor, C. Brewster Rhoads, and the unanimous approval by formal resolution, of the current board of governors of the association."[4] A copy of the letter, which amounted to a reaffirmation of the bar association's resolution, was fired off to each of the attorneys who had participated in the Smith Act trial. Sawyer also reviewed from Chancellor Rhoads his "enthusiastic endorsement of the fine job which you and your associates performed in your representation of the defendants in the Smith Act trial last year. I can only repeat the appreciation of the officers, board of governors and members of the Philadelphia Bar Association....You performed a difficult task with dignity and energy and in the fine tradition of the Philadelphia bar, and all of us who followed your performance are indebted to you for a job well done."[5]

One week later, Segal wrote to Supreme Court Justice Felix Frankfurter, "knowing of your interest in such matters."[6] Segal enclosed the newspaper release and his letter to Bill Green, indicating that they had been in response to a "violent attack by the head of the local branch of the Veterans of Foreign Wars upon a highly regarded Philadelphia lawyer." Segal also noted that "apparently [the letters] served their purpose, as I am told that...as a result of the favorable publicity resulting from the statement, the party leadership adhered to their endorsement [of Sawyer]."[7]

On April 1, 1955, Justice Frankfurter responded: "How thoughtful of you to bear in mind my interest in such situations as those raised by the indefensible attack on Mr. Henry W. Sawyer III, because of his recognition of the public duty of the bar and his high-minded response to it. I thought your statements were admirable and it is cheering to have you tell me that they brought even politicians to recognition of the fact that lawyers who act as did Mr. Sawyer are entitled to the commendation and not the condemnation of the community."[8]

Speaking in 1994, Henry Sawyer recalled a "hearing" in 1955, when several prominent citizens were "called down to Bill Green's office" to discuss the attack on Sawyer. At the time, Congressman Green was also the long-time Chairman of the Democratic City Committee. According to Sawyer, in addition to Bill Green and himself, those present included the politically powerful "Jack" Kelly, Sr.; two mayors-to-be, Richardson Dilworth and James Tate; and two leaders of the American Legion and the Veterans of Foreign Wars, Colbert McClain and John Capitola. Sawyer remembered "Jack Kelly, in the course of the meeting, saying, 'You know that I believe that everybody has the right to a lawyer—even murderers—but not those guys. They want to destroy our very foundations.' Later when McClain shouted, 'We even have a transcript here of Sawyer defending the Fifth Amendment,' Bill Green called McClain 'a tin-horn Hitler' and in the classic dismissal, flipped to the switchboard with, 'I'll take calls now.'"

As part of a Reform Democratic movement sweep, Henry Sawyer III was elected to the City Council of Philadelphia in November 1955.

On June 15, 1955, Judge Ganey denied the pending motions—a decision later described by Joe Lord as "gutless" and by Ben Reed as "asinine." Ganey also let it be known that the defendants would be sentenced five days later; almost two years had passed since our arrests. The following is excerpted from the pre-sentencing remarks I prepared:

> Your Honor, I am deeply concerned, as are all my co-defendants, about serving time behind prison walls. You see, I cherish my freedom. My desire to help protect and preserve our liberties, my desire to extend these liberties to all sections of our people and my warnings to my neighbors that one by one their liberties are rapidly vanishing, has made me the evidence, ironically, that those who fear freedom in our great land today will jail freedom's advocates.
>
> I stand before you today because I am afraid. Afraid of war. Afraid that because of war I, my wife, my two sons, my mother and brothers and everyone I love dearly may die too soon. I stand before you today because this fear moved me again to speak to my neighbors who can halt the drive to atomic destruction just as they helped to win the truce in Korea. I stand before you today because the real advocates of force and violence, the would-be war makers, who fear and hate the ability of my neighbors and others like them throughout this nation to impose their will, will today jail the advocates of peace.
>
> The prosecution would have you believe I was arrested solely because I advocate the principles of scientific socialism, of Marxism-Leninism. What a hoax! Suppose for a moment, Your Honor, I had suggested in 1951 the bombing of Manchuria. Or suppose just a few short weeks before my arrest, instead of rejoicing at the immediate possibilities of ending bloodshed in

Korea, I actively campaigned for the position of General MacArthur and Senator Knowland, a position aimed at spreading the war. Would I be standing before you today? I would not.

It is difficult for me to believe, however, that my few chosen words will influence Your Honor one way or the other. You have listened to the most expert, eloquent and convincing arguments on my behalf by Mr. McBride, Mr. Lord and the other able attorneys for the defense. You heard the barren, parrot-like arguments of my prosecutors. You saw the prosecution's case strung out by sick, perverted witnesses, and you also heard Dr. Aptheker and Dr. Somerville for the defense. In saner times, Your Honor, would I have been convicted? What court would have even tolerated the indictment? Would I have had to speak? Since I chose not to testify, I speak today lest you and others construe my silence as acceptance of guilt.

Let me first say, I deny everything that has been said by the prosecutors and the creatures they placed on the witness stand. At the time of my arraignment, I pleaded innocent. I am still innocent. I deny that it was my intention, or the intention of any of my co-defendants, to at any time advocate anything that was not in the best interest of the American people....

What have I done these past years? My neighbors can tell you. That is, those who can speak freely, who do not fear for their jobs. Most, for the time being, watch these proceedings silently, confused. The politically ambitious prosecutors did not produce one of my neighbors to testify against me. Why not? These are the people with whom I live. These are the people who have watched my family grow. These are the people with whose children I played. These are the people I have tried to influence. These are the people who know I am a communist. Some of my neighbors, I learned recently, addressed themselves to you, Your Honor. "Mr. Labovitz is a communist, but Mr. Labovitz is a good man," they said. I say to my neighbors and to you, Your Honor, I am a good man because I am a communist.

Yesterday, the conspiracy gimmick gained a conviction of the National Committee of the Communist Party. The Justice Department then moved to the alternate national committee, then to various state and district committees. With my indictment, they moved into a new level of communist leadership. What was the damning evidence to link me to the alleged conspiracy? I was responsible for the circulation of the party's press; I bought and sold newspapers! Sure, it was the Pennsylvania edition of *The Worker*. Certainly, it is a newspaper that the administration finds distasteful..... But because they fear our newspaper's message, they strike at the paper's salesmen. The record in this trial shows how interested our Justice

Department is even in the readers of *The Worker*. The informers, Thomas and Mosher, testified as to how they were paid for
names of people who even looked at a copy.
    You yourself...at the close of the prosecution's case, said that
you realized your position on the alleged conspiracy might
encompass thousands. How many thousands, Your Honor?
Who, Your Honor, will cancel the citizenship of thousands of
Americans as they begin to express their disgust with the
administration's foreign policy and speak out for peace? Who,
Your Honor, will send to prison every dissenting voice against
whom the conspiracy gimmick can be used? Where will they
build the new prisons, not to hold thousands, but millions, Your
Honor? I have nothing more to say.

Those feelings engulf me whenever I recall that last encounter with Judge
Ganey, captured only on the yellowed onionskin paper upon which they
were expressed. The defense attorneys recommended, and we all agreed,
that none of the defendants would add anything to the court record.

The conduct of the trial and the persuasiveness of the defense team
apparently had a bit of an impact on Judge Ganey's conscience. The sentences he handed down were more lenient than those imposed on defendants in earlier Smith Act trials. Four of my co-defendants were to serve
three years in prison and the remaining five of us were to be jailed for two
years. Our bail was revoked and we were immediately taken to holding cells
above the courtrooms. Our attorneys promptly filed prepared motions for
an appeal and for new bail with the Third Circuit Court.

I spent the best part of that day worrying about whether enough of the
dysfunctional aspects of bureaucracy could be satisfied before our keepers
would decide to transfer us again to Holmesburg Prison. Not the least of
those aspects, after the appeals court agreed to continue bail in the same
amounts, was to bring the people who originally placed bail for us to the
courthouse in order to sign new papers. Bob Klonsky, whose bailor was
nowhere to be found, did get out late that afternoon "on credit." His release
was a tribute, I suppose, to the importance of informal structures in bureaucracy. A relationship had developed between the federal court bail clerk and
the Civil Rights Congress Bail Fund administrator that permitted Congress
Director Jack Zucker to produce the missing bailor and his signature on the
next day.

There is another reason that I will never forget that special day in the
holding cell. One month earlier, for the first time on national television, the
link between the incidence of lung cancer and cigarette smoking was given
a public hearing by the noted newscaster Edward R. Murrow. The evening
following that telecast, I was with two physician friends who provided me
with "scientific" evidence that smoking was "purely a social habit" which

required only "will and determination" to break. Here I was, about 30 days into trying to kick a two-pack-a-day habit. Once again I was separated from my wife and children. The emotions tied to incarceration were surfacing. The ex-con in the hallway didn't make me feel any better when he noted rather incredulously, "Two years? I can do that standing on my head." Nor was my anxiety lessened by recalling how I once heard the author Howard Fast, commenting on his own period in jail for "contempt of Congress," infer that six months behind bars could be good for the soul. Frayed nerves, tension, qualms, misgivings, worry and apprehension all demanded amelioration by nicotine, and my cellmate that day, the ever-kidding, lovable, chain-smoking Chick Katz, was playfully teasing me with offers of cigarettes. I was determined; I willed that no matter what or how long it would take, I would not succumb to temptation. And I suspect that in teasing me, Chick was, in his own special way, helping me with my "will and determination." In any event, I haven't smoked since that day and I credit my success to jail without bail and—with very fond memories—to Chick Katz.

By the time we were presenting our own case to the Third Circuit Court of Appeals, the government had managed 86 Smith Act convictions. An additional 41 defendants were still under indictment. I went back to selling lamps and waited as things began to brew in Cleveland, where the bar association, together with the judge assigned to their Smith Act case, had drawn heavily on the Philadelphia experience. After almost two years and with considerable difficulty, they eventually put together a similarly impressive broad-based defense team. When the 11 Smith Act defendants in Cleveland were finally put on trial late in 1955, some of the national hysteria had dissipated. And the Cleveland trial dealt the government's prosecutors another setback. The judge directed acquittal for one defendant; and, after deliberating for 10 days, the jury freed four more.

The Philadelphia defense team had already stung the Justice Department. It had also significantly influenced the developments in Denver, Pittsburgh and Connecticut. This combination of events, plus the results from using the Philadelphia approach in Cleveland, appeared to be too much for the Justice Department to tolerate. The United States Attorney General's office lashed out at the support that was growing within several of the nation's bar associations for guaranteeing Smith Act defendants the right to counsel, and the resultant number of court-appointed attorneys that slowed down plans to bankrupt the Communist Party with legal expenses. During March 1956, in conversations with Robert Coll of the United Press, Assistant Attorney General William Tompkins and other representatives of the Justice Department referred to "the dupes of communists, [lawyers who were] foiling one of the objectives of the government to force the party to expend its resources on legal expenses."[9]

There were sharp reactions and rejoinders from prominent national civil libertarian lawyers; they defended the right of communists to counsel of their choice, and they were critical of the government's use of the paid, professional "false witness." Just a few years earlier, there would have been serious ramifications for those critics, but these were the beginnings of new times, and conditions were ripening for a growth in the number of supporters of the Bill of Rights. The more the civil libertarians made their voices heard and forced meetings with Justice Department officials, the quieter became the barking from the Attorney General's office. Tompkins eventually denied making the derogatory remarks; Coll and the United Press stood firm; and the net result was a Justice Department retreat from its attack on the lawyers who had been involved in the Smith Act cases.

By this time, President Eisenhower had appointed the former Governor of California, Earl Warren, as the new Chief Justice of the U.S. Supreme Court. Under his stewardship and with staunch support from Justices Hugo Black and William O. Douglas, the Warren Court began to repair a bit of the damage that had been inflicted upon the United States Constitution and its Bill of Rights. Two of the decisions reached by the Court during its 1956-57 term had a dramatic impact upon future prosecutions of American communists. In one of those decisions, the Court required that government prosecutors make available to the defense all FBI reports that were used in any particular trial.

The other decision dealt directly with the Smith Act itself. On June 17, 1957, the Supreme Court delivered its opinions regarding *United States v. Yates*. Oletta Yates and 13 additional West Coast communists charged with conspiring to violate the Smith Act were arrested in July 1951, immediately after a previous Supreme Court upheld the convictions in New York of the first group of party leaders in *United States v. Dennis*. Oletta Yates and her co-defendants were convicted in California in August 1952. The California Smith Act case became only the second trial of communist leaders to reach our nation's highest tribunal. Arguments were presented to the Supreme Court in October 1956, at a time when identical issues were being deliberated by the Third Circuit Court of Appeals considering the Philadelphia case.

After pondering the Yates appeal, the Supreme Court ruled in 1957, with Justice Harlan writing for the five-to-two majority, "that the term 'organize,' as used in the Smith Act, refers only to acts entering into the creation of a new organization; since the Communist Party was organized in 1945 and the indictment not returned until 1951, it was also held that prosecution on this charge was barred by the three-year statute of limitations." In other words, as to the organizing charge, the three-year period of time to bring the charge had elapsed prior to the indictment and the statute of limitations had run out. In so finding, the Supreme Court rejected the prosecution's contention that the Smith Act meant the term "organizing" as ongoing.

In addition, the Supreme Court's decision in the Yates case was an implicit rejection of the precedent-setting opinion written in 1950 by Judge Learned Hand for the Second Circuit Court of Appeals concerning *United States v. Dennis*. In regard to the clause in the Smith Act indictments that stipulates actions to be taken *"as soon as circumstances would permit,"* Judge Hand's finding as to a *"clear and present danger"* had an impact on all subsequent Smith Act trials.

Judge Hand put a judicial stamp of approval on the prevailing mythology that communist literature and teachings precluded any possibility of a lawful and peaceful attainment of power. Despite widespread evidence to the contrary in the writings of Marx and Engels and in those of numerous contemporary American communist leaders, Judge Hand was referring to communist doctrine when he wrote in that opinion: "The violent capture of all existing government is one article of the creed of that faith, which *abjures* [my emphasis] the possibility of success by lawful means."

It was this inaccurate charge that was at the root of Judge Hand's test and interpretation regarding the existence of a "clear and present danger." And it was Hand's interpretation that the Supreme Court upheld in 1951 in the Dennis case: If the seriousness and the gravity of the charge—"teaching and advocating force and violence"—were to be joined together with the degree of the possibility or probability of its occurrence—"clear and present danger"—"as speedily as circumstances would permit"; and if they were placed on one side of the scales of justice, those factors should then be weighed against any incursion into the "free speech" guarantee of First Amendment rights that would be found on the other side of those scales.

It was this kind of rationale that led to the earlier judicial opinions, and it demonstrates the extent to which even a renowned interpreter of the Constitution and its Bill of Rights like the venerable Judge Learned Hand could give voice to McCarthyism.

In the Yates case, however, the Warren Court narrowed the interpretations that had been given to the Smith Act in earlier decisions. Particularly, it distinguished between statements about an idea that *might* result in an action and the *advocacy* of such action. Of the seven justices who deliberated (two others did not participate), six concurred in the following: "We are thus faced with the question whether the Smith Act prohibits advocacy and teaching of forcible overthrow as an abstract principle, divorced from any effort to instigate action to that end, so long as such advocacy or teaching is engaged in with evil intent. *We hold that it does not* [my emphasis]....The statute was aimed at the advocacy and teaching of concrete action for the forcible overthrow of the government, and not of principles divorced from action." In a separate opinion, Justices Black and Douglas added, "The proposed instructions under which the defendants would be punished for advocating action were *constitutionally not permissible*" [my emphasis]. In other words, the six justices were saying that for the government to get a conviction even under the Smith Act, the prosecution had to produce evidence of teaching "concrete action" leading to force and violence, and the government failed in that task. But in addition to adding their names to that position, Justices Hugo Black and William O. Douglas also concluded that the Smith Act itself was in violation of the First Amendment, and was therefore unconstitutional. All of these positions had been previously delineated in arguments to the district court during the course of the Philadelphia Smith Act trial, and in further pleadings before the Third Circuit Court of Appeals.

During a second interview with Henry Sawyer on September 19, 1994, he reflected a bit about the review of the Dennis case by the Second District Court of Appeals. Sawyer mused about the "extremely bad and very faulted written opinion by the highly respected Judge Learned Hand." Sawyer noted that it was not until the somewhat cooler days of 1957 that another Supreme Court reversed the lower courts in the California Smith Act trial. Henry Sawyer referred to that decision as "sub silencio," meaning, "They never said that they were overturning Dennis, but in fact, their decision in the Yates case did overturn First Foley."

On September 7, 1957, the Philadelphia attorneys submitted a supplemental brief to their Smith Act case appeal to the Third Circuit Court, referring to the Supreme Court's new definition of "organizing" in their Yates decision. "While the decision on the 'organizing' point unquestionably requires the grant of a new trial," our attorneys wrote, "the insufficiency of the evidence in the light of the standards laid down in the Yates case requires judgment of acquittal for all appellants."

On October 16, 1957, the government responded to our supplemental brief by requesting of the Third Circuit Court of Appeals that Walter Lowenfels and I be acquitted. On November 13, 1957, the Appeals Court did in fact acquit Walter and me, along with Ben Weiss and Chick Katz. While doubting that the government could produce a case against the remaining five defendants under the new rules of evidence established by the Supreme Court, the Court of Appeals, nevertheless, allowed the Justice Department to proceed, if it wished, with a new trial. Seven months later, on May 16, 1958, the government finally decided against this course of action, and dropped all charges against the remaining defendants.

Chapter 17

DEBT-FREE

Not only were we free, we were free of debt. The trial and appeal had cost in the neighborhood of $90,000, a veritable fortune in those years. However, the fact that the prosecution forced us to spend that amount did not satisfy another government objective: to have the costs of the defense totally bankrupt the Philadelphia Communist Party. Unlike what happened in other parts of the country as a result of Smith Act expenses, the party in Philadelphia was in relatively good shape financially.

During my Communist Party years, one of my co-defendants, Ben Weiss, was always the party's treasurer. Somewhat of a maverick, he was both tolerated and respected by the many party leaders who frequently came to Philadelphia, because of the unusual degree of success he brought to developing and implementing fundraising plans. Ben was bright, articulate, a bundle of energy and the consummate salesman committed to selling socialism. He loved fine art, the theater, music and especially gourmet food. Ben could hold folks captured and enraptured in discussions on any of those subjects for hours on end. At the time of our arrests, he and his wife, Helen, lived with their six-year-old daughter and two sons aged eight and 10, in an appropriately lovely home on Parkside Avenue just across from Fairmount Park and down the hill from the Mann Auditorium, the present site of the Philadelphia Orchestra's summer outdoor programs.

Ben often spoke with me, admiringly, about how the numbers and strength of the Italian communists could be directly correlated with the fact that their party "owned and operated banks." When it came to fundraising, Ben's commitment to socialism was sprinkled with the pragmatism of Italian Marxism as well as aspects of American capitalism. Some of his money-raising tactics have become legend. And as in most undocumented history, the view one holds about a particular course of events is frequently the result of how one was personally affected. Scores were involved in Ben's very unusual fundraising ventures. All had expectations, many profited and some did not.

Ben had access to those we used to call the "Island playboys and playgirls." They were those "filthy rich" heirs of many millions of dollars who were ready, willing and able to sell portions of their inheritances at a fraction of their values in order to have immediate access to ready cash so that they could maintain their lavish lifestyles.

One member of that group with a need for immediate cash inadvertently helped finance the defense in the Philadelphia Smith Act case. Almost all of the costs involved in that trial were paid as a result of the sale of assignments to a portion of the Horace Dodge estate. In his will, the founder of the Dodge Motor Company had provided for his widow who was, at the time of our trial, an octogenarian. Upon her death, however, there was to be a distribution of millions of dollars to numerous heirs. It was one of those future beneficiaries who sold a substantial piece of what she expected to receive to an investment counselor at approximately 25 percent of its projected value upon the death of Mrs. Dodge. The counselor was a long-time friend and associate of Ben Weiss and made the total assignment available to Ben in his capacity as the party's treasurer.

Perhaps as many as 100 people were convinced that they could help defray the costs of the Smith Act trial by making relatively substantial loans to the party. These were secured by reassignments of the Dodge estate, worth more than double the value of the loan, and would be paid whenever Mrs. Dodge succumbed to the already existing ravages of her old age. I don't know that records of those transactions still exist, but I was peripherally involved with the process, approved of the method, identified potential clients and even sold the "investment" to a few. Some of my potential clients called it "sound and sophisticated financial investing"; others thought it was a case of "beating the enemy at his own game." Quite a number dismissed it as "absolutely ghoulish."

Whatever people thought of our plan, it worked. Even before the trial had ended, the defendants paid in full the $65,000 we had contracted as the trial costs from funds that were mostly derived from reassignments of the Horace Dodge estate. In addition, a large part of the cost of the subsequent appeal was met when several of our lawyers purchased into the plan.

There were other estates, assignments and investments, and I've learned since that some individuals did indeed profit. But the big one was the Horace Dodge caper, and Mrs. Dodge fooled everyone. She hung on for many years. Afterwards a court challenge by the original heir resulted in a reduction of the amount of the initial assignment. No one made money on Dodge; no one lost money in Dodge. Everyone, however, had the satisfaction of having helped the Smith Act defendants.[1]

Chapter 18

WHAT THE TRIAL MEANT

It was a historic defense of the Bill of Rights that took place in Philadelphia during 1953-54, the result of a merging of mixed-interest positions and long-held traditions arising from broadly different perspectives. The many contributions from these sources, some minor and a few quite significant, led to the end of the Smith Act trials and to the eventual demise of McCarthyism. What follows is a chronological summary of those developments and contributions.

The four great traditional groups in Philadelphia—Reformers, Quakers, Main Line aristocrats and Philadelphia lawyers—had historical roots that inevitably led some of them into modest confrontation with those less concerned about civil liberties. The nation was suffering through a period of ultra-conservative reaction; it was the height of repressive McCarthyism. Yet there were some—among Philadelphia's Society of Friends, for example— who were rekindling their commitment to long-affirmed moral values of conscience, caution, temperance and tolerance. And in a rebirth of reform in the City of Brotherly Love, "Young Turks" were reconstructing the Democratic Party and successfully leading an increasingly progressive, grassroots-supported, "kick out the rascals" political movement. At the same time, a few of the Main Line aristocrats, many of them long-time leaders of the Philadelphia bar, seemed sufficiently secure to give voice to some of their civil libertarian concerns about the excesses of McCarthyism. In addition, they had a special interest in protecting a particular historical perception, one which held that ever since the days of Andrew Hamilton and Peter Zenger, there really was such a thing as a "Philadelphia lawyer" who was not the "corrupt shyster" stereotype, but who was indeed a dedicated counselor always ready to safeguard the right to freedom of speech.

During the early years of McCarthyism, the significance of those traditional ideas was recognized by a handful of Philadelphia communists who were bent on developing relationships with others in the broader community, based on positions of common interest. Over several years, they reached out to members of the traditional groups; several of them became board members of the local branch of the Civil Rights Congress. Small meetings and discussion groups were held, and in a couple of those get-togethers, one or two nationally known communists participated. While no commitments were sought, it was nevertheless an effort to increase consciousness and concern regarding the dangers inherent in the assault on dissent and to pique and hone a growing awareness about the need to defend the Bill of Rights.

All of these factors were at play in Philadelphia during the Korean War as anti-communist hysteria intensified. There were arrests for circulating peace petitions and for alleged perjury concerning loyalty oaths; there were inquisitions into the public schools and the universities; there were also the planned visits of Senate and House investigators. But those unique Philadelphia distinctions had a mitigating impact on subsequent developments, and what eventually unfolded in the city was significantly different from what took place earlier in other parts of the country. Not the least of those developments was a series of actions taken by local leaders of the American Civil Liberties Union and the Philadelphia Bar Association that culminated in the June 1953 bar association resolution. As if anticipating the Smith Act arrests in Philadelphia one month later, that resolution was an affirmation of the right to counsel for unpopular defendants.

All of the foregoing provided a set of expectations when exorbitant bail was set for the Philadelphia Smith Act defendants and when counsel was not forthcoming. Notwithstanding initial resistance from the national offices of the Communist Party and the Civil Rights Congress, first the wives and then the defendants themselves became convinced of what should be done. Instead of proceeding with a strategy aimed at explaining and advancing the position of the Communist Party, as was done in previous Smith Act trials, we decided that our best course of action was one that could lead to a much broader First Amendment defense even if, at first, that meant more weeks in Holmesburg's prison cells.

With the Philadelphia Bar Association resolution as its rationale, the defendants' wives pressed for appointments and visited every prominent law firm in the city while a number of additional meetings took place involving committees of the bar association, the American Civil Liberties Union and senior partners from the major law offices in the city. The process resulted in the emergence of Tom McBride and Joe Lord, and the selection of a defense team of young attorneys from among the most prestigious law firms in Philadelphia. This remarkable implementation of the bar association's intent to guarantee the right to counsel, as well as the composition of the team that actually came forth, became the pattern for subsequent Smith Act trials elsewhere.

As noted earlier, Philadelphia's Smith Act case was far from the first, nor was it to be the last in the country. However, the dramatic steps in defense of the Bill of Rights that took place during preparation for the trial, notably the manner in which the Philadelphia Bar Association eventually responded and rose to the occasion, was a turning point. Together with the conduct of the trial and some of its outcomes, those steps established new patterns and experiences for people in other cities to build upon in the defense of First Amendment rights.

As early as the month of our arraignment, September 1953, Tom McBride received an inquiry concerning the selection of counsel for the Philadelphia defendants. The request came from a Los Angeles law firm, purportedly on behalf of the chief editorial writer for the *St. Louis Post-Dispatch,* whom the writer described as a "wonderful friend of the First Amendment," wanting information upon which he would editorialize "in view of the fact that the defendants in the St. Louis Smith Act case had no such counsel."[1] McBride sent the request to the Executive Director of the American Civil Liberties Union, Spencer Coxe, who in a letter to James Brittain, Chairman of the bar association's Civil Rights Committee, suggested that Brittain respond to both A.L. Wiren, the Los Angeles attorney, and Irving G. Dilliard, the *St. Louis Post-Dispatch* chief editorial writer.[2] Two weeks later, Coxe himself sent Irving Dilliard an account of the developments: "Those of us concerned with civil liberties here are proud of the actions of the Philadelphia Bar Association and hope it will receive the publicity and commendation it deserves in other areas."[3]

Even before the Philadelphia trial started, in a series of letters in February 1954, the President of the Cleveland Bar Association, H. Walter Stewart, asked of his Philadelphia counterpart, Bernard Segal: "It would be of great service to us if we could have the benefit of your experience in this kind of situation."[4] Noting that the defendants in Cleveland claimed indigence, could not find counsel and were "screaming that their constitutional rights have not been protected," Stewart wanted to know, "What did the Philadelphia Bar Association find its obligation to be?"[5] And three months after Philadelphia's responses were shared: "Judge Charles J. McNamee and I will not forget soon...the splendid way in which you and your association handled a very grievous situation existing in Philadelphia."[6]

The defendants' inability to secure counsel in Cleveland took almost two years to be resolved. Eventually, one year after the conclusion of the trial in Philadelphia, Judge McNamee in Cleveland drew heavily upon what was learned from the Philadelphia model and experiences. In consultation and cooperation with the Cleveland Bar Association, the judge appointed six attorneys, one each from six leading law firms.[7]

In a letter to Congressman William J. Green, Chairman of the Philadelphia Democratic City Committee, Chancellor Segal noted that following our trial the Philadelphia Bar Association had "inquiries from judges and lawyers in other parts of the United States, asking us to give them details of our handling of the situations here as a guide to them, so that they might be assured the same representation in Smith Act cases in their communities as was made possible by the counsel here."[8]

Still others gained from Philadelphia having paved the way; a member of our defense team, Joseph M. DuBarry IV, was assigned the task of responding to the many inquiries. As the trial in Philadelphia ended in August 1954, the "Colorado Seven" were being indicted and the defendants were unable to secure counsel. Leading law firms in Denver communicated with Joe

DuBarry. In a March 1955 letter to Chancellor Segal, DuBarry quoted attorney Jay W. Tracey: "Based on the procedure which was followed in the Philadelphia case, the United States District Court here in Denver appointed, October 21, 1954, 11 attorneys from 11 firms as a team to defend the seven defendants."[9]

Early attacks on attorneys in civil liberties cases, Congressional investigation committee hearings, deportation proceedings and prosecutions under the State Sedition Act made Pittsburgh a hotbed of anti-communism for years. In 1956, Henry Foster, secretary of Pittsburgh's American Civil Liberties Union, wrote to Spencer Coxe: "700 members of the local Bar had refused to defend Steve Nelson in the Smith Act case."[10] Coxe advised him to seek out Tom McBride for details about how Philadelphia went about selecting and paying for counsel. On May 24, 1957, Coxe was informed of results; the Pittsburgh Bar Association had "lined up attorneys for all Smith Act defendants, including Nelson, and they will be paid by contributions received from the local bar."[11]

Philadelphia even made an impression on New York City. Harrison Tweed wrote to Bernard Segal: "Herbert Goodrich [Judge of the Third Circuit Court] has just been telling me of the organization set up to represent the more or less impecunious who have been accused of more or less unpopular offenses....I was wondering [if that] could not be done by the Association of the Bar of the City of New York. Could you...write me...about the Philadelphia set-up and how it was financed?...You did a wonderful job which has been of real value. I hate to see Philadelphia get so far ahead of New York."[12]

Segal sent Tweed a copy of his earlier reply to H. Walter Stewart and added, "Publicity on the matter has been excellent. Locally, the attorneys have the respect rather than the condemnation of the community. Nationally, the bar association and the attorneys who are trying the case have been accorded by columnists and commentators the credit they merit."[13]

The precedent-setting, broad-based nature of the defense in Philadelphia's Smith Act trial could not have emerged had not the communist defendants agreed, at the very outset, with advocates for a new kind of defense strategy. This new approach rested on the proposition that freedom of speech had been arrested in Philadelphia and it was this, not the Communist Party program, which needed to be defended. It was a strategy that also demanded that our own defense be adjusted to the unique opportunities Philadelphia presented.

Consequently, the Philadelphia trial would not become still another attempt at vigorously presenting Communist philosophy and ideology. Instead, it was the time to affirm that attacks taking place on the rights of communists were attacks on the rights of all Americans; a defense of those rights was a defense of the United States Constitution.

Given the breadth of community represented in the lawyers who came forth, an almost certain outcome could be predicted; a decision and a determination by the defendants and counsel together to make the *right* to free speech, instead of an *interpretation* of its content, the central point of the trial in Philadelphia. This change in emphasis influenced and shaped the focus of all subsequent Smith Act trials.

This new approach to the defense of communists who were prosecuted under the Smith Act, together with ongoing developing relationships between the highly regarded counsel and the defendants, had a salutary effect upon the very conduct of the trial in Philadelphia. The prosecutors and judge could not, with impunity, bait and attack the defense lawyers. As a result, the "circus-like" atmosphere, prevalent at previous Smith Act trials, was absent in Philadelphia.

The quality and skill of the defense team, their use of time and their ability to do the required research resulted in exposing and discrediting all of the prosecution's paid false witnesses during cross-examinations. One of the witnesses, Paul Crouch, was so badly damaged that he could never again be used, and the government's employment of paid informants like him became the subject of national questioning and investigation.

To this day, the summations to the jury by the chief defense counselors, Tom McBride and Joe Lord, remain as classics in their defense of constitutional rights. Although those summations did not change the built-in guilty verdicts for all of the defendants, the jury did take longer to deliberate than its counterparts in previous trials. The judge then pondered for almost a year before he meted out sentences that were lighter than any given before. Given his deportment, his rulings and his obvious interventions on behalf of the prosecution during the course of the trial, the sentences were clear indications that the composition and nature of the defense team had an impact. Those sentences also made it easier for a subsequent court and jury in Cleveland to acquit half of the defendants, and for the Supreme Court opinion in the Yates case in California, which essentially put an end to that particular episode of the Smith Act's major infringement upon the United States Constitution.

Judge Edmund Spaeth reminded me that there was still another important contribution of the Philadelphia Smith Act defense. It provided the basis for the establishment of precedent for intervention by the bar association in cases involving unpopular defendants and causes. The quality of that type of intervention continued for defendants needing counsel because of their involvement and activities during the civil rights, Black power and peace movements of subsequent years.

In 1953-54, the constitutional guarantee of the right to counsel continued to depend upon one's ability to afford a lawyer. The costs for the defense in Philadelphia were borne by friends and sympathizers of the Smith Act defendants. However, that was not necessarily so in the subsequent interventions into "unpopular" cases by representatives of the bar. Around the nation, mounting pressures as a result of uncompensated (pro bono) services contributed to an atmosphere which culminated in the 1963 Supreme Court ruling in *Gideon v. Wainwright,* widely interpreted as meaning that government must supply counsel where it cannot be afforded. The way was opened for the establishment of government-funded public defender systems. While questions still remain as to the "adequacy of counsel" provided, the public defender system seems clearly superior to the even grosser inequities of prior years.

Whatever the reasons that motivated the Philadelphia Bar Association, its involvement with the defense in the city's Smith Act trial in 1953-54 started paving the road toward a much more favorable interpretation of the constitutional guarantee of the right to counsel.

What did we accomplish in Philadelphia during the McCarthy era? John Rogers Carroll, who for many years has been one of the city's leading criminal defense attorneys and who was then one of the young lawyers on the team, reflected some 40 years later: "We had an impact; we established the right to fight McCarthyism. Not only was it okay to fight McCarthyism. Eventually, there was honor in it."

Chapter 19

AFTERWORD

Defending communists had no negative consequences for any of our attorneys. Each of them viewed the Philadelphia Smith Act trial as a highlight in a very successful career. In 1956, Tom McBride was appointed Pennsylvania Attorney General. Among other things, he prosecuted the Pennsylvania Turnpike scandals, established a civil rights division in the Department of Justice and was an outspoken opponent of wiretapping and capital punishment. He was appointed to the Pennsylvania Supreme Court in December 1958. Shortly before McBride's death at age 62 in 1965, the Smith Act trial's chief prosecutor, W. Wilson White, was charged in another case with illegally withholding information. Ironically, White engaged Tom McBride to represent him.

Joseph S. Lord became the Editor-in-Chief of *The Shingle* and *The Practical Lawyer*. In 1961, after a short term as a United States attorney, Lord was appointed to the federal district court in eastern Pennsylvania, became its chief judge in 1971 and served a dozen years before assuming senior status on the court.

Shortly before his death, Lord said that the Philadelphia Smith Act case was "absolutely a highlight of my career. Before I became a judge, I had well over 500, maybe even 1,000 cases, and the communist case was one of three that stands out."[1]

A past editor of *The Shingle*, Charles C. Hileman has been a member of the Philadelphia Bar Association Board of Governors and chairman of its disciplinary board. He is presently a retired partner at Schnader, Harrison, Segal and Lewis, the same firm that provided him to the defense team in 1953.

Robert W. Sayre became active with the Lawyers Committee on Civil Rights and the Public Interest Law Center. Sayre served as Chairman of the United Fund of Greater Philadelphia, and remains a senior partner with the firm of Saul, Biddle and Saul.

John Rogers Carroll, who along with Joe Lord prepared and filed our briefs to the appeals court, represented many clients before investigating committees. He became one of Philadelphia's most highly regarded defense attorneys and for years was the counsel of record in many of the area's most publicized cases. For many years Carroll has generously made his time available to lawyers in need of personal counseling.

Benjamin H. Read went to Washington, D.C., where he joined the staff of Senator Joseph S. Clark, frequently defended clients in civil liberties cases and founded a crisis counseling center. Read was a member of the American-Canadian Heavy Industry Environmental Control Commission and served on the Commission on Environmental Controls with scientists from the United States and the former Soviet Union. During the Carter Administration, Ben Read was Undersecretary of State.

After a stint in Philadelphia City Council, Henry Sawyer was counsel in numerous cases involving wiretapping, First and Fifth Amendment rights, draft card burning and church/state separation issues. He went to Mississippi to assist in voter-registration campaigns and later headed a group of lawyers opposed to the war in Vietnam. Sawyer has been an officer of the Fairmount Park Art Association, Commissioner of the Delaware Port Authority, a member of the Board of Directors of the Philadelphia Orchestra, Chairman of Americans for Democratic Action and Chairman of the Board of Trustees of Philadelphia College of Textiles and Science.

Judge Edmund B. Spaeth, Jr. was co-chair of the Citizens Charter Committee and a common pleas judge. He was Chairman of the Board of Directors and President of the Board of Trustees for Bryn Mawr College, a member of the Board of Directors of the Curtis Institute of Music and a member of the Philadelphia Commission for Effective Criminal Justice. For 20 years he was a judge of the Superior Court of Pennsylvania and is presently "of counsel" in the law firm of Pepper, Hamilton and Sheetz.

David Cohen has been a long-time consumer advocate and reformer. Elected to Philadelphia City Council in 1967, he resigned in an unsuccessful primary bid for mayor in 1971. Since his re-election to City Council in 1979, he has served continuously and has sponsored, among other things, bills for recycling, billboard controls, asbestos removal, senior citizen discounts and shelters for the homeless.

My little more than one decade of intensive activity and leadership in the Communist Party coincided with the years of its rapid decline. No single factor can be isolated as most responsible for that deterioration. The Cold War, the Red Scare, McCarthyism and the government's systematic persecution of Communist Party leaders should not be the only reasons cited. While certainly destructive, those factors also served in a perverse way to unite the party and to help it overcome other adversities.

While many quit the Communist Party as a result, the repressive atmosphere of the times and the government's prosecutions had nothing to do with my decision to leave. The intense factionalism and inner-party theoretical disputes that had been constant during the previous 10 to 12 years had taken its toll on the party's ability to provide effective leadership. If Philadelphia were the measure, then scores of members must have been expelled nationwide. As a member of the party's review commission in Philadelphia, I can recall participating in the expulsion of at least a half dozen local leaders for questionable behavior or activity. Mendy was believed to be too nationalist; he was called "anti-party." Max W. and Ted W., while opposed to Earl Browder's "American exceptionalism," also had questions about William Z. Foster's leadership; they were considered to be "revisionists." Bob F. had "unexplainable" friends and contacts; he was expelled as an "enemy agent." There were also those who were ferreted out for maintaining a relationship with Samuel Adams Darcy, a former district chairman expelled as a "revisionist." While a decade later I offered apologies to a few that I felt I had wronged, those acts of contrition never succeeded in overcoming my sense of culpability.

In February 1956, the Communist Party of the Soviet Union held its Twentieth Congress. The crimes against socialism committed during the years of Stalin's rule, the mass imprisonments and executions that had previously been denied and called libelous and the widespread anti-Semitism within the Soviet leadership were revelations that shook the world communist movement—nowhere more than in the United States.

The party here was rocked to its foundations by the Soviet admissions. The divisions and splits among us were sharply revealed during the subsequent months of intensive discussions, soul-searching questioning and deep criticism. However, whatever opportunity remained for American communists to chart a new and independent course seemed to vanish by the end of that year. The Soviet Union flexed its muscles in Poland, threatened in Hungary and then, in order to reverse a decision of the Hungarian government to withdraw from the Warsaw Pact, sent in its tanks and troops to depose the dissident leaders. What was left of the Communist Party leadership in the United States responded by using the questioning of that latest series of events as a reason for ending crucial discussion. They closed ranks and reverted to the "axiom" that any criticism of the Soviet Union was an undermining of the development of socialism.

The convergence of these developments led to my decision to leave the party sometime later in 1957. I no longer believed that the Communist Party of the United States could be the vehicle for bringing about socialism in this country. Mine was to be a dream deferred.

The final "t" was crossed at a meeting in 1959, shortly after the victory of the Castro-led revolution in Cuba. Gus Hall, the national head of the Communist Party, was in Philadelphia. He let it be known that he would like to meet with the Philadelphia Smith Act defendants. I do not know for certain how many of us were still members of the party at the time. In any event, those of us still alive and in Philadelphia obliged. Neither Bob Klonsky nor Tom Nabried was present; Bob was no longer a resident of the city and, a couple of years earlier, Tom had died on the operating table during open heart surgery. In Gus Hall's appeal to us to rejoin the party, what I heard was a repetition of past indefensible positions, an overestimation of the strength and influence of American communism, and one absolutely absurd and unbelievable assertion. Hall credited the U.S. Communist Party for the success of Fidel Castro in Cuba. It was an embarrassment!

That was the last time I met with my co-defendants as a group, although I saw Chick Katz and Ben Weiss frequently, and crossed paths with the others from time to time.

Shortly after the death of Tom Nabried's wife, Gladys, in the mid-1950s, he married another activist, Eleanor Williams. Tom remained a leader of the Communist Party for the short period of time that he lived following the Smith Act trial.

Before cancer claimed the life of Chick Katz at age 50 in 1969, he was a loving, doting, hard-working husband and father who successfully supported his family through buying and selling antiques. He and his wife, Vi, continued expressing their social action concerns within the secular-humanist Sholom Aleichem Club, a group in which Pauline and I also maintained membership.

After the revelations of the Soviet Union's Twentieth Party Congress in 1956, I saw very little of Dave Davis. The final years of his life were difficult ones for the feisty former union leader. Unable to return to his position as business agent for Local 155, he turned to his almost-forgotten training in bookkeeping and eked out a livelihood servicing sympathetic friends.

Walter Lowenfels, until his death in 1976, continued to be a prolific poet and writer. Still sporting a beret, he was a frequent lecturer and reader on college campuses throughout the country. Much of his material remains in print and a collection of his work is maintained in the poetry and rare books section of the library at the State University of New York in Buffalo.

After 1957, Joe Roberts was employed by a friend who had a roach and termite exterminating company. In the early 1960s, Joe and his family moved to California where he and his wife, Barbara, were divorced. I saw Joe only once thereafter when, recuperating from a mild stroke, he was visiting friends in Philadelphia. I've been told that Joe rejoined the Communist Party in the late '70s and remained a member for several years before he died.

Bob Klonsky moved to Berkeley, California, where he opened a bookstore near the college campus. On occasion, I saw him when his business brought him east and he visited with friends in Philadelphia. Bob's wife, Helen, died very early, a victim of Hodgkin's disease. In the late '60s, their son, Michael, made news as a national leader of Students for a Democratic Society and the Revolutionary Youth Movement. At one point, Bob rejoined the Communist Party and was later involved in more inner-party factional fighting in California. He married again in 1980 and subsequently moved to New

Mexico for a few years before returning to California. When I last spoke with him during the spring of 1997, Bob was recuperating from a stroke.

Ben Weiss continued at what he knew best as he raised money for causes in which he believed. In the immediate aftermath of our trial, Ben was instrumental in getting a group of small investors to develop a business—supplying tables, chairs and whatever else was needed for any kind of meeting or affair—that at the same time provided employment for some of the victims of the McCarthy period. Joe Kuzma, unable to find work elsewhere, became the firm's operations manager. On the rare occasions I saw Joe after we left the party, he remained the quiet, introspective, hard-working family man who stayed at his job until illness forced him to retire shortly before his death early in 1983. Over the years, Ben Weiss became increasingly involved with fundraising activities on behalf of the American Civil Liberties Union. The Philadelphia branch eulogized him after a massive coronary took his life in 1986.

When I left the Communist Party toward the end of 1957, I continued to manage my brothers' store where I had worked since the end of the trial. Employing a few of my older skills, I helped organize a topical forum under the aegis of the Federation of Jewish Agencies' Neighborhood Center. Unfortunately, the residual impact of McCarthyism was still too strong, even for the left-leaning professional staff of the center. Although I judiciously avoided being personally credited with any of its success, the forum was sabotaged by quiet and behind-the-scenes "red-baiting" concerned with my connections to the series.

Then came a time when, in addition to the long hours that work in a retail store demanded, I became fully involved in wonderful and hectic parental responsibilities: umpiring little league games, monitoring springboard diving and music instruction, and the accompanying performances of my rapidly maturing sons. Pauline and I became active in ethnic cultural programs and social action events—especially those dealing with relationships between Blacks and Jews—during the growth and development of the Sholom Aleichem Club.

Our two sons, Marc and Gary, entered college and high school respectively in September 1965. Pauline went back to work the following February, and I went off to Temple University to add to the 24 credits I had earned years before and to satisfy a promise to my sons that I would someday return. With much to accomplish in a hurry, I became engulfed in classes, study and internships; I also worked to help Pauline cover expenses and made time for civil rights and peace activities.

During the summer of 1969, I was appointed Assistant Professor of Social Welfare at Temple. Three years later I was recruited as a full professor and given the opportunity to establish a new program in social work at the Richard Stockton College of New Jersey. In the interim, I had earned a bachelor's degree from Temple and master's and doctoral degrees from the

University of Pennsylvania. My community activities and sense of social responsibility remained much the same with particular interests in social welfare policy, community organizing and the focus of my doctoral dissertation: Black/Jewish relations.

I have never attempted to hide or deny my past Communist Party affiliations or my continued adherence to socialism. As a professor I shared my perspective with my students, and they honored me in turn. It has also been my pleasure to serve my academic community and colleagues in many ways, beyond establishing a highly regarded program in social work, that included a period as President of Stockton's Faculty Union. When I chose to retire in 1994, the Richard Stockton College Board of Trustees named me the college's first professor emeritus.

When I left the Communist Party in 1957, I had finally come to recognize that the Soviet Union's concept of "socialism" had been distorted by criminal acts, authoritarian rule and an absence of civil liberties and democracy. It may have taken me longer than some, certainly longer than it should have, but I continued to have high hopes that the Soviet Union would find its way. The early days of Gorbachev's "openness" (Glasnost) looked very promising to me. To my dismay, the Soviet Union's "restructuring of the society" (Perestroika) turned from early moves to create a truly democratic socialism to policies of privatization and "free market" consumerism that appear today to be headed toward catastrophe.

As in capitalist countries elsewhere, in Russia some people have become extremely wealthy while many more are becoming impoverished, encouraging organized criminal behavior and social disintegration. In Russia today everything seems permissible; old restraints have disappeared and extreme manifestations of nationalism, anti-Semitism and ethnic hatred are not only tolerated, they flourish in the guise of democratic reform.

The breakup of the Soviet Union has been packaged and marketed by gloating Western I-told-you-so's as the triumph of capitalism. But wherein lies the victory? I believe it is fair to evaluate an economic and social system by the manner in which it benefits everyone within its boundaries. For the millions of people throughout the world over which it claims hegemony, capitalism has never been a force for societal change and human achievement. Even in a nation as great as our own, there is no capitalist social policy aimed at providing homes for the homeless and low-cost housing for the disadvantaged, affordable health care and insurance for everyone, jobs for the unemployed and income security for our millions in abject poverty.

Is socialism dead? I do not believe so. The lesson to be learned from the Soviet experiment is that the process of building socialism can be perverted and ultimately sabotaged if not pursued within perimeters that are free and democratic. The process will die aborning if it does not rely on the popular rule and the popular dictates of its constituents.

What failed in the Soviet Union was not the concept of socialism; the nation itself failed. The experiment, which was undoubtedly hindered by its origins, its timing and a world full of enemies, started out with serious encumbrances. And it collapsed under a tremendous burden of internal contradictions, corrupt leadership and a murderous distortion of democratic and humanistic socialist principles. There were previous experiments with socialism, but none compared with what developed in the Soviet Union, and its downfall was most distressing to those of us who wanted socialism to succeed. But capitalism also had a few miscarriages before it eventually replaced the thousand years of feudalism that preceded it. Capitalism has since shown a propensity for pulling itself together, calling upon its resources and then manipulating them, sometimes hideously, to work its way through crisis after crisis. History demonstrates how poorly capitalism has served so many of the world's people with never-ending cycles of economic recessions and depressions, nuclear disasters, wars and holocausts; and it remains unsuitable for coming to grips with environmental and ecological concerns and for living in concert with nature.

There are many who continue to believe that socialism is a realistic and realizable alternative to capitalism and will look for ways to reassert that proposition. The collapse of a tyranny-ridden Soviet Union and the demise of other unscrupulous and criminal regimes—those that too many of us, for far too long, accepted as models for socialism—is a phenomenon for which we pay dearly. But given the very serious limitations of capitalism, I believe people will continue to be on the lookout for another way to solve their problems, for another economic and social system to replace it. Socialism can go on representing a rational and humane alternative to capitalism, a system that holds out the hope that there can be a society at peace—with itself, with others and with nature. I continue to believe that to be a most beautiful proposition.

In May 1949, in his essay "Why Socialism?" Albert Einstein had this to say:

> I am convinced there is only *one* way to eliminate these grave
> evils [of capitalism], namely accompanied by an educational
> system which would be oriented toward social goals. In such an
> economy, the means of production are owned by society itself
> and are utilized in a planned fashion. A planned economy
> which adjusts production to the needs of the community, would
> distribute the work to be done among all those able to work
> and would guarantee a livelihood to every man, woman and
> child. The education of the individual, in addition to promoting
> his own innate abilities, would attempt to develop in him a
> sense of responsibility for his fellow men in place of the glorifi-
> cation of power and success in our present society.
> Nevertheless, it is necessary to remember that a planned soci-
> ety is not yet socialism. A planned economy as such may be
> accompanied by the complete enslavement of the individual.
> The achievement of socialism requires the solution of some
> extremely difficult socio-political problems: how is it possible, in
> view of the far reaching centralization of political and economic

power, to prevent bureaucracy from becoming all-powerful and overbearing? How can the rights of the individual be protected and therewith a democratic counterweight to the power of bureaucracy be assured?

I share those concerns of Albert Einstein as I remain convinced of the desirability of socialism and the inevitability of the creation of the proper democratic forms for its attainment and achievements.

The fragility of democratic forms and processes was never more evident than during the peak of anti-communist hysteria that marked the McCarthy era. The Smith Act trials were but one in a set of manifestations pointing out the extent to which any power, when it perceives a threat—contrived, real or imagined—can resort to tyrannical methods in order to maintain control, and how American civil liberties can never be taken for granted. The manner in which officialdom and policymakers reacted to the threat of a "red menace" rocked the very foundation of our Constitution as those in power attacked its guarantee of the rights to assembly, speech, thought and dissent. At the height of the Cold War, the leaders of the Communist Party and other dissenters suffered unjustly, and the Bill of Rights and the American people suffered along with them.

When the Smith Act prosecutors reached Philadelphia, the pendulum was about ready to move in another direction; we were ripe for helping that process along. Some of Philadelphia's history, traditions and relationships, together with the defendants, combined to produce a new approach. Instead of defending the platform of the Communist Party, it was a defense that emphasized the protection of the Bill of Rights, a most important turning point upon which others were to build.

One could reasonably argue that it was precisely the strength and flexibility of political democracy, as we've come to know and appreciate it in the United States, that allowed for the demise of McCarthyism. Nevertheless, during the McCarthy era, all three branches of the government permitted people who were merely believed to be communists or communist sympathizers to be investigated, harassed and cited for contempt of Congress and perjury. And as a result, untold numbers of them were fired from their jobs, deported or convicted and sent off to jail. But in particular, the prosecution of the leadership of the Communist Party was made possible by laws that continue to exist to this day. Through the use of the Smith Act at a time when socialist ideology had very little popular support in the United States, communists were imprisoned for advocacy of its principles. It was political demagoguery at its apex and underscores why, today, we must remain concerned about and ever alert to any attempt to use old or enact new "anti-terrorist" legislation, even though we know that some of today's dissenters wear fearsomely frightening faces, spew venom and exhibit a kind of hatred we abhor. It is in the guise of "protecting our national security from dangers within our midst" that constitutional rights frequently become compromised and endangered.

One can only wonder to what lengths true prosperity might extend if an American majority chose to embrace a system that would bring together already existing democratic forms, rights and liberties with creative economic plans, further extending democracy—a system that would assure the satisfaction of individual and social needs instead of bowing to multinational corporate demands for ever greater private profits. And given its past performance, one can only worry about what other abridgments of our constitutional rights the existing power structure might devise to prevent such a likelihood.

While my illusions have been tempered by today's realities, the dream of a planned and well-ordered world, governed by the maxim, from each according to ability, to each according to need, remains very much alive— "a consummation most fervently to be desired."

GLOƎƎARY OF NAMEƎ

(Where no dates are listed, most references will relate to the 1950s.)

Alexander, Sadie (1898–1989).	Philadelphia African-American civil rights and community activist, educator, lawyer, member of the Fellowship Commission and an officer of the ACLU.
Allesandroni, Walter (1914–1966).	Noted Philadelphia anti-communist, prominent in the Philadelphia Bar Association and leader of veterans' organizations.
Alsop, Joseph (1910–1991).	National newspaper columnist together with brother, Stewart (1914–1974).
Amter, Israel (1881–1954).	A founder of the U.S. Communist Party, its New York state chairman in the '30s and '40s and a frequent candidate for public office. Lost 1938 bid for Congress with 106,000 votes.
Aptheker, Herbert (1915–).	Historian, lecturer, editor of *Political Affairs* and *Masses and Mainstream*, director of American Institute of Marxist Studies and the author of numerous articles and books on African-American history.
Bard, Guy (1895–1953).	Judge, U.S. District Court, Eastern Pennsylvania.
Beitscher, "Hank" (1916–1982).	Chief organizer for the Philadelphia Progressive Party.
Black, Hugo (1896–1971).	U.S. Supreme Court Associate Justice, 1937–71.
Blumberg, Albert (c. 1906–).	A communist leader who was indicted under the membership clause of the Smith Act.
Bridges, Harry (1901–1990).	Long-time labor leader and President of the International Longshoremen's Association.

Brittain, James (1893–1976).   Chairman of the Civil Rights Committee of the Philadelphia Bar Association, 1954–55.

Browder, Earl (1891–1973).   General Secretary, U.S. Communist Party, 1930–45.

Brownell, Herbert (1904–1996).   U.S Attorney General, 1953–57.

Budenz, Louis (1891–1972).   Professional informer and witness for the prosecution; former editor of the *Daily Worker*.

Capitola, John.   An officer in Philadelphia chapter of Veterans of Foreign Wars.

Carner, Lucy (1886–1983).   Peace, civil rights and pioneer women's rights activist.

Carolan, Thomas (1916–1983).   Prosecution witness.

Carr, Henry (1895–1979).   U.S. Commissioner.

Carroll, John Rogers (1926–).   Attorney for the defendants.

Cary, Stephen (1915–).   Society of Friends, leader and activist.

Charry, Elias (1906–1983).   Rabbi, Germantown Jewish Community Center.

Clark, Joseph Sill (1901–1990).   Mayor of Philadelphia, 1952–56. U.S. Senator from Pennsylvania, 1957–68.

Cohen, David (1914–).   Attorney for the defendants.

Cohn, Bernard (1908–1985).   Philadelphia lawyer.

Coll, Robert (1903–1977).   United Press representative.

Coxe, Spencer (c. 1918–).   Executive Secretary of the Philadelphia ACLU.

Cronin, James.   Special U.S. Prosecutor with Smith Act trial experience.

Crouch, Paul (1903–1955).   Professional informer and witness for the prosecution.

Darcy, Samuel A. (1917–1993).   Merchant and past chairman of Eastern Pennsylvania Communist Party.

Davis, Benjamin, Jr. (1903–1964).   African-American lawyer, twice elected to New York City Council, 1943–47. Served prison sentence after Smith Act conviction.

Davis, David and Sophie.   Philadelphia Smith Act defendant and wife.

Dennis, Eugene (1905–1961).   General Secretary, U.S. Communist Party, succeeding Earl Browder and at the time of his Smith Act conviction for which he served several years in prison.

Dilliard, I.G. (1905–1985).   *St. Louis Post-Dispatch* chief editorial writer.

Dilworth, Richardson (1898–1974). Philadelphia District Attorney, 1952–55 and Mayor of Philadelphia, 1955-62.

DiMaria Sam. Union organizer, witness for the prosecution.

Dodge, Henriette (1867–1970). The wife of automobile magnate Horace Dodge.

Donner, Frank (c. 1915–1995). New York attorney and Smith Act defense consultant.

Douglas, William O. (1898–1980). Associate Justice, U.S. Supreme Court, 1939–75.

Drinker, Henry (1880–1974). Prominent Philadelphia attorney, senior member of Drinker, Biddle & Reath law firm.

DuBarry, J.N., IV (1916–1993). Attorney for the defendants.

Du Clos, Jacques (1897–1975). French Communist Party and Comintern official.

Dunham, Barrows (1905–1995). Philosopher, Temple University professor and author of *Heroes and Heretics* and *Giants in Chains*.

Eckert, Kenneth (1913–1975). Prosecution witness.

Ernst, Morris (1888–1976). Author-educator, chief counsel and spokesperson for the American Civil Liberties Union.

Fast, Howard (1914–). Prolific and popular author, political and social activist.

Flanders, Ralph E. (1880–1970). U.S. Senator from Vermont, 1946–58.

Forbes, Kenneth (1910–1990). Prominent Philadelphia Protestant minister.

Ford, James W. (1894–1957). African-American leader, two-time Communist Party candidate for U.S. Vice-President.

Foster, Henry (1902–1969). Pittsburgh attorney.

Foster, William Z. (1881–1961). Long-time union leader, socialist activist, co-founder and Chairman of the U.S. Communist Party.

Frankfurter, Felix (1882–1965). Associate Justice, U.S. Supreme Court, 1939–62.

Frazier, Elizabeth (1902–1983). Activist in church, civic and women's organizations.

Ganey, J. Cullen (1899–1972). Presiding judge in the Philadelphia Smith Act case.

Gates, John (c. 1914–). Spanish Civil War veteran and U.S. Commmunist Party national committee member who served time in prison after Smith Act conviction.

Goodrich, Herbert (1889–1962).   Justice of the Third Circuit, U.S. Court of Appeals, 1940–62.

Green, William J., Jr. (1910–1963).   Chairman of the Philadelphia Democratic Party who served in U.S. House of Representatives, 1945–65.

Greenfield, A.M. (1887–1967).   Real estate broker and financier, active in national and local affairs. Recipient of numerous honors and awards.

Grim, Alan (1904–1965).   Judge, U.S. District Court, 1949–65.

Hall, Gus (1910–).   Became Acting General Secretary of U.S. Communist Party (1950) while Eugene Dennis was in prison. Since 1959, he has been the General Secretary.

Hamilton, Andrew (1676–1741).   Colonial legislator and jurist who, in 1735, defended a New York printer charged with sedition; the prototype for the Philadelphia Lawyer.

Hand, Learned (1872–1961).   Justice, U.S. Court of Appeals, Second Circuit, 1924–51.

Harlan, John M. (1899–1971).   Associate Justice, U.S. Supreme Court, 1955–71.

Harrison, Earl (1899–1955).   Prominent Philadelphia Quaker leader and attorney with numerous federal government appointments. Dean of University of Pennsylvania Law School, 1945–48.

Hartley, Frank (1903–1969).   Congressman from New Jersey, 1929–49 (see Taft).

Hays, Will (c. 1915–).   American songwriter and folksinger.

Haywood, Harry (1898–1985).   African-American communist theoretician, author of *Negro Liberation* and an autobiography, *Black Bolshevik*.

Heltzinger, Ralph (1905–1991).   Prosecution witness.

Hildenberger, J. (1911–1968).   U.S. attorney in Philadelphia at the time of Smith Act arrests.

Hileman, Charles (c. 1923–).   Attorney for the defendants.

Hopkinson, F. (1885–1966).   Financier and investor. Trustee of the University of Pennsylvania, the Free Library and Wistar Institute. Chairman of Philadelphia City Planning Commission, 1943–56.

Johnson, Arnold.   National Legislative Director, U.S. Communist Party.

Katz, Irwin (Chick) and Vi.   Philadelphia defendant and wife.

Kelly, John B. (1889–1960).   Former Olympic sculler, successful

Klein, Max (1885–1973).

Klonsky, Robert and Helen.

Kuzma, Joseph and Marion.

Labovitz, Sherman and Pauline.

Lautner, John (1902–1977).

Leopold, Harry (1898–1983).

Levinson, David (1904–1970).

Levinthal, Louis (1892–1976).

Levitan, Harry (c. 1912–).

Lewis, John F. (1899–1965).

Lord, Joseph S., III (1912–1991).

Lowenfels, Walter and Lillian.

Mann, Frederick (1903–1965).

Maynard, Larry (1918–1972).

McBride, Thomas D. (1903–1965).

McCabe, Louis (1896–1964).

McCarran, Patrick (1876–1954).

McCarthy, Joseph (1908–1957).

McClain, Colbert (1889–1975).

McClosky, Jack (1910–1990).

McCustey, William.

McNamee, Charles (1890–1964).

building contractor and political patriarch. The father of John B., Jr. and Princess Grace.

Rabbi, Congregation Adath Jeshurun.

Philadelphia defendant and wife.

Philadelphia defendant and wife.

Philadelphia defendant and wife.

Professional informer and witness for the prosecution.

Teacher at Congregation Adath Jeshurun, c. 1935.

An attorney in civil liberties cases, 1930s and '40s.

Judge, Philadelphia Common Pleas Court.

Attorney in numerous civil rights and civil liberties cases and a defender against deportation of foreign-born citizens.

Prominent figure in Philadelphia civic and cultural affairs.

Attorney for the defendants.

Philadelphia defendant and wife.

Philadelphia civic leader and philanthropist.

Prosecution witness.

Chief attorney for the defendants.

Philadelphia attorney in *U.S. v. Dennis*; among those who, at its conclusion, served several months in jail for "contempt of court." Counsel for Philadelphia Democratic Party, Vice-President of National Lawyer's Guild and, after 1960, Philadelphia Assistant District Attorney for appeals.

U.S. Senator from Nevada, 1933–54.

U.S. Senator from Wisconsin, 1947–57.

A leader of the American Legion and the Veterans of Foreign Wars.

Successful Philadelphia building contractor.

Special U.S. prosecutor with Smith Act experience.

Presiding federal judge in Cleveland Smith Act case.

Medina, Harold (1888–1990).   Served on Federal District and Circuit
                                     Courts, 1947–80. Presided at the first
                                     Smith Act trial of communists.
Mosher, Harold (1922–1992).   Prosecution witness.
Murrow, Edward R. (1908–1965).   *See It Now* and *Person to Person* televi-
                                     sion news commentator; Director of
                                     U.S. Information Agency.
Nabried, Thomas and Gladys.   Philadelphia defendant and wife.
Nelson, Steve (1903–1989).   Pittsburgh communist leader whose 20-
                                     year state sedition sentence was super-
                                     seded by a federal Smith Act conviction.
Nix, Robert N.C. (1908–1987).   African-American congressman,
                                     1957–78. Chaired Philadelphia
                                     Democratic Party Campaign
                                     Committee.
Oakes, John (1883–1972).   *New York Times* editorial staff
                                     member.
Olmsted, Mildred (1921–1990).   Philadelphia social worker, church
                                     lay-leader and women's leader.
Oursler, Fulton (1893–1952).   American journalist, author and play-
                                     wright.
Philips, Helen (1910–1995).   Philadelphia women's rights activist
                                     and social worker.
Phillips, Walter (1894–1965).   Leader in the Philadelphia reform
                                     movement.
Pickett, Clarence (1884–1965).   Executive Secretary of the American
                                     Friends Service Committee, 1929–50.
Pollit, Harry (1890–1960).   General Secretary of the Communist
                                     Party of Great Britain.
Randolph, John (c. 1917–).   Television and screen actor. Peace and
                                     civil liberties activist.
Read, Benjamin H. (1925–1993).   Attorney for the defendants.
Reed, John (1887–1920).   American journalist, poet, revolution-
                                     ary associate of Lenin and author of
                                     Ten Days That Shook the World.
Reivich, Isadore (c. 1919–).   Historian, Philadelphia public high
                                     school teacher.
Rhoads, C. Brewster (1892–1973).   Vice-Chancellor and subsequently
                                     Chancellor of the Philadelphia Bar
                                     Association, 1953–55.
Roberts, Joseph and Barbara.   Philadelphia defendant and wife.
Robeson, Paul (1898–1976).   African-American scholar, athlete,
                                     actor and bass-baritone. World-
                                     renowned performer, political and
                                     civil rights activist.
Rogge, O. John (1903–1981).   Lawyer and author. Assistant U.S.
                                     Attorney General for Criminal Division,

1939–40. Special Assistant to Attorney General, 1943–46.

Rosenberg, Ethel and Julius. Husband and wife executed in 1953 as Soviet agents.

Rotenberg, Sol (1911–1973). Communist political activist and a leader of the Jewish People's Fraternal Order's efforts to prevent the deportation of foreign-born political "undesirables."

Sawyer, Henry W., III (c. 1918–). Attorney for the defendants.

Sayre, Robert W. (c. 1920–). Attorney for the defendants.

Segal, Bernard (1907–1997). Chancellor of Philadelphia Bar Association, 1952–53.

Sharfsin, Joseph (1898–1979). Former Philadelphia City Solicitor.

Smith, Howard, W. (1883–1976). Congressman from Virginia, 1933–66.

Somerville, John (1905–1994). Non-communist authority on Marxism who appeared as a defense witness in Philadelphia trial.

Spaeth, Edmund B. (1920–). Attorney for the defendants.

Stewart, H. Walter (1895–1987). A lawyer in Cleveland, Ohio.

Strong, Edward (c. 1918–1955). African-American Chairman of the Communist Party of Eastern Pennsylvania and Delaware.

Taft, Robert (1889–1953). U.S. Senator from Ohio, 1939–53. Co-author, with Frank Hartley, of Taft-Hartley Act.

Tate, James J. (1910–1983). Mayor of Philadelphia, 1955–62.

Thomas, Herman (c. 1915–1983). Prosecution witness.

Thompson, Robert (c. 1912–1965). Chairman, New York State Communist Party.

Thorez, Maurice (1900–1964). Leader of the French Communist Party; Minister of State in several French governments.

Togliatti, Palmiro (1893–1964). Secretary General of the Communist Party of Italy; Vice-Premier and Minister of Justice, 1944–45.

Tompkins, William (1913–1989). Assistant U.S. Attorney General, 1954–58.

Tracey, Jay W. (1925–1995). Attorney in Denver, Colorado.

Trowbridge, George. Philadelphia religious leader.

Tweed, Harrison (1885–1964). President of New York Bar Association.

Vinson, Fred (1890–1953). U.S. Secretary of Treasury, 1945–46; Chief Justice of the U.S. Supreme Court, 1946–53.

Waldbaum, Saul (1905–1991). Philadelphia lawyer and associate of Harry Levitan.

Wallace, Henry (1888–1965).

Secretary of Agriculture, 1933–40; Vice-President of the United States, 1941–45. Progressive Party candidate for President, 1948.

Walter, Francis E. (1894–1963).

U.S. congressman from Pennsylvania, 1933–62.

Warren, Earl (1891–1971).

Governor of California, 1943–53; Chief Justice of the U.S Supreme Court, 1953–69.

Weiss, Benjamin and Helen.

Philadelphia defendant and wife.

Welsh, George (1878–1970).

Eastern Pennsylvania Federal District Court Judge, later Senior Judge, 1932–70.

White, Harry Dexter (1905–48).

Economist with various U.S. Treasury appointments after 1934; Executive Director, International Monetary Fund, 1946.

White, W. Wilson (1906–64).

U.S. Attorney for Eastern Pennsylvania, 1953–57; Assistant U.S. Attorney General, 1957–59.

Williamson, W.C.

Philadelphia Protestant minister.

Winston, Eric (c. 1919–).

Defendant in loyalty oath perjury trial. Case dismissed when FBI would not make files available to defense.

Winston, Henry (1911–1986).

African-American leader and long-time national officer of U.S. Communist Party.

Wiren, A.L. (1901–1978).

Los Angeles attorney who was the first full-time lawyer employed by the American Civil Liberties Union.

Woolston, William.

Attorney for the defendants.

Yates, Oleta (1907–1976).

California Smith Act defendant.

Zenger, Peter (1697–1746).

Colonial printer and founder of *Weekly Journal*. Tried for libel, 1734–35. Defended by Andrew Hamilton.

Zucker, Jack S. (1910–).

Executive Secretary, Philadelphia Civil Rights Congress.

NOTES

INTRODUCTION

1. Harry S Truman, Presidential Executive Order No. 9835, March 25, 1947.
2. Fear of communist infiltration into the State Department reached a peak with the perjury conviction of a former official, Alger Hiss. Shortly thereafter, on February 9, 1950, an unrenowned senator from Wisconsin, Joseph McCarthy, claimed in a speech to have "here in my hand a list" of communists "known to the Secretary of State" and "still working and making policy." The inference was that the "list" was huge, perhaps greater than 200 names. That the Senate found it to be a "fraud and a hoax" did not keep the allegation from launching McCarthy's scurrilous career.
3. Joseph McCarthy, *New York Times*, June 15, 1951, 3:1, regarding George C. Marshall, and again on August 31, 1951, referring to Dean Acheson as the "Red Dean of Fashion."
4. Richard Nixon, *New York Times*, October 14, 1952, 1:6, accusing the administration of covering up a communist conspiracy, and Joseph McCarthy, on October 28, 1952, 1:7, referring to Adlai Stevenson.
5. There were several attempts in the early 1950s to demonstrate the pervasiveness of fear by circulating petitions that quoted sections of the Declaration of Independence. At least one of those experiments was undertaken by one of the Philadelphia newspapers.

CHAPTER 2

1. Front-page stories, Philadelphia newspapers, July 30 and 31, 1953.
2. Philadelphia *Evening Bulletin*, August 1, 1953, p. 1.
3. Ibid.

CHAPTER 3

1. Saul Waldbaum, interview with Fred Zimring, Temple University Urban Archives.

2. Ibid.
3. Robert N.C. Nix, August 10, 1953, and Bernard Cohn, September 10, 1953: letters to Bernard Segal.
4. Bernard Segal, interview with the author, Philadelphia, August 16, 1989.
5. James M. Brittain, press release, August 1953.
6. Walter Lowenfels, *The Prisoners* (Philadelphia: Whittier Press, 1954), p. 14.
7. Letters between Sadie Alexander and Bernard Segal, August 14 and 18, 1953; ACLU files, Temple University Urban Archives.
8. Helen Weiss, letter to Bernard Segal, August 1953.
9. James M. Brittain, as recorded in *The Legal Intelligencer*, October 16, 1953.

CHAPTER 4

1. Abraham Lincoln, First Inaugural Address, March 4, 1861: "This country with its institutions belong to the people who inhabit it. Whenever they shall grow weary of the existing government, they can exercise their constitutional right of amending it, or their revolutionary strength. The Declaration of Independence: "We hold these truths to be self-evident, that all men are created equal, that they are endowed by their creator with certain inalienable rights, that among these are Life, Liberty and the pursuit of Happiness....that whenever any form of Government becomes destructive of those ends, it is the Right of the People to alter or abolish it, and to institute new Government,...it is their right, it is their duty, to throw off such Government, and to provide new Guards for their future security."
2. V.I. Lenin, *Selected Works*, vol. 6, p. 1, and *State and Revolution*, p. 34; Karl Marx and Frederick Engels, *Das Kapital*, Vol. 1, Preface.

CHAPTER 8

1. George Gallup, *The Gallup Poll: Public Opinion, 1935–71* (New York: Random House, 1972), vol. 2, p. 1191.
2. Temple University Urban Archives, ACLU, Box 10.
3. Joseph S. Lord III, interview with the author, Philadelphia, June 31, 1989.
4. David Cohen, interview with the author, Philadelphia, August 8, 1989.
5. Benjamin H. Read, interview with the author, Washington, DC, December 1, 1989.
6. A survey of these can be found in Jerold S. Auerbach, *Unequal Justice: Lawyers and Social Change in Modern America* (New York: Oxford University Press, 1976), pp. 233–246.
7. Milnor Alexander, "The Fight for the Right to Counsel," *Law in Transition* 22:19–45, 1962.

8. John Rogers Carroll, interview with the author, Philadelphia, July 10, 1989.
9. American Civil Liberties Union, *Weekly Bulletins*, July 1948 through July 1954.
10. Harrison E. Salisbury, "The Strange Correspondence of Morris Ernst and John Edgar Hoover, 1939–1964," *The Nation*, December 1, 1984.
11. Spencer Coxe, op. cit.
12. Spencer Coxe, interview with Fred Zimring, Temple University Urban Archives.
13. Edmund B. Spaeth, interview with the author, Philadelphia, July 10, 1989.
14. Henry W. Sawyer III, interview with the author, Philadelphia, June 22, 1989.
15. Henry W. Sawyer III, op. cit.
16. Spencer Coxe, interview with the author, Philadelphia, September 20, 1989.
17. Jack S. Zucker, interview with the author, Philadelphia, February 1, 1991.
18. Ibid.
19. Temple University Urban Archives, ACLU files, 7/III-99.
20. Ibid., 7/III-98.
21. Temple University Urban Archives, ACLU files, 7/III-98 (1953).
22. Ibid.
23. Spencer Coxe, interview with the author, Philadelphia, September 20, 1989.
24. Spencer Coxe, interview with Fred Zimring.

CHAPTER 9

1. James M. Brittain, *The Legal Intelligencer*, October 16, 1953.
2. Judge Alan Grim, Philadelphia *Evening Bulletin*, September 14, 1953, p. 1.
3. Judge George Welsh, in *United States v. Winston*.
4. Philadelphia Smith Act defendants, press release, September 16, 1953.
5. Temple University Urban Archives, ACLU files, 7/III-98.
6. From the files of Bernard Segal.
7. J. Cullen Ganey, as reported in the Philadelphia *Evening Bulletin*, December 17, 1953, p. 1.
8. *United States v. Kuzma*, transcript, vol. 1, opening statement.

CHAPTER 10

1. Walter Lowenfels, op. cit., p. 16.
2. Philadelphia Smith Act trial, transcripts, vols. I and II.

CHAPTER 11

1. Printed in the Philadelphia edition, *The Afro-American*, April 17, 1954, and signed by Franklin I. Sheeder, Executive Director, Board of Christian Education; Blanche Nicola, Head Worker, St. Martha's Settlement House; Mildred Olmsted, Administrative Secretary, Women's International League for Peace and Freedom; George A. Trowbridge, Rector, St. Paul's Church; Elias Charry, Rabbi, Germantown Center; Stephen G. Carey, Head, American Friends Service Committee, Philadelphia; D. Wilmot Gateson, Rector, Church of the Savior; F. Snyder Thomas, Rector, St. Barnabas Church.
2. Robert W. Sayre, interview with the author, Philadelphia, October 25, 1989.
3. Charles C. Hileman III, interview with the author, Philadelphia, August 16, 1989.
4. Benjamin H. Read, interview with the author, Washington, DC, December 1, 1989.
5. Joseph S. Lord III, interview with the author, Philadelphia, June 23, 1989.
6. Henry Sawyer, John Rogers Carroll, Edmund Spaeth, Charles Hileman and Joseph Lord each made reference to Ben Read's meticulous efforts.
7. As reported in the Philadelphia *Evening Bulletin*, April 16, 1954.
8. Ibid.
9. Joseph S. Lord III, interview with the author, Philadelphia, June 21, 1989.
10. Benjamin H. Read, interview with the author, Washington, DC, December 1, 1989.
11. Joseph S. Lord III, interview with the author, Philadelphia, June 21, 1989.
12. Joseph and Stewart Alsop, Philadelphia *Evening Bulletin*, May 18, 1954.
13. Ibid.
14. "Crouch Charges Brownell Frame-up," Philadelphia *Evening Bulletin*, June 21, 1954.

CHAPTER 12

1. Philadelphia Smith Act trial, transcript, p. 692ff.
2. Ibid., p. 431.
3. Ibid., pp. 444–449.
4. Ibid., p. 463ff.
5. Ibid., p. 547ff.
6. Ibid., p. 798ff.
7. Philadelphia Smith Act trial, transcript, p. 609ff.
8. Philadelphia Smith Act trial, transcript, p. 736ff.
9. Ibid., p. 741ff.
10. Ibid., p. 741.

CHAPTER 13

1. Philadelphia Smith Act trial, transcript, p. 897.
2. Ibid., p. 1199.
3. Ibid., p. 1059.
4. Ibid., pp. 1202–1204.
5. Ibid., p. 1239ff.
6. Ibid., pp. 1247–1251.
7. Ibid., p. 1254ff.
8. Philadelphia *Evening Bulletin*, May 21, 1954.
9. Philadelphia Smith Act trial, transcript, vols. 6 and 7.
10. Philadelphia Smith Act trial, transcript, p. 1400.
11. Ibid., pp. 1401–1406.
12. Ibid., p. 1435ff.
13. Ibid., p. 1437.
14. Ibid., p. 1458ff.
15. Ibid., p. 1497.
16. Ibid., pp. 1504–1567.
17. Ibid., p. 1749.
18. Ibid., p. 1748.
19. Ibid., pp. 1748, 1768, 1901–1902.
20. Ibid., pp. 1856, 1869–1879.
21. Ibid., pp. 1847–1856.

CHAPTER 14

1. Philadelphia Smith Act trial, transcript, p. 1940.
2. Ibid., p. 1956.
3. Ibid., p. 1968.
4. Ibid., p. 1982.
5. Ibid., p. 1986ff.
6. Ibid., p. 1988.
7. Ibid., p. 2011.
8. Ibid., p. 2004.
9. Ibid., pp. 2017-2025.
10. Ibid., p. 1982.
11. Ibid., pp. 2027–2029.
12. Ibid., p. 2045.
13. Ibid., pp. 2049–2050.
14. Ibid., p. 2072.
15. Ibid., pp. 2103–2104.
16. Ibid., p. 2158.
17. Ibid., p. 2162.
18. Ibid., pp. 2173–2174.
19. Ibid., pp. 2181–2182.

20. Ibid., p. 2247ff.
21. Ibid., p. 2258.
22. Ibid., pp. 2265–2270.
23. Ibid., p. 2380.
24. Ibid., p. 2386.
25. Ibid., p. 2408.
26. Philadelphia Smith Act trial, transcript, p. 2994.
27. Ibid., p. 2297.

CHAPTER 15

1. Joseph S. Lord III, interview with the author, Philadelphia, June 21, 1989.
2. Edmund Spaeth, interview with the author, Philadelphia, July 10, 1989.
3. Philadelphia Smith Act trial, transcript, vol. 9.
4. Ibid.
5. Ibid.
6. Philadelphia Smith Act trial, transcript, p. 2792.
7. Ibid., p. 2793.
8. John Sommerville, *Communist Trials and the American Tradition* (New York: Cameron Associates, 1956).
9. Philadelphia Smith Act trial, transcript, vol. 10.
10. David Cohen, interview with the author, Philadelphia, August 8, 1989.
11. Joseph S. Lord III, interview with the author, op. cit.
12. These and all subsequent quotes regarding the summation of Joseph Lord to the jury can be found in Criminal No. 17418, *United States v. Kuzma et al.* Argument to the jury by Joseph S. Lord, August 11, 1954.
13. These and all subsequent quotes regarding the summation of Thomas McBride to the jury can be found in Criminal No. 17418, *United States v. Kuzma et al.* Argument to the jury by Thomas D. McBride, August 11, 1954.

CHAPTER 16

1. Bernard Segal, letter to William J. Green, March 15, 1955.
2. Ibid.
3. Ibid.
4. Ibid.
5. C. Brewster Rhoads, letter to Henry Sawyer, March 1955.
6. Bernard Segal, letter to Justice Felix Frankfurter, March 22, 1955.
7. Ibid.
8. Justice Felix Frankfurter, letter to Bernard Segal, April 1, 1955. In 1994, Henry Sawyer told me that he had neither seen nor known about the existence of this letter. I made certain that he received a copy.

9. A more detailed account of these events and subsequent references to them can be found during March and April 1956 in the *St. Louis Post-Dispatch*, the *New York Times*, the *Cleveland Press* and *The Nation*.

CHAPTER 17

1. $65,000 was the amount we paid for the trial counsel representation we received in the district court. An additional $20,000 to $25,000 was involved in legal fees for the appeal, and there were printing charges for copies of the court transcripts and scores of "incidentals" that I've made no attempts to verify. The recollections of the attorneys I interviewed were similar to mine. I turned up 10 receipts signed by Tom McBride, or for him by his secretary. I have an additional three receipts from a duplicating company for printing the court transcripts. The total amount of all these is greater than $67,000. Since, as I remember, all financial obligations were satisfied, I assume that whatever balance existed, particularly pertaining to the appeal, was met with assignments from one of the beneficiaries of the Horace Dodge estate.

CHAPTER 18

1. A.L. Wiren, Temple University Urban Archives, ACLU files, 7/III-98, letter to Thomas McBride, September 29, 1953.
2. Ibid., Spencer Coxe, letter to James Brittain, October 6, 1953.
3. Ibid., Spencer Coxe, letter to Irving Dilliard, October 20, 1953.
4. H. Walter Stewart, letter to Bernard Segal, February 11, 1954.
5. H. Walter Stewart, letter to Bernard Segal, February 22, 1954.
6. H. Walter Stewart, letter to Bernard Segal, May 18, 1954.
7. Reported in *Cleveland Bar Association Journal*, September 1955.
8. Bernard Segal, letter to William J. Green, March 15, 1955.
9. Jay W. Tracy, quoted in a letter from Joseph M. DuBarry IV to Bernard Segal, March 18, 1955.
10. Letter to Spencer Coxe, Temple University Urban Archives, ACLU files, 7/III, folder 39, Henry Foster, March 1956.
11. Irving R. Murray, letter to Spencer Coxe, May 24, 1957. Temple University Urban Archives, ACLU files, 7/III, folder 39.
12. Harrison Tweed, letter to Bernard Segal, June 15, 1954.
13. Bernard Segal, letter to Harrison Tweed, June 18, 1954.

CHAPTER 19

1. Joseph S. Lord III, interview with the author, Philadelphia, June 21, 1989.